RICHARD MELZER

ERNIE

IN THE AMERICAN SOUTHWEST

· PYLE ·

Ernie Pyle relaxing in the living room of his Albuquerque home. Courtesy of the Museum of New Mexico, #161828.

RICHARD MELZER

ERNIE PYLE

IN THE AMERICAN SOUTHWEST

· PYLE ·

SUNSTONE PRESS

SANTA FE
New Mexico

To Kam,
whose early love of books
led us to the Ernie Pyle Public Library
and into Ernie Pyle's world

Special thanks to The American Legion,
Department of New Mexico,
and The Albuquerque Historical Society.

First Edition

Printed in the United States of America

10 9 8 7 6 5 4 3 2 1

Library of Congress Cataloging in Publication Data:
Melzer, Richard
   Ernie Pyle in the American Southwest / Richard Melzer.
      p. cm.
   Includes bibliographical references and index.
   ISBN: 0-86534-243-1 (pbk):
   1. Pyle, Ernie, 1900-1945. 2. War correspondents—United States—Biography.
   3. Southwest, New—Description and travel. I. Title.
   PN4874.P86M45   1996
   070.4'333'092—dc20
   [B]   95-40232
                                                 CIP

Published by SUNSTONE PRESS
              Post Office Box 2321
              Santa Fe, NM 87504-2321 / USA
              (505) 988-4418 / *orders only* (800) 243-5644
              FAX (505) 988-1025

COVER:
Ernie Pyle in his favorite Stetson hat, Albuquerque, New Mexico. Photograph by Ferenz Fedor. Courtesy of the Museum of New Mexico, #103612. The background artwork is taken from a full-color silkscreen image, "Winter Solstice," by Kate Krasin.

TABLE OF CONTENTS

PREFACE

I first encountered Ernie Pyle, or at least his former home, years ago while still a graduate student at the University of New Mexico. His home was by then a branch of the Albuquerque Public Library. Living nearby, I sometimes visited this intriguing place of small rooms and many books, my young daughter in tow. Kam enjoyed the children's section, while I took in the aura of a building I knew little about, but which always drew me back. From the beginning, I wanted to know more about the humble white house and its famous first occupant. But, faced with the demands of post-graduate study, time did not allow such extracurricular curiosity. Years passed before I had the opportunity to unravel the mysteries of Ernie's private world through his house, his newspaper columns, his friends, and his voluminous correspondence. No author could have hoped for a more fascinating delayed journey.

Many have generously offered their time and assistance in my look at Ernie Pyle's world of the 1930s and 1940s. Foremost among these helpers were Evelyn Hobson, curator of the Ernie Pyle State Historic Site in Dana, Indiana; the reference staff of the Lilly Library at Indiana University; Stephany A. Eger and her staff at the Ernie Pyle Public Library; Kris Warmoth and Judy Marquez of the University of New Mexico-Valencia Campus Library; Edward Padilla, Denise W. Warren, and Barbara S. Rosen of the University of New Mexico's Zimmerman Library; Terry Ann Gugliotta, University of New Mexico archivist; Janet H. Johnson at the University of New Mexico Medical Archives; Susan Berry of the Silver City Museum; Jake W. Spidle, Jr., of the Department of History and Fred Bales of the Department of Communication & Journalism at the University of New Mexico; authors David Nichols and Dolly Cave; playwrite Bill Derringer; History students KenAaron and Joel Granger; attorney James R. Toulouse; SisterAnita Marie Howe of the Sisters of Charity in Cincinnati, Ohio; and Peggy Errera of the Zippo Lighter Company in Bradford, Pennsylvania.

Nelson Van Valen, Charles Davis, Jack M. Campbell, and Archie Westfall lent additional support and encouragement. Henrietta Loy, Sarah Mount, and Mo Palmer of the Albuquerque Historical Society read drafts of the manuscript, making helpful comments and suggestions.

I am especially grateful to Ernie Pyle's New Mexican friends and acquaintances who graciously answered my countless questions in oral histories. The Shaffer and Shoemaker families were particularly generous in sharing their personal memories and family correspondence.

Finally, I would like to thank my parents, my wife, Rena, and Kam for their never-ending support in every venture I attempt in life. The task of writing history is far easier and more pleasant when you are surrounded by loving hands that never let you fall.

—Richard Melzer
Belen, New Mexico
1995

INTRODUCTION

Most Americans who lived through the Second World War remember Ernie Pyle as the greatest war correspondent of their generation. Fewer Americans recall Pyle's earlier career as a roving reporter during the six and a half years prior to the bombing of Pearl Harbor in 1941. Accompanied by his wife, Jerry, Pyle traveled approximately 250,000 miles in search of human interest stories to fill his syndicated column six days a week, 52 weeks a year. In the process, the Pyles visited every state in the Union at least three times, slept in about 800 hotels, wore out two cars, and wrote enough copy to fill approximately twenty books. Calling himself the "constant voyager,"[1] Pyle maintained this grueling pace by combining a great talent for writing with an even greater love of the freedom he found on the road.[2]

In the course of their gypsy lives, Ernie and Jerry Pyle visited the Southwest on a number of occasions, becoming more fascinated with the region with every trip. When they finally decided to settle more-or-less permanently, they "didn't even have to take a vote." According to Pyle, "we both knew without asking. The place was New Mexico."[3]

And so they moved to Albuquerque after years of living out of six suitcases and the back of a car. The couple had a small house built on the outskirts of town where they could enjoy beautiful sunrises over the Sandia Mountains to the east and breathtaking sunsets on the distant horizon to the west. Unfortunately, the Pyles' happiness in their new home was short-lived. War and personal tragedy marred the four-and-a-half years they called New Mexico home.[4]

Ernie Pyle's attraction to the Southwest and brief life in Albuquerque has been described in broad terms by the reporter's two biographers, Lee Miller and David Nichols.[5] As we commemorate the fiftieth anniversary of Pyle's death, a fuller description of this famous author's days in New Mexico seems long overdue. When did he first visit New Mexico, and what were his early impressions of the state, as reflected in his newspaper columns and private correspondence? What drew Ernie and Jerry Pyle to this place, rather than to any other state or region of the country? What were their hopes and expectations once they arrived? What happiness did they realize, and what sadness plagued their lives at 700 Girard Avenue in southeastern Albuquerque?[6] Once the world war began, what contributions did they make to the war efforts of New Mexicans on the home front and abroad? Finally, what impact did New Mexico have on their overall lives, and what imprint did Ernie Pyle leave on his adopted state? The answers to these several questions reveal much not only about a famous journalist's life, but also about New Mexico in the 1930s and 1940s, as seen through the eyes of an expert observer at the height of his professional career.

1

EARLY YEARS TO 1935

New Mexico was far different from Ernie Pyle's native state of Indiana. Born on August 3, 1900, Ernest Taylor Pyle was raised as an only child on a family farm outside Dana, Indiana. Although Dana (population 850) was small by any measure, Pyle claimed that he "never felt completely at ease [there] .... [f]or I was a farm boy, and town kids can make you feel awfully backward when you're young and a farm boy."[1] Uncomfortable in Dana and hardly fond of farming (an aunt claimed that he squirted more milk on his sleeve than in the bucket while milking), Pyle sought to broaden his horizons by enrolling at Indiana University in 1919. Four years later he was just shy of completing a Bachelor's degree in journalism when he left school to take his first job as a cub reporter on the *La Porte (Indiana) Herald*. Pyle only worked on the *Herald* for a short while before moving on to a series of newspaper jobs farther east, in Washington, D.C., and New York City.[2]

Pyle's professional duties ranged from copy editor to managing editor. Although successful at every task he attempted from 1923 to 1935, he was not content with the direction his newspaper career had taken by the mid 1930s. Showing clear signs of what is now called professional burnout, he wrote to a friend that his indoor office jobs had become "hard and fatiguing," leaving no time to pursue the work that gave him his "greatest satisfaction": writing.[3]

Relief arrived in an unusual manner. Prone to catching colds, Pyle was suffering from a particularly bad case of the flu in late 1934. A

Washington physician advised him to convalesce in warmer weather. Following thousands of health seekers who had gone before them, Ernie and Jerry Pyle dutifully packed a few bags in their Ford coupe and journeyed southwest in search of a cure. This was not their first such extended car trip. After marrying in July 1925, they had impulsively quit their respective jobs to drive "around the rim" of the United States in a Model T roadster the following year. Ten weeks, 9,000 miles, and thirteen tire changes later, they returned east penniless, but with good memories of life on the road and an especially good impression of the American Southwest.[4]

The Pyles' trip of early 1935 was quite different from their adventure of 1926. Although they found more rain than warmth on the highways and side roads from Texas to California, the Pyles encountered many interesting subjects and sites. The couple also found great comfort in a warm new friendship they established as they passed through New Mexico. Stopping at an Albuquerque hotel, Pyle had placed a courtesy call to the editor of the city's evening newspaper, the *Albuquerque Tribune*. Amicably know as "Shafe," editor Edward H. Shaffer and his wife Liz dined with the Pyles that same evening, beginning an enduring friendship that would change both families' lives forever.[5]

Ernie Pyle returned east to write a series of eleven columns on his travel experiences of 1935. Using an appealing, conversational style, Pyle wrote four columns on fascinating places he and Jerry discovered, ranging from the casinos of Las Vegas to the ancient cathedral in church-banned Juarez, Mexico. Two articles dealt with unique individuals, including an Arizona rancher who specialized in doing "absolutely nothing" and a world traveler who seemed "more nearly what I would like to be ... than anyone I have ever known." A seventh column described Southwestern public opinion of the New Deal, a curious choice of topics given Pyle's general aversion to politics.[6]

Pyle's four remaining columns addressed miscellaneous topics of particular appeal in his travels. Several had to do with New Mexico. Writing about the books he read recently, Pyle recalled a "wave of enthusiasm ... on books about the Southwest," including Harvey Fergusson's *Rio Grande*, Ross Calvin's *Sky Determines*, and Mary Austin's *Land of Little Rain*. While reporting on the best and the worst of everything on his trip, Pyle unfortunately found one of his least favorite hotels in New Mexico. "Dirty, cold and bleak" with torn wallpaper, no curtains, and an unshaded light bulb "hanging miserably" from the ceiling, his room in this hotel was declared "an abominable place in such an otherwise perfect state."[7]

Back on the road, the Pyles ran out of gas only once in their 8,000-mile journey. As luck would have it, the couple had just passed a ranch house "far off the main highway some place in New Mexico" when their motor stopped for lack of fuel. Undaunted, they simply "coasted back 100 yards to the ranch house, got some gas from the rancher, and drove away, having [barely] escaped a twenty-mile walk." Pleased by his good fortune and amazed by the "spaceless, free ... land of humility and good taste," Pyle concluded that "I love the Southwest."[8]

In the most philosophical of his eleven original columns, Pyle quoted a woman from Washington, D.C., who had written him that

My roommate and I feel that one of the paradoxes of modern civilization is the fact that so large a part of humanity is condemned to the treadmill of toil, and is deprived of life's joys and beauty. Most of one's waking hours are spent in a struggle for mere existence, for the bare necessities of life. All else must be put aside until that far off and all too distant day when one can realize the fruit of his life's labors, if he is fortunate. Having worked thru [sic] the seven years of the depression it had been impressed upon me the futility of striving to get more than one jump ahead of the wolf. Today one may be working and thinking that he is well on the way to success and security. Tomorrow brings the awakening, and all too soon the hope and peace that one nurtured within the heart is gone forever and a substitute of bitterness and despair is left to console.

Pyle said that he felt free to quote so much of this woman's letter because "she practically took the words right out of [not only] my mouth ...., but out of thousands and maybe millions of other people's," as he had discovered in his recent travels. He had learned that Americans felt the futility of "thrift and self-sacrifice for some nebulous and sort of holy 'rainy day'" "when maybe we'll have a revolution and it'll all be taken away from us." Or "why waste the good years preparing for the far-off years of old age, when maybe things will be so different by then we won't need money or it wouldn't do us any good if we had it? And anyhow, we'll have old-age pensions by then." Pyle doubted that this was "the same 'what the hell' feeling that led us dancing and shouting into night clubs after the war. That was a release. This one is more thoughtful, more resigned, more somber. We don't know what's coming, so why count on a plan of life which may never unfold?"[9]

Pyle ended his column by answering a question that his letter writer from Washington had posed regarding whether she and her roommate should "strike out to see the world" or "be content to grow old and dreary and forfeit our desire to travel?" Pyle replied that, given the nation's economic condition and drastically changing attitudes, he could only suggest "to any one with the gypsy foot and the gleam in his eye ...., [s]ure, why not?"[10] As he put it years later, "if in your soul you've got to do a certain thing, then it's right for you to do it."[11]

Ernie Pyle's eleven columns were judged an "instant hit" when they appeared in the *Washington Daily News* from April 2 to 13, 1935. Encouraged by this early success, Pyle grew determined to abandon his "man-killing" desk job and take his own advise to "strike out and see the world" before he grew too "old and dreary" in his life and career. Pyle boldly proposed to the Scripps-Howard Newspaper Alliance (which owned the *News* and 23 other papers) that he be allowed to "go where I please and write what I please" in a syndicated human-interest column to run six days a week.[12] George B. Parker, editor-in-chief of all Scripps-Howard newspapers, agreed to a trial run. Calling his new assignment "just the kind of job I always wanted," Pyle enthusiastically entered the second major phase of his professional life in mid 1935.[13]

Ernie Pyle launched this new phase of his career a day short of his 35th birthday. Joined by Jerry, he traveled extensively and truly enjoyed his new-found freedom. "That girl who travels with me" (as he referred to Jerry in his increasingly popular columns) proved an ideal traveling companion. Although they often went hours without speaking and she never drove (Pyle described her as more "poetic than mechanical"), their mutual silence was far from awkward and her moods usually matched his, at least in these early years.[14] A perennial non-conformist, Jerry seemed as delighted with her husband's new job and her role in it as he was. According to a newspaper friend, Jerry was "of major help with the column, sometimes retyping it for him, always ready with advice and, when Ernie was down in the mouth about the quality of his stuff, [ready] with reassurance."[15]

Traveling also appealed to Jerry. After growing up in a traditional Minnesota home where she'd learned the piano, sang in the church choir, graduated from high school, and gone to business school, Jerry had traveled far from home in 1918. Answering the government's call for more wartime clerks in Washington, D.C., she and a friend had journeyed from Stillwater, Minnesota, to take Civil Service jobs in the nation's capital when only 18. Jerry Siebolds met Ernie through a mutual friend; they married on July 7, 1925. Despite her lack of higher education, Jerry was described as well-read, well-spoken, and intellectually curious.[16] Her talents and interests would prove ideal in Pyle's new venture, although, given her private nature, she seemed most comfortable in her anonymous role as "That Girl." When inquisitive readers asked for information about her, Pyle responded in "a masterly piece of spoofing":

> She's a Russian princess who escaped with a pack of wolves in 1917. I met her while working as a drug-store cowboy on a dude ranch in Wyoming. She is six feet eight and weighs 43 pounds. She writes books under the nom de plume of Ernest Hemingway. She sits and stares at spiders on the wall.[17]

Kidding aside, Pyle privately praised his wife, calling her "the original Pyle fan." Friends remembered Jerry as her husband's "most ardent" supporter.[18]

With "That Girl" at his side and the entire nation to explore, Pyle set off across the country. His newly syndicated column appeared for the first time in August 1935. When Scripps-Howard decided that his trial run was a success, the newspaper chain made Pyle's column a regular feature and raised his salary by five dollars, bringing it to exactly a hundred dollars a week.

Pyle soon developed a great ability to track down unusual subjects by scouring local newspapers, talking to local acquaintances, and keeping small black pocket books with valuable leads indexed by states.[19] Tips listed in one such black book ranged from the ridiculous to the sublime. In his notes on tips in Virginia, for example, Pyle reminded himself to visit Jasper Davis, known for his super human ability to spit 12' 9" "in high wind." Elsewhere in his book, Pyle jotted down that Charles D. Raymer would be an interesting subject because he ran a "post office" for a thousand homeless men and women from the back of his bookstore in Seattle, Washington. Pyle also noted that he needed to visit God's Mercy Store in Waller, Texas, "where customers wait on [them-]selves and set [their] own prices."[20] By 1937, Pyle wrote of "getting a hell of a lot of letters from New Mexico [in particular] .... giving tips on swell stories in their territory.... I'm delighted to get them and it makes me feel good."[21] Pyle never had time to meet all the people or visit all the places listed in his black books, but the opportunities seemed unlimited and exciting in his early years on the road.

The reporter became increasingly adept at interviewing the unique subjects he met in his travels. Employing a friendly, disarming manner, Pyle created an almost instant rapport with his subjects; relaxed and at ease, they were usually eager to share information with this small (5'8", 110 pound), unassuming stranger. He was, moreover, a "born listener." Not needing to take notes during interviews, he relied on his remarkable memory when it came time to write his columns hours and sometimes days later.[22]

But it was Pyle's writing style that made his columns especially popular in the mid and late 1930s. As one journalist put it, Pyle wrote with a much-admired "eloquence, compassion, and simplicity."[23] Editors from coast to coast echoed the *Rocky Mountain News's* appraisal that "your feature is without a doubt the most widely read thing in [our] paper."[24] By writing of far-off places and unusual people, Pyle appealed to the wanderlust in many Americans. Thousands traveled vicariously with the successful writer and "that girl who travels with me."[25] As one Albuquerque woman wrote to Pyle in 1936, when his column "isn't in the paper her evening is spoiled."[26] Another fan remarked that Pyle's column was "about the only doggone thing" he read in the *Albuquerque Tribune* because Pyle's words were such "good medicine."[27] To most, his daily columns seemed like wholesome letters sent by a personal friend or relative who enjoyed the freedom of the open road, while most of his readers remained "farm-bound or pavement-bound" during some of the hardest years of the Great Depression.[28]

In fact, given the upbeat content of most of his columns, it would be hard to believe that there was even an economic depression going on in the nation.[29] Pyle's tone and wry humor made his column increasingly popular at a time when Americans strove to escape their troubles, not dwell on them. If writing style can be compared to photographic style, Ernie Pyle's vignettes were carefully focused, pleasing snap shots rather than profound depictions of life in the Great

Depression, as perfected by contemporary photographers like Russell Lee and Dorthea Lang.[30]

But Ernie Pyle's carefully focused vignettes required concentrated, time-consuming effort. According to one observer, his "homespun, sometimes corny, sometimes eloquent style" came naturally, but it did not come easily. He wrote "slowly at best, often rewrit[ing] a column three or four times" before he was satisfied with its content.[31] Time was in fact Pyle's greatest enemy. Reflecting his frustration with time, he exaggerated by swearing that it took him half a day to "dig up" a story, half a day to write and rewrite it, half a day to travel, half a day to visit old friends, and the rest of the day to catch up on his sleep.[32] Faced with the constant pressure to mass produce good copy, Pyle often checked into hotels and subjected himself to "writing sieges" in which he wrote as many as 34 columns in a two-and-a-half week span; thirteen columns in two days was his personal record.[33]

2

TRAVELING NEW MEXICO 1935-42

Despite the hectic pace of his work, Ernie Pyle continued to relish his life of travel and freedom. He especially enjoyed traveling through his favorite states, including Hawaii, Idaho, Washington, Oregon, and New Mexico.[1] The Pyles visited New Mexico in particular as often as their schedule allowed. Once there, Pyle wrote columns on some of the state's most famous or unusual sites. He was particularly awed by two of its natural wonders: Carlsbad Caverns and White Sands.

Although Ernie Pyle had traveled through Carlsbad several times before, he and Jerry arrived to see the town's famous caverns for the first time in April 1938. After touring the caverns with the park superintendent for most of a day, Pyle wrote to his family in Dana that the place was without question "one of the most wonderful sights I ever saw."[2] While he was certainly impressed with the caverns' rocks and formations, Pyle seemed particularly struck by the darkness he encountered when the park superintendent put the lights out far below ground.

You have never known darkness until you have sat in it 800 feet below the surface. You look around for a faint glow somewhere, a shadow, a movement. There is nothing. You are in a complete solid of blackness. And the silence is as thick as the darkness. Your soul creeps, and you sit there in mental obeisance.[3]

18

The traveling journalist was visibly relieved when the lights were turned back on and his party surfaced "out into the hot, blinding sunshine of the New Mexico desert." Pyle concluded that "Life is suddenly real again, and it is impossible that this gray, rolling plain can conceal another world so near. But you will dream about it for a long time."[4] Years later, when he was listing the best and the worst of every place he had seen in the country, Pyle claimed that Carlsbad Caverns were "the best one-day National Park in America."[5]

Ernie Pyle was similarly impressed by White Sands a year and a half later. In sharp contrast to the darkness he found in Carlsbad Caverns, Pyle wrote of White Sands' "dazzling light" in which "you must wear dark glasses or ... tears will come to your squinty eyes and there will be nothing in your vision but glare." Much like the darkened caverns, "out on the sands there is no sound, no perspective, no single thing to break the vast whiteness." Concluding with words reminiscent of what he thought of Carlsbad Caverns, Pyle declared that this "ocean of utter white" could both "astound you and ... give you the creeps."[6]

Pyle also used his descriptive talent to portray whole towns, including Lincoln, northwest of Carlsbad and northeast of White Sands. Made famous by the exploits of Billy the Kid, Lincoln was found to be "remarkably preserved," although in Pyle's estimation it had begun its decline on April 28, 1881, the day of Billy's famous escape from its two-story courthouse. Eager to preserve the area's rich history, Pyle suggested that the entire townsite be made into a state or national monument.[7] Pyle later wrote to Shafe that he had gotten the idea for such a monument in Mexico where the entire town of Taxco was made a national monument so that all buildings had to be "in tune with the old." Pyle liked the same concept for Lincoln, but thought that building regulations would have to be strict so that some "smart" businessman couldn't ruin everything by putting up a "Hollywood curio shop" ten feet from the town's famous courthouse.[8] Ed Shaffer agreed wholeheartedly. While confessing that he didn't "know exactly how you go about making a monument of an entire community," Shafe editorialized in the *Albuquerque Tribune* that he could "think of nothing more unfortunate" than seeing Lincoln become "commercialized and cheapened" like a "western Coney Island."[9]

As taken as Ernie Pyle was with places like Carlsbad Caverns, White Sands, and Lincoln, it would be a mistake to conclude that he liked all parts of New Mexico with equal enthusiasm. Thus, while he was generally impressed by Chaco Canyon, he confessed to his readers that he had no desire to "go see any more Indian ruins" because, with so many unanswered questions about their origins and demise, they all seemed quite "exasperating."[10]

Pyle showed little more enthusiasm for the four-corners marker at the only spot in the United States where the boundaries of four states (New Mexico, Arizona, Utah, and Colorado) meet. The famous reporter explored the four-corners region on a rare two-week vacation taken with Shafe in mid 1939. As Pyle later wrote in a column about the unique intersection of boundaries, few people ever ventured there, if only because few knew it existed and others had a hard time locating it since the last eight miles were "just an old Navajo wagon trail" that didn't even appear on road maps.[11] Privately, Pyle wrote of how he and Shafe were "amazed at how blank and worthless" this region appeared.[12]

Despite his disappointment in finding the four-corners marker in such desolate terrain, Pyle could not resist the temptation to get "kind of silly" once he arrived there. In a series of antics reflecting his wry sense of humor, Pyle proceeded to lean over the monument so that one of his feet was in Utah and the other was in Colorado, while one of his hands was in Arizona and the other was in New Mexico; he could thus claim to have been in all four states at the same time. Next, Pyle insisted on driving around and around the marker in his car so that he could say that he had traveled through four states in record time. At lunch, the reporter "had to sit on top of the point, which made my rather scant behind repose in four states simultaneously." When done eating, he threw his banana peels and some pieces of bread into the air so that they fell into all four states; he could thereby assert that the "dirtiest tourist can't out-desecrate me."[13]

Pyle was hardly more impressed with the New Mexico terrain he encountered while traveling alone from Albuquerque to El Paso two years later. The reporter told his readers that there was so little to see on this route that "you don't even have fence posts or telephone poles to count, much of the time." Pyle grew so bored with his surroundings that he wanted to carve his name on a rock at every curve (they were so rare), play solitaire on the front seat as he drove along, and ride on the hood of his car, "yelling and waving my old hat at all the cacti." South of Hot Springs, Pyle reached "the end of my rope," becoming so sleepy that he had to pull off the road and nap in the back seat of his 1941 convertible—a car he praised "for slumber purposes" far more than he praised his surroundings for their stimulating scenery.[14] Kidding aside, Pyle fully realized the great danger of growing tired on long hauls. On one occasion, he and Jerry "came across a car hanging by two wheels over the edge of a cliff" somewhere in New Mexico. "The driver," explained Pyle, "had simply gone to sleep."[15]

Ernie Pyle revealed his disappointment in other parts of New Mexico with less good-natured humor than he employed in describing his travels from Albuquerque to El Paso. Taos certainly received little praise in a pair of columns written in the spring of 1938. Pyle began his description of the northern village by asserting that Taos was "rather picturesque, but not ... enchanting." Its plaza was said to be "crammed with Mexicans, Indians and poor-looking whites," while its streets were unpaved, its street lights were non-existent, and its three hotels were small. Fires were frequent, according to Pyle, and some of the town's old adobe houses were falling apart. Taos was so inactive that it was "like a grave" by nine o'clock each evening.[16]

Pyle claimed that not even the town's famed artists thought much of Taos or its future by 1938. The reporter wrote that "You might hang around Taos for a month and never see an artist" because most only lived in their "fashionable ... adobe shack[s]" a few months a year, while others, like Ernest Blumenscheim, discovered they "couldn't stand Taos" any longer. As a result, only two "big 'name'" artists or authors remained: Mabel Dodge Luhan (who was in New York when Pyle arrived) and D.H. Lawrence's widow, Frieda. "The rest," according to Pyle, "might just as well be [named] Smith or Jones to you and me."[17]

Ernie Pyle used even less flattering words to describe his experience at the Taos Pueblo. Pyle was struck by the pueblo's grand view and impressive architecture when he and his "traveling partner" drove up. However, he grew steadily disenchanted with the pueblo once he and Jerry paid a quarter each for a tour led by a guide dressed in white deerskin moccasins with a "bed-sheet ... draped around his shoulders." Their Indian guide spoke little English, lacked keys to open the local church, and refused to allow them to enter any dwellings other than curio shops filled with "home-made drums, crude pottery, moccasins, [and] ears of colored corn." Little girls followed the tourists from shop to shop, calling, "Gimme a nickel," while younger children "kept saying 'Penny, penny.'"[18]

When the tour was half over, Pyle asked what more their guide had left to show them. The Indian replied, "Fine curio shops," to which Pyle responded, "No you won't." The Pyles "furiously ... abandoned" their befuddled host, got into their car, and drove away. Feeling like he'd been made a "sucker," Pyle told his national reading audience that he had seldom "been so mad" in his life. He concluded his blistery column by advising all future tourists to simply "Drive out to the Pueblo, stop right between the two big buildings, sit in the car and look around for five minutes, ... and then turn around and drive away. You will have seen everything."[19]

Ernie Pyle was no more considerate of Native Americans on the few other occasions he mentioned them in his columns on the Southwest. When referring to a tribe that lived at the bottom of the Grand Canyon, he impertinently "asked an old cowboy about them— whether they were smart or not." The cowboy answered that he thought that the Indians were "just about average," a response that Pyle interpreted to mean that "there weren't any Einsteins down there."[20] On his 1939 vacation with Shafe, Pyle wrote of "loafing Indians" with "sinister" faces who stood around an Arizona trading post, staring at strangers "like so many animal eyes around a campfire."[21] Back in Albuquerque, Pyle went to a local hotel's basement washroom and found it locked. After acquiring a key upstairs, he inquired why the washroom was kept closed. "Because of the Indians," he was told. "We can't keep them out of there. They're in there all day and all night. They even go in ... and take baths." Rather than trying to understand why these people might need a public source of running water, Pyle simply concluded that he "had always supposed the Indians sitting in the lobby were paid by the hotel" to add atmosphere to the Southwestern surroundings.[22]

Pyle made little effort to understand Indian life and had little respect for others who did. He belittled Ernest Thompson Seton's deep respect for Indian ways, as reflected in Seton's efforts to teach whites to appreciate native culture at his Institute of Indian Lore outside Santa Fe. Rather than enroll in an institute where whites were supposedly told "that they're mere punks compared to Indians,"[23] Pyle preferred to agree with an old-timer in Taos who proudly declared that he didn't know any more about Indians "than any other white man. Talking to Indians is just like writing a note and putting it in a prairie dog hole."[24] In a private moment, Pyle remarked that "We didn't pay much attention to the Indians, as they are hard to talk to, and I don't like Indians anyway."[25]

Pyle's remarks did not go unnoticed in Taos and the Taos Pueblo. The *Taos Review* printed a copy of the roving reporter's fault-finding column on the town, but offered little in local reaction beyond its own suggestion that residents "take it on the chin.... This is the way the other half of the world sees us."[26] Pyle may well have received far more angry feedback had Mabel Dodge Luhan, the so-called matron of "Mabeltown," been in town to respond.[27] Present and infuriated, the Indians of Taos Pueblo were vehement in their reaction to Pyle's column about their ancient community. Pyle wrote Shaffer that

the Taos Indians got out an ultimatum threatening to cut my dolliper off if I ever showed up there again.... But that's one complaint I didn't brood much over, because I think the column was exactly right even if I do say so. Spud Johnson, who is sort of Taos' literary set (and who, in fact, wrote the resolution for the Indians at their request) wrote me that he thought the column was justified, and he had tried to get them to change [their minds] but they wouldn't do it.[28]

Blinded by his own ethnocentrism, Pyle was unable to see beyond his own expectations of what the Taos Indians should have shared of their private lives and beliefs. His blatant disregard for the Indians' privacy would come back to haunt him when his own private world was repeatedly compromised in the coming years.

Ernie Pyle's observations regarding Santa Fe were even more critical than his disparaging remarks regarding Taos. The Pyles visited the state capital early in their many years on the road. Although the couple was generously "wined and dined," and Pyle pronounced Santa Fe's architecture to be "the most beautiful ... in the world," he readily admitted his aversion for much of the community and many of its residents.[29] His several columns on the "city different" reveal the reasons for his bias and distaste. Thus, while he admired Santa Fe's adobe architecture, he found "a lot of old 1890-type brick buildings oozing tastelessness .... [and] hideously out of place." Moreover, while he discovered some of the finest shops west of Dallas, he also found "some that are the worst." Politics in the capital were judged even more unsavory than in his home state of Indiana.[30]

But these were minor criticisms compared to Pyle's chief complaint regarding Santa Fe: its acclaimed artists and authors. The town's 150 artists and authors were described as "an awful gob of genius" with a badly inflated image of themselves, despite the fact that none of them were "world-famous figures" and there were only about twenty "who were downright and permanently interesting." While a few were considered to be "genuine people," most were seen as "freaks and pretenders ... who ... like to sit on the floor and talk about 'composition' and dress up like Indians and stare into fireplaces." These pretenders had gone "to pot," in Pyle's estimation, because they were known to avoid baths, ride to parties on spotted ponies, and spend conspicuous hours at La Fonda, "the very classy Harvey house [sic] right in the center of town."[31] In an unusual triad, Pyle warned his many readers that

the art circle (if you participate) is a deadly thing. You're so in danger of losing your head and getting into the groove of thinking all is art, and drinking too much and looking down upon common people too much and getting to believe you're a genius and the world is a fool for not recognizing you and isn't fit to recognize you if it did, and after a while you're all washed up and nothing interests you except yourself and Good Old Art.[32]

Not satisfied with this broadside of early 1937, Pyle returned to Santa Fe to employ biting satire to describe the city's snobbish art colony. In a syndicated column that appeared in the *Albuquerque Tribune* on April 29, 1938, Pyle assumed the persona of a pretentious artist who told how he spent a typical day in Santa Fe. Before breakfast, this fictional character claimed to have "painted a magnificent study" laden with symbolism that not even he was intelligent enough to understand. He then "rushed to La Fonda's bar in my paint-streaked overalls" where he could gaze into space "so that the rich tourists could see I was a great painter thinking about something ... far over their heads."[33]

In the course of the day that followed, Pyle's hypothetical artist began a highly symbolic 1,500-foot mural around the governor's chicken house, had an "immensely successful" discussion on the "The Future of Futurism" (in which "nobody knew what anybody else was talking about"), made a "striking sculpture in shaving cream of an [upside down] adobe shack," and inspired "a detachment of pupils from Miss Oogalawa's Exclusive School for Stupid Millionaire

Girls" with eight-syllable words that described "the forces [of] creation that are boiling within me." By dawn the next day, Pyle's artist had written an "ageless epic" (with time to spare) before returning to La Fonda, "spent, exhausted, sanctified by the fire of my own genius," and ready for another self-absorbing day.[34]

Like most satire, Pyle's was more than half factitious. For two consecutive years Pyle had depicted the intellectuals of Santa Fe as cultural elitists who took themselves and their art far too seriously for anyone's good, including their own. Pyle may well have been attacking cultural elitism in any part of the country, for he hated pretension wherever he found it. Santa Fe was simply a natural target for Pyle's accumulated wrath because it boasted more artists and authors per capita than most any city of its size in the late 1930s.[35]

However, unlike Taos Pueblo, the residents of Santa Fe hardly protested Pyle's caustic description of their art colony. Many non-artists may have secretly agreed with the reporter's appraisal of their creative neighbors, while many artists may have kept their silence for fear they would be identified with the "freaks and pretenders" Pyle described in such detail. Pyle predicted that his "completely insane, nasty" column of April 1938 would probably "cause me to be exiled from Santa Fe forever more," but noted only a single reference to his satire in the capital city's press.[36] According to Pyle, the *New Mexico Examiner* stood alone in its charge that "millions are charmed by my vitriolic pen."[37] Santa Fe's largest newspaper, the *New Mexican*, simply reprinted his column on the city and its faults with neither resentful comment nor spirited defense.[38]

Having expressed his bias against certain groups and places of the Southwest, Ernie Pyle proved far kinder in his treatment of individual New Mexicans featured in his daily columns. The roving reporter interviewed at least 29 individuals or couples in the course of four trips through the state from 1936 to 1942. His subjects ran the gamut from the rich and famous to the poor and obscure. Most, including a hitchhiking poet and a song-writing couple who lived "at the end of nowhere," could be classified as eccentric.[39] Some were unusual based on the dwellings they called home: a boxcar in the case of Irene Fisher in Albuquerque and an elaborate man-made cave near Silver City in the case of Cornelious Cosgrove Whitehill.[40] All of Pyle's New Mexicans, from a ten-year-old cowgirl to Roswell's rocket scientist, Robert H. Goddard, were undeniably interesting.[41] Six examples illustrate this point.

Ernie Pyle wrote two columns about New Mexico's most colorful governor of the 1930s, Clyde Tingley. The Pyles were invited to dine with Tingley and his wife at the governor's mansion in the spring of 1938. Dress was informal, as was dinner (fried chicken eaten with fingers) and conversation (peppered with Tingley's notoriously bad grammar). Pyle described the governor as "loud and blunt," but a person "you enjoy listening to" even if most of the conversation was one-sided. According to Pyle, "what little ice there was quickly melted away, and after that it was just as if we lived there."[42]

Not surprisingly, most of Governor Tingley's monologue centered on politics. He took many phone calls at the table during dinner and boasted of frequent calls from President Franklin Roosevelt, who liked to call him "Clyde." Tingley seemed especially proud of getting "the best of his [political] enemies"; one of his parrots was trained to say "'Republican morning paper,' which tickles the Governor because he is always in fights with the Republican papers." Pyle wrote that Tingley looked like a machine politician, which was exactly what he was, as he was the first to admit; in Tingley's words, "that's the only way you can get anything done." As a result, there was "always a line of people at his office wanting something," and he "had as many as 200 callers a day."[43]

Pyle reported that Clyde Tingley was "probably the money-gettingest man in New Mexico," securing New Deal funds for countless state projects, including his personal favorite, the million-dollar hospital for crippled children located in Hot Springs and named after his wife, Carrie. Carrie Tingley was said to be as popular as the governor, especially based on her charity work for children. The couple was generous to an extreme; piles of ready-to-be-distributed presents cluttered many tables in the governor's mansion. The governor was, in fact, so generous and gregarious that he insisted that the next time the Pyles were in Santa Fe Ernie should "just drive right into the garage back of the mansion, get out your bags and ... stay here til you get tired of it." Ernie Pyle appreciated the invitation, but, with little interest in politics, never took Tingley up on his offer.[44]

Ernie Pyle had interviewed an equally generous, but far less political individual just prior to his visit to the governor's mansion in 1938. In sharp contrast to Mr. Tingley, this deeply humble young woman remained anonymous to Pyle's readers. Referred to simply as "my friend," this professional nurse's job was to personally assist many of the over 300 health seekers who regularly arrived in Albuquerque to "chase the cure" each year. A majority of her patients suffered from tuberculosis. In Pyle's mind, his devoted friend had "one of the most interesting jobs in the [entire] city."[45]

It was also one of Albuquerque's most demanding jobs. Corresponding with health seekers before their arrival, she briefed them on everything from living conditions to the cost of living (equaling "$60 a month and up"). Later, she greeted new arrivals at the train depot, helped them select housing, made sure their utilities were all on, and often went so far as to "get blankets [from] her own bed to keep the new health-seekers warm the first night." Depending on their needs and condition, Pyle's friend was known to stay with her newcomers "anywhere from a few hours to three days." But that was not all. Considering the "whole batch as her own family," she kept track of them in the coming months, sending doctors to those in danger and freely "cussing" those who gave up on their chances of recovery too soon.[46]

Sadly, some in her care were unsuccessful in their battle for improved health. In fact, some, like a seriously ill gentleman who traveled from abroad, died en route, in this case only an hour from his destination by rail in Albuquerque. Pyle's friend would then use her expertise in funeral arrangements, knowing "all the rates, rites and rituals" for everything from a military funeral to a Masonic burial. Fortunately, many of her patients won their personal battles and either returned to their homes elsewhere in the world or stayed, often to make major contributions in their adopted state. With some exaggeration, Pyle stated that Albuquerque's "commercial and civic reins" were, by the late 1930s, securely in the hands of the same people who had first come to the city with little hope of even surviving. Their recovery and success were due in part to Pyle's friend, the health seekers' hostess.[47]

Ernie Pyle had particular admiration for a health seeker who had first come to Silver City for three months in 1927, but stayed on in the Southwest for the rest of his life. Dr. Ross Calvin was a "learned" minister of the Episcopal Church who developed a nervous disorder while serving in a parish back East.[48] Thinking that the Southwest's climate plus several months of rest would cure his ills, Calvin journeyed to New Mexico "down and out and broke," in his own words.[49] Once there, Calvin grew more and more interested in the region. Indeed, by the time he was summoned to the *Silver City Daily Press* office to meet Ernie Pyle on November 7, 1939, Calvin had become so fascinated with New Mexico that he became an expert on its natural surroundings.[50] His nervous disorder still caused "dreadful insomnia" and serious depression, but his love of the land soon outweighed his physical and mental condition.[51] Following his doctor's orders that he "spend as much time as possible out of doors, Calvin rambled over the foothills of Silver City, penetrating deeper and higher into the Gila wilderness. Stopping to rest, he would observe and contemplate, and then make notes on the ... cards he carried with him."[52] Calvin also became a "photographer of almost professional ability" and "an authority on the plant growth of the whole Southwest." In the process, he got to know "ranchers and miners and trappers and desert-rats for scores of miles around," winning so much of their respect that they continually told Pyle that "If Dr. Calvin tells you something you can put it down as correct. He knows."[53]

Calvin developed such a keen knowledge of the Southwest that he eventually wrote a classic volume entitled *Sky Determines*. Pyle described *Sky Determines* as an "essay on the sand and air and cactus and white sun of the Southwest" with particular focus on "the effect of the climate on the land." Calvin's book was so insightful and valuable that the Pyles carried it with them as "our Southwestern Bible" for years.[54] Still important in the late twentieth century, *Sky Determines* remains in print with Ernie Pyle's words of praise quoted on the cover of its most recent edition.[55]

Ross Calvin took Ernie Pyle to meet another unique health seeker thirty miles outside Silver City. Father Roger Aull was originally from Cincinnati, Ohio, but, came to New Mexico when his health deteriorated as a result of injuries suffered while serving as an Army chaplain in World War I.[56] While his original goal was "to read and write and think and get ready for the hereafter," Father Aull managed to do these and many other deeds that Pyle admired. Despite continued poor health, the Jesuit priest built a large stone house, all his own furniture, a little chapel, several outbuildings, plus "lots of porches and walks and bridges and fancy arches." When the Pyles arrived, he was busy constructing an addition to his house while dressed in "bibbed blue overalls," rather than priestly garb, as one might expect.[57]

Most importantly, Father Aull received as many as a thousand visitors a year, or an average of about three a day. Pyle wrote that some arrived even before breakfast, staying as little as an hour or as long as several weeks. Without hanging out a counselor's shingle to announce his vocation, the priest drew Mormons, Jews, agnostics, Protestants, and, of course, Catholics. All sought direction from this wise, universally respected man whom Pyle found to be "bluff but not gruff .... and ... awfully easy to talk with." To the scientists, fellow priests, troubled youths, and countless others, his simple words of advice were often, "Let's just start over." Pyle clearly admired this man of the cloth, less for his religious ideals than for his ability to treat all callers fairly and equally.[58]

Ernie Pyle interviewed an Isleta Pueblo Indian for yet another column about New Mexicans. Despite his earlier comments regarding Indians in the Southwest, Pyle truly respected Pablo Abeita, writing that he was "smart" and "spoke better English than I do." Pyle nevertheless questioned the authenticity of a remarkable story attributed to Abeita. Abeita told Pyle that he had met President Theodore Roosevelt when he went to Washington, D.C., on one of his eighteen trips to the capital to serve as an interpreter and to represent Southwestern Indian interests. After a prolonged conversation in the White House, Roosevelt supposedly promised Abeita that he would someday travel to Isleta and "visit you in your home." Roosevelt eventually kept his promise, arriving in Albuquerque and sneaking off to Isleta after Abeita disguised him in a Indian blanket wrapped "clear up over his head." Following his visit to the pueblo, Roosevelt returned to his Albuquerque hotel where people "were running around ... because they couldn't find the President." Abeita reported that he "gave a big war whoop and jerked the blanket off the President's head, and you should have seen the people stare." According to Abeita, TR reassured the worried crowd, saying, "Boys, I was just as safe in Pablo's hands as I am with anybody in the world."[59]

Ernie Pyle interviewed a final example of his New Mexico subjects if only because "So many people for so many years [had] pester[ed] him to ... see Pop Shaffer that I finally got sick of the pestering" and decided to visit this unique individual in April 1942.[60] Clem "Pop" Shaffer (no relation to Shafe) was unique not only because of a "special gift," but also because he was the only New Mexican to leave a complete written record of the brief time Ernie Pyle spent interviewing him in the years prior to Pyle's career as a famous war correspondent.

Pop Shaffer was 62 when he met Pyle. Pop had lived in Mountainair, New Mexico, since 1908 and had opened the town's only two-story brick hotel in May 1924. His special gift was his ability to transform odd-shaped branches and roots into "perfect caricature[s]" of animals ranging in size from a "little 'dog' you could hold in your hand, clear up to 'dinosaurs' forty feet long." His 300 finished works were placed on display at his ranch south of Mountainair where thousands of tourists had come to see them over the years. Although generous to a fault with his money, Pop was seldom willing to part with his creations. Only President and Mrs. Roosevelt ever received "animals" from Pop's "zoo" as gifts.[61]

Pop Shaffer's recorded memories of Ernie Pyle's visit reveal a great deal about Pyle's modus operandi as a reporter. According to Pop, the famous writer arrived at the Shaffer Hotel where he found the hotel's proprietor sitting in front of a big fireplace in the hotel lobby. Pyle opened the conversation, commenting on the cool morning air and joining Pop near the fire. Pyle said he was "looking for a man named Pop Shaffer," to which Pop replied, "You don't have to go any farther." They shook hands, and Pyle explained that he had heard so much about Pop that "I came over to have a talk with you ... about your hobby." The two men soon discovered a common bond: they were both originally from Indiana, which of course led to a comparison of names and memories from their respective pasts.[62]

Pop showed Pyle around his 32-room hotel and served him lunch in the hotel's large dining room. A gracious guest, Pyle finished the meal by saying it was "the best food I have eaten since my mother's [cooking]." After lunch, Pop took Pyle to his 240-acre ranch south of town to see his famous handiwork. Pyle was reportedly shocked to see Shaffer's "Rancho Bonito" with its hundreds of animal sculptures and its patriotic log cabin painted in red, white, and blue inside and out. Pop recalled that his new friend asked him "so many questions [that] I can't remember a quarter of them," although he "answered them as best I could."[63]

Once back in town, Pop mentioned that he still had the first two dollars that he had made when his hotel opened in 1924. Pyle reportedly said, "Now, Pop, you have told me so many things about yourself that I had my doubts about[,] ... how [are] you going to prove ...

this story?" Shaffer proceeded to lead Pyle up the hotel's main stair-well; on the second floor he pointed to two silver dollar coins and a note tacked on a high window. Unable to read the note from a dis-tance, but eager to humor his host, Pyle climbed up on a couch. Still unable to see the note from this vantage point, Pyle put a chair on the couch, climbed up the couch and chair, and confirmed that yes, Pop was right. Pyle was supposedly so impressed with this bit of proof that he declared himself ready to believe anything Pop would now tell him.[64]

Obviously pleased, Pop led the reporter downstairs to the lobby where they "set down and talked some more" before Pyle announced that he needed to be on his way back to Albuquerque. It was after 4:00 p.m. when the two men shook hands and Ernie Pyle departed, having gathered sufficient mental notes for two columns under his byline.[65] Delighted with these stories and the publicity they brought Mountainair, the town's newspaper reprinted them on the front page of its April 17, 1942, edition.[66] Memorabilia of Pyle's brief visit is still proudly displayed in the Shaffer Hotel, though Pop Shaffer has long since passed on, having died of a heart attack 22 years after his his-toric encounter with Ernie Pyle.

If Pyle's style in interviewing Pop Shaffer was typical, it is possible to identify several key techniques employed by the well-known jour-nalist. Having established common ground (their common roots in Indiana), Pyle was friendly (joining Pop at the fire), complimentary (comparing Pop's hotel cooking to his mother's), patient (while Pop answered his questions the best he could), and agreeable (climbing high up a wall to verify Pop's first-two-dollars story). It appears that Pyle skillfully worked with his subject less to manipulate Pop Shaffer than to relax, humor, and encourage him in the interest of ultimately writing a good column. In the process, Pop was pleased with the attention he received, Mountainair was happy with the positive pub-licity it reaped, and Ernie Pyle was content with the information he gathered and later presented in column form.

Pop Shaffer and Ernie Pyle's other New Mexican subjects shared several characteristics that Pyle clearly admired in others. Five com-mon threads are especially evident. First, Pyle's subjects were usually fiercely independent and often quite eccentric. This was certainly true of Clyde Tingley (who reportedly locked every door and win-dow in the governor's mansion rather than allow access to it by his successor),[67] but it was also true of Pyle's health seeker hostess, Ross Calvin, Father Aull, and Pop Shaffer in their different ways. Some, like Tingley, had strong, assertive spouses, although their wives' unflagging support usually served to enhance their husbands' independence, rather than compromise it. With this and similar support, most of Pyle's subjects were free of contemporary social anchors, often living in isolated rural locales and very nearly self-sufficient.

Pablo Abeita clearly demonstrated his bold independence on the day he assisted Teddy Roosevelt in his concealed escape to Isleta Pueblo, as reported by Ernie Pyle (with some scepticism) in 1936. Abeita provided an equally bold example of independent action four years later, during the dedication of the Coronado Monument in Bernalillo, New Mexico. On May 29, 1940, after many hours of laudatory speeches regarding Francisco Coronado's glorious deeds as a Spanish conqueror, Abeita took the crowd by surprise by damning Coronado rather than praising him. According to one observer, Abeita presented "a short and cutting debunking of white man's history, which he said [was] 90 per cent wrong." "Electrified" by these words, the audience "broke into the heartiest applause of the afternoon" as most agreed that "a little blunt truth telling had added to the occasion, rather than detracted [from it]."[68] While Ernie Pyle never commented in writing on Abeita's interpretation of early Spanish-Indian relations (and may well have harbored a quite different opinion), he undoubtedly admired the Isleta Pueblo Indian for his courage of conviction and consistently bold actions.

Next, Ernie Pyle's subjects in New Mexico were almost always naturally talented or self-taught. Some, like Ross Calvin and Father Aull, had received formal educations, but their traditional schooling often had little to do with the new talents they developed once they arrived in the Southwest. Indeed, in keeping with their fierce independence, most had educated themselves in relation to their newfound interests and skills. Clyde Tinley, for one, had come to New Mexico trained as a machinist, but taught himself the art of politics, first as an alderman from Albuquerque's Second Ward, then as the ex-officio mayor of Albuquerque, and finally as governor of the entire state.[69]

Third, Ernie Pyle's subjects were generally unpretentious and humble. With the exception of Tingley, most were genuinely surprised by their fame and did little to actively promote it. In keeping with their individualism, they usually shunned publicity for fear it might compromise their independence and well-guarded privacy. Most were unmaterialistic, living either in small homes or, if more elaborate, in dwellings they had artfully built themselves. The importance was in the process of building more than in the actual use of home or property, which was judged to be only temporary anyway. In Father Aull's indicative words, he had built his house of stones on borrowed land, "But it's mine as long as I'm here, ... and when I pass on I won't want it anyhow."[70]

Fourth, Ernie Pyle's subjects were almost always committed to long-term, admirable goals. In most cases, their goals involved helping others. In addition to writing about Father Aull and the health seekers' hostess, Pyle devoted whole columns to Jim Terry (who guarded the savings of more than two hundred neighbors in Estancia when the local banks "went broke"), Dr. Richard Stovall (who saw up to 35 patients a day but "never sent a bill"), and Mary Boyd (who ran a truckers stop in Santa Fe but never charged truckers for the hundreds of gallons of coffee they consumed at her roadside cafe).[71] Based on their highly respected talents and universal good nature, Pyle's subjects were constantly sought out by others, whether they made their homes in the governor's mansion (in the case of Clyde Tingley) or "so far off the road that originally you had to stop and open nine gates to get [there]" (in the case of Roger Aull).[72]

Finally, few of Ernie Pyle's featured subjects were native New Mexicans. The vast majority had migrated to the state from elsewhere in the world. Some, like Conrad, the head chef at La Fonda, came from as far away as Europe, while the rest had arrived from all parts of the United States.[73] A good many first came for their health or the health of a close relative, and some were still actively "chasing the cure" when they met Ernie Pyle.[74] All but the ten-year-old cowgirl, the health seekers' hostess, and Irene Fisher were males, and all but Oliver La Grone (a Black sculptor in Albuquerque) and Pablo Abeita were white.[75] Hispanics were conspicuously absent from Pyle's list of subjects; only Señor Miranda, the postmaster, Ramon Maes, who owned the local bar, and 84-year-old Francisco Maes, who shared memories of Billy the Kid, were briefly mentioned in Pyle's column on the town of Lincoln.[76]

But it would be unfair to chastise Ernie Pyle for his lack of political correctness in choosing subjects to write about in the 1930s and early

1940s. It is far more important to consider Pyle's subjects in relation to their main qualities, qualities that Pyle both admired and aspired to in his own life. Like the New Mexicans he wrote about, he worked hard to maintain his independence and individualism by remaining on the road where he felt most free. He thought of himself as a largely self-taught reporter, having refined his art long after attending his classes in journalism at Indiana University. Like his subjects, Pyle was not pretentious and, as proven by his columns on the Santa Fe art colony, he could not bear the company of those who were. Personally, he owned few clothes, wore shoes until they were completely worn, lacked expensive taste in liquor, liked to roll his own Bill Durham cigarettes, and was generally frugal.[77]

Pyle also employed self-effacing humor to mask his "inherit modesty."[78] Pyle thus kidded himself when two successive New Mexico governors (including Tingley) named him an honorary colonel "in some kind of civic convulsion," making him twice the colonel of anyone else with the same rank in the state. Pyle wrote that he especially liked going to lunch with his fellow colonels because

They must defer to me in all things. They dare not start eating till I have taken the first bite. When they address me, I insist on being called "Double Colonel." At the end of each sentence, they not only have to say "sir" to me, they have to say "sir-sir".... And of course it would be akin to treason if they ever let me pay the bill.[79]

Without making false claims to privilege, Pyle still hungered for the respect of those he respected most; Pyle measured his increasing success by how many newspapers ran his syndicated column, rather than by his accumulated material possessions. In 1937 these newspapers numbered less than two dozen; by 1941 there were 47.[80]

The same characteristics that Pyle admired most in the New Mexicans he interviewed were the personal characteristics that had helped to make him a successful journalist nationwide. Little wonder that when it came time to choose a state in which to settle, he and Jerry "didn't even have to vote."[81] It had to be New Mexico.

3
WHY NEW MEXICO?

Ernie Pyle's admiration for those he wrote about was only one of the many reasons why he and Jerry decided on New Mexico for their new home. Frequently asked just why they chose New Mexico, Pyle may well have felt like an inn keeper of the Old West who was so inconvenienced by countless questions about his background that he reportedly posted a question and answer sheet with his personal history for all newcomers to read—and stop annoying him.[1] Resorting to a similar solution, Pyle wrote a now-famous article for the *New Mexico Magazine* entitled, "Why Albuquerque?" Written at the request of editor George Fitzpatrick, the article served such a beneficial purpose for Pyle—and Albuquerque—that the reporter refused compensation for his labor.[2]

Pyle began his explanation of "why Albuquerque" with a rather romantic response. Pyle wrote that "probably the main [reason] is simply a deep, unreasoning affection for the Southwest" that began as early as his first trip to the region in 1926. In Pyle's words, his affection for the Southwest was "like being in love with a woman.... You just love her because you love her and you can't help yourself. That's the way we are about the Southwest."[3]

Becoming more specific, Pyle explained that he and Jerry also chose New Mexico because they had "made personal friends" there. He was, of course, referring to Ed and Liz Shaffer and their children, Edward, George, and Stella Mary. Pyle had liked Shafe from the first time they met in 1935. Two years Pyle's senior, Shafe had been born and raised in Kansas, with brief childhood intervals in New Mexico. He had fought bravely in World War I, earning the Army's Oak Leaf Cluster as well as a Purple Heart. Shafe graduated from Northwestern University with a degree in journalism in 1923, before starting his news-paper career at a small town newspaper, the *Lima (Ohio) News*, much like Pyle had started at the *La Porte Herald* in neighboring Indiana.[4]

Still suffering from the aftereffects of mustard gas from the war, Shafe moved to Albuquerque for his health in 1923. He worked for the *Albuquerque Herald* first, but soon moved on to the *New Mexico State Tribune*, later known as the *Albuquerque Tribune*, of the Scripps-Howard newspaper chain. After four years with the *Tribune*, Shafe was promoted to editor in 1927, becoming the youngest editor in the entire Scripps-Howard organization. As editor, he was known for his humorous daily column, the "Pie Line," which he authored under the pen name Ezra Egg. In a more serious vein, he also wrote many fine editorials, including one on the Gallup coal miners' strike of 1933 which won him honorable mention in the Pulitzer Prize competition that year.[5]

Ernie Pyle admired Ed Shaffer because Shafe possessed many of the same attributes that Pyle admired most in those he wrote about in New Mexico. Shafe was, first and foremost, "fiercely independent." Never afraid to "call ... them as he saw them," his famous editorial on the Gallup strike strenuously objected to the sending of National Guard troops to end that labor protest.[6] His editorial of August 31, 1933, declared that while he had little sympathy for the miners' issues, he had "even less ... sympathy with the frantic mobilization of guardsmen to watch over men and women who are peacefully picketing mines, for we believe in the right of workmen to strike." Governor Arthur Seligman, according to Shafe, "remains the tool of the old feudal capitalism accustomed to yell for government in every dispute with [labor]. His conception of the [only] way to end controversy between capital and labor is to involve armed troops."[7] This vehement protest was hardly an isolated event. Shafe's family still recalls their father's thunderous phone conversations with Clyde Tingley, debating one controversial issue or another long into the night. Well aware of these heated debates, Ernie Pyle jokingly cautioned his friend that he'd "probably stand less of a chance of getting shot [at in a war] than in the same town with Mr. T[ingley]."[8]

Next, like others Pyle admired, Shafe was naturally talented both as a journalist and, earlier, as a soldier. Too young to have fought in the First World War, Ernie Pyle looked up to others of his generation who had seen combat and had demonstrated great courage.[9] In Shaffer's case, he was wounded twice in Europe, including at the Battle of Argonne Forest where "he lay in a muddy shell hole for 36 hours before being found by stretcher bearers." Reported killed in action, his hometown newspaper had printed his obituary before news arrived that he had miraculously survived.[10]

Shafe was also well-respected, humble, and as unpretentious as Pyle himself. In typical fashion, he lived in a modest house, seldom spoke of his wartime experiences, and only received his combat awards years later when friends insisted that he complete the required forms. Like Pyle, he shunned the public spotlight and hated all forms of snobbery. Kindred spirits, Shafe and Pyle preferred evenings of intelligent conversation, mixed drinks, and good-natured humor to long nights at garish parties with large, boisterous crowds.[11]

Elizabeth Shaffer befriended Jerry Pyle almost as easily as her husband had befriended Ernie. An accomplished author in her own right, Liz's work appeared in *The New Yorker* and other publications; the Pyles encouraged her efforts with warm praise throughout their friendship.[12] The Pyles also enjoyed the Shaffer children. Childless themselves, they doted over Edward, George, and Stella Mary, sending the "little Shaffers" presents from across the nation and around the world. Stella Mary received a set of ivory dominos from Mexico and a doll from Guatemala, among other interesting gifts. Postcards arrived at the Shaffers' home, as did letters for the whole family and unusual stamps and rocks for "the rock-mad Shaffer children."[13]

In typically humorous fashion, the Pyles played a joke on the Shaffer family when the vagabond couple arrived in Albuquerque bearing gifts in early April 1938. To Liz, "we took a small box full of rocks, each wrapped up in tissue paper like candy." For Shafe, "we took a ginger aile bottle full of water," while Edward received "an old oil can we picked up along the road," George got a stick found in the desert, and Stella Mary opened her package to find a cigar. Always generous, the Pyles followed up their prank by delivering real presents to each good-natured family member.[14]

The Pyles stayed with the Shaffers on several occasions, and Jerry stayed with the Shaffer children at least once while their parents traveled out-of-town. Jerry also accompanied Liz and Stella Mary to the Mayo Clinic in Jerry's home state of Minnesota when it was feared that the Shaffers' daughter might have a brain tumor. Fortunately, the danger proved to be a false alarm.[15] In less critical moments, Liz used her talents as a gourmet cook to prepare special meals for her famous friends, including several during a memorable Christmas holiday in 1936. The Pyles would refer to this refreshing holiday season for years to come.[16] According to Pyle, he and Jerry "never had such a good time anywhere."[17] According to Jerry, there was "No place else in the country where we'd have felt 'at home'—free to be up or down—or where we'd have felt so really included."[18] They would want to be near their closest family friends when they chose to settle down. As Pyle put it in October 1938, "We hardly dare go to Albuquerque, we hate so badly to leave."[19]

The Shaffers were not the only "grand people" who drew Ernie and Jerry Pyle to Albuquerque "like a magnet." Pyle wrote that the city (population 35,449 in 1940) was "still small enough that you always see somebody you know when you go downtown." "You can cash a check almost anywhere ... without being grilled as though you were a criminal," and "after your second trip to a filling station the gas-pumper calls you by name."[20] Long known as a western city with a small-town atmosphere, Albuquerque was a welcome relief compared to the large, impersonal cities the Pyles had known back East.

Pyle was especially pleased because the people of this friendly city were kind enough to know when to "leave you alone."

People in Albuquerque realize that our life and work is one of seeing thousands of people a year all over the world, and that, when we come to Albuquerque to rest, we do want to see a few people, but not thousands. And so they are considerate of us.[21]

The Pyles' problem of dealing with intruding fans had become increasingly difficult by the late 1930s. By the nature of his informal-sounding column, many readers assumed a natural friendship with the couple, taking great liberties with their time and privacy.[22] As Pyle wrote to the Shaffers in October 1939, the *San Diego Sun*

didn't give out where we were staying, still enough got through that it was like being a fugitive in a nightmare with fingers pointing at you and people "just wanting to shake hands" and people wanting "just two minutes" and just half an hour and "just two hours." It was wonderful of course but at the same time it was awful and it really scared the living daylights out of me and I kinda had the sweats at night from being scared of it all....[23] Pyle felt "badly frightened" and "disillusioned with fame" as he left southern California.[24] The situation hardly improved as the Pyles traveled east across the Southwest to towns like Silver City and Lordsburg.

In none of these places did I ever come down from the room, or come in from the outside, but that there were people waiting to see us—just to say how much they enjoy the column. The first night in Silver City we tried to eat in the coffee shop, and never did get to finish our dinner. After gathering my columns I had planned to stay in Silver [City] a couple of days and write them out, but it was impossible—we simply had to leave.[25]

Ernie Pyle did not hold this enthusiastic reception against the people of Silver City or Lordsburg. In fact, he wrote a most complementary column about the former town, saying that it suffered so little class distinction that the only thing that prevented every resident from attending every social function was room enough to fit them all. He seemed particularly impressed that Catholics and Protestants had packed the home of a Jew to witness the marriage of a "popular young Chinese couple," while "some ne'er-do well with a good heart" drew record crowds to his funeral in town.[26]

The Pyles also had fond memories of Lordsburg where one of their favorite photographs of themselves was snapped by businessman Willard E. Holt outside the town's Chamber of Commerce building. Pyle liked the picture so much that he and Jerry featured it on the 250 Christmas cards they had printed in 1939; with typical humor, the saying next to their photo read: "The Rolling Stones wish you lots of Holiday moss."[27] As Pyle told Holt, his only regret was that the "dirty dog" printers cut off the Lordsburg Chamber of Commerce sign when they produced the holiday card.[28] But Pyle recalled Holt's kindness most of all. Unfortunately, the same unmitigating kindness that characterized the residents of towns like Silver City and Lordsburg also wore the Pyles out, forcing them to seek refuge elsewhere.

The Pyles' friends in New York and Washington, D.C., were nearly as demanding of the couple's scarce time and energy. When the Pyles visited New York or stopped by their rented apartment in Washington for rest and relaxation, they often faced their "big-city problem" of imposing friends who typically thought of Ernie Pyle's job as nothing less than a "perpetual holiday."[29] Happy to see the "prodigal sons," acquaintances habitually visited the Pyles at all hours, usually overstaying their welcome, and, worse, encouraging Ernie and Jerry to drink far beyond moderation.[30] The Pyles experienced much the same problem among friends in California.[31] Ironically, relaxing during these brief intervals was so difficult that the Pyles often had to escape their vacations in order to vacation. "It isn't the job that's [killing us]," wrote Pyle, "it's the people and harassment and no time to think."[32] Increasingly exhausted from the strain of work and the imposition of friends, the Pyles searched for a safe haven. Albuquerque, where people "are considerate of us," was the natural choice.

Ernie Pyle also disliked the East because it included "too much of everything," from "too damn many people" to too much violence and too much activity and excitement.[33] As early as the second month of his column's syndication, Pyle wrote of hating New York with its "inhuman tempo," "piled-up skyscrapers," "rude" crowds and rivers of "filth."[34] After seeing two men shot outside a New York hotel in 1940, Pyle declared that "This is a terrible place."[35] Though less scathing, he had few kind words for life in the nation's capital. By 1938 Pyle noticed that his friends in Washington led "a sort of unnatural life ... full of furious sticking to habit, dashing day after day to the same places, serious about the same old things...."[36] In sharp contrast, Pyle found that "Each time, after leaving [the East], I realize that in the West my spirit has been light; I've felt freer and happier."[37] He also felt better able to write "because I'm always in better spirits and more interested out there."[38]

Ernie Pyle particularly liked the "overwhelming warmth of feeling" he encountered in the Southwest's "empty space."[39] After escaping the overbearing attention he received in San Diego, he wrote Shafe that "When we came out of the pass and down into the desert and wide open spaces ..., that ... old empty desert looked so good we could have got out and kissed it."[40] Pyle was sure that the rich benefits he reaped in the Southwest could be enjoyed by others as well. In an unpublished column about the Southwest, Pyle went so far as to predict that

> If it were possible to bring here the millions that live in cities, the lives of caged canaries, giving to each three months of contemplation and real thought in these wide spaces, the human average of this country might be pushed ahead several centuries.[41]

Even urban Albuquerque was more country than city in Pyle's appreciative eyes. After moving to Albuquerque, he wrote of his unobstructed view that stretched "as far as you can see" without being "stifled and smothered and hemmed in by buildings and trees and traffic and people." While only seven minutes from downtown, he still had a "country mailbox instead of a slot in the door," a dirt street in front of his house, and a "tempo of life [that was far] slower than in the big cities." Pyle also wrote of rabbits and quail that wandered through his yard and meadow larks that "sing us awake in the summer dawn." On Sunday afternoons he could "take a ... spin into the [nearby] mountains and see deer and wild turkey" from the road.[42]

Downtown, Albuquerque was free of the "smoke and soot" of eastern cities. Its atmosphere was so relaxed that "you see lots of men on Central Avenue in cowboy boots." Pyle preferred to wear overalls to the Cocina Cantina, the Alvarado Hotel's rather elaborate restaurant, but happily noticed that "nobody raises an eyebrow" when he did. He discovered that Albuquerque's favorite pastime was standing by the railroad tracks outside the Alvarado, watching for the arrival of celebrities on the ten transcontinental trains that went by daily.[43] There weren't any streetcars in Albuquerque, and traffic jams were rare. Despite a "comfortable sense of isolation," Pyle claimed "not [to] suffer from over-isolation." He confidently told his readers in the *New Mexico Magazine* that "people here ... live lives that are complete and full. We want for little, even in the nebulous realm of the mind." Free of most formal or informal restraints, Pyle felt nearly as free as he had felt on the open road. In his phrase, "you can do almost anything you want to, within reason."[44]

Finally, Ernie and Jerry Pyle were attracted to Albuquerque "because the days are warm and the nights are cool." Describing themselves as "hot weather fiends," both hated the cold they experienced in places like New England, Canada, and parts of South America.[45] Both noticed that cold climates adversely affected their spirits to the point that Pyle, suffering a cold spell in December 1938, complained that "nothing interests me, [not] even trying to write a good column."[46] Cold weather affected not only their emotions, but also their health. Pyle's propensity to catch colds (and other illnesses) increased greatly in cold climates, forcing him to remain in bed for days at a time. The reporter claimed to have caught no fewer than seven colds in a fifteen-month period from 1936 to 1937.[47] Pyle in fact claimed "to have been sick in more hotel rooms than any man on earth."[48] These setbacks slowed his writing because "I just can't write when I'm cold," making it necessary for him to catch up in tiring bursts of labor.[49] On November 12, 1938, he reported that he and Jerry both had bad colds in Rio de Janero. "I am very weary," he told his close friend, Paige Cavanaugh, "and seek only a little adobe shack in New Mexico" even if it were "full of rattle-snakes."[50]

These, then, were the main reasons why the Pyles were repulsed by the East and drawn to New Mexico by 1940. But there were other reasons that a very private person like Pyle would never address in print. Actually, most of these other reasons had less to do with New Mexico and its people than with the Pyles and larger events in a troubled world.

Ernie Pyle suffered increasingly dramatic mood swings during his years of almost constant travel. At various times he experienced "dark helpless moods" when "Life looks pretty glum ... and I see less sense to it than I ever did [before]."[51] Some of his gloom was caused by growing older, in what modern therapists now call a mid-life crisis. Turning forty in 1940, he visited his parents' home in Dana and reported to Cavanaugh that "seeing my own folks—so old, so disappointed, so ... helpless— ... it kind of throws me. There's no sense to the struggle, and there's no choice but to struggle."[52]

At other times, Pyle grew depressed because, given his own high standards, he felt "that my stuff at its best is only just barely good enough."[53] While he received great praise from many readers and editors,[54] he was extremely sensitive to criticism in any form, including an article written by fellow-columnist Westbrook Pegler in 1939. Pegler described Pyle as a "tumbleweed reporter blowing this way and that across the land" and writing "pieces [that] are strictly T-bone medium all the time."[55] Pyle may have recognized a grain of truth in this commentary; even he admitted that his work seemed trivial compared to the serious events occurring all around him. In September 1939 he wrote to Cavanaugh that "For the last two weeks I've been so goddam bored writing silly dull columns ... that I think I'm going nuts."[56] On at least one occasion, he seriously thought of quitting his column, settling down, and opening a custom-jewelry business.[57] Liz Shaffer later remembered she and her husband sitting up with the Pyles "until early morning discussing his column. He was tempted to quit several times, and go to work on what he called a 'menial job.'"[58] When he learned that Cavanaugh had built a house in southern California, he told his friend that "I believe you're set for life and have a fine little house and are a mighty happy man. I congratulate you and wished I was in your shoes. For me—there's nothing but misery ahead as far as I can see."[59] While Pyle always bounced back, his mood swings were often so traumatic that they helped cause a serious drinking problem, frequent illnesses, and, perhaps, his long-term impotency.[60] Pyle became convinced that only a long overdue respite would allow him time to think and recover. To friends and relatives he expressed a persistent longing to do little more than sit and read for months at a time—in Albuquerque.[61]

As extreme as Ernie's mood swings became, Jerry's seemed even worse. Increasingly left behind as Pyle traveled to remote regions, Jerry suffered terribly from colds and headaches and deep depression. While Pyle had his work to motivate him, Jerry had little to fall back on when alone. As early as 1937, when Pyle left her while he traveled in the backlands of Alaska, Jerry wrote to the Shaffers that she was "glad for him, since the Alaska trek will do him a lot of good—but sorry for poor *ME*! We've been together so constantly these past few years—or perhaps it's age—for I never used to mind."[62] No better in later separations from Pyle, "sinister moods" drove her to private drinking and to the use of both sedatives and stimulant drugs.[63] In August 1937, Pyle confided in Cavanaugh that Jerry had become "even less interested in living than I am."[64] By mid 1938, Jerry was temporarily committed to a private sanitarium back East.[65]

Jerry's condition had deteriorated to such an extent by 1940 when Pyle left for a trip to London that she complained to the Shaffers about "internal fainting spells" and a "constant jabbing from something in my brain that cut me off from even the small comfort of sleep."[66] As a family friend recalled, doctors

were unable to isolate a specific origin of her trouble. Perhaps there was a remote and forgotten incident or situation of earlier days that bedeviled her subconscious. Perhaps it was something in her relationship with Ernie.... Conceivably Jerry was affected by an unrealized jealousy of Ernie's growing importance; in a way, she had for years been the dominant member of the household, on whom Ernie leaned for comfort and morale; but now, in print at least, she was simply that anonymous "girl who rides with me." Whatever the cause, something malevolent was gnawing at her.[67]

Entangled in his own emotional problems and unschooled in the skills to help resolve her's, Ernie Pyle desperately searched for ways

43

to assist his ailing wife. By 1940 he believed that part of the solution, if not the whole panacea, lay in relocating to New Mexico. On September 17, 1940, he wrote to Paige Cavanaugh that he and Jerry were going to build in New Mexico.

It's foolish and an utter luxury, and yet I have a feeling it is gravely important for us.... Jerry, desperate within herself since the day she was born, has seemed to become more so. I have a feeling that the only possible peace for her, even tho [sic] it may only be temporary, is a new interest and then an opportunity for solitude.... I am terribly afraid for our future as we're going now; if ... New Mexico can offer her a minute of contentment, I'll jump at it.[68]

Less than two weeks later, in a letter to Jerry about his desire to move to New Mexico, Pyle included a paragraph about the editor of the *San Francisco News* who had jumped off the Oakland Bay Bridge shortly after hearing that he'd lost his job. Pyle concluded that William N. Burkhardt's "life was in such a mess it couldn't be straightened out." Pyle may well have been thinking of Jerry's life—and his own—when he wrote these telling words. New Mexico represented an "opportunity for solitude" that might literally save their minds and, ultimately, their lives before they also deteriorated into "such a mess" that they could never be "straightened out."[69]

World events made Pyle's decision to build in New Mexico even more urgent than it might have been during a less complicated period of history. The Second World War had broken out in Europe in 1939, and, while the United States remained officially neutral, it seemed increasingly evident that the country could be drawn into the conflict at any time. The Roosevelt Administration's preparedness campaign of 1940-41 caused Americans to consider their collective fate, while families, including the Pyles, considered their individual best interests. In the spring of 1940 Pyle wrote Shafe that he'd "been so saturated with horror and despondency over [the war] that I couldn't see much point in living. The slaughter has been so terrible and the Allied efforts so discouraging."[70] Jerry shared Pyle's concern "about the war and [its] aftermath, and feels more than ever that we ought to get some property, because we'll likely lose everything else."[71] Given their joint pessimism about the future, the Pyles requested that Shafe "resume your looking around" for property they might purchase before conditions grew much worse.[72]

These, then, were the main reasons for the Pyles' decision to move to New Mexico. In many ways, they were *drawn to* the state: by the nature of the people Pyle interviewed, by a "deep, unreasoning affection," by the close friends they had made, by the considerate residents who generally left them alone, by Albuquerque's small town atmosphere, and by the state's salubrious climate. In other ways, they were *fleeing from* various aspects of their quickly darkening world: from the overly complex East, from Pyle's well-meaning but intrusive fans, from the mood swings that accompanied his arduous job, from the "sinister moods" that increasingly plagued Jerry, and from the rapidly escalating international conflict.

But how could the Pyles trade the freedom they enjoyed on the road for the burdens of home ownership? As late as November 1940 Ernie Pyle used his daily column to list the serious (and less serious) advantages of "all this travel."

> You don't have to make your own beds. You don't have to buy coal. You can make new friends and go on before they find out how dull you are. You don't have to get up at 4:00 a.m. and milk the cows. And then, too, lots of people write us nice letters, and there are even fanatics who thrill me by vowing that there is a certain quality in my writings that on some days actually makes sense.[73]

On another occasion, Pyle wrote that his travel represented an "escape complex." This "cowardly" complex gave him the freedom "not to have to stay and face anything out.... If something happens that isn't pleasant, we can leave, and settle it later by letter ... or just let it go forever."[74] Above all else, Ernie Pyle still enjoyed the thrill of getting up in the morning, packing his bags, filling his car with gas, and "light[ing] out into open country."[75]

Pyle reconciled the glory of this personal freedom with the need to settle down by thinking of his planned new home as "a sort of home plate," a place where he and Jerry "could run to on occasion and then run away from" when the "cloak of responsibility" grew too heavy, and the "sweet taste" of friendship and community "turns to vinegar."[76] According to Pyle, "the house will not change our life, nor our profession .... for we will be here no more than one month of the year."[77] In short, the Pyles sought the best of both worlds: the open road as well as a refuge in the form of a home of their own. After years in which "we were like trees growing in the sky, without roots," the couple yearned for at least temporary stability.[78] The question remained if they could find their coveted balance in humble New Mexico.

4
BUILDING IN NEW MEXICO, 1940-41

Ernie Pyle began the task of building a home in New Mexico by visiting Santa Fe in June 1940. Despite the "nasty" columns he had written about Santa Fe in 1937 and 1938, he had admired the city's beauty, writing in 1939 that the "country around Santa Fe always fills me with an elation that wipes out smaller things."[1] Pyle even liked some members of Santa Fe's often-maligned art colony. Carlos Vierra was described as a "gentle man" whose paintings were the kind Pyle appreciated "because they look like the subject, not what some arty brain 'interprets' them to look like."[2] Sculptor Allan Clark was likewise praised for living in a self-made adobe home, avoiding Santa Fe's elitist social life, and talking about art "in your own language."[3] Moreover, as little as Pyle thought of Ernest Thompson Seton's Institute of Indian Lore, he undoubtedly admired Seton's use of Santa Fe as a "home base" where he spent about half the year when not otherwise booked on lecture tours. Pyle hoped to use his Santa Fe "base" in a similar fashion when not away on writing trips.[4] Most importantly, Ernie Pyle first thought of Santa Fe, rather than Albuquerque or any other town in New Mexico, for Jerry's peace of mind. He wrote to Paige Cavanaugh of a spot near Santa Fe where Jerry had "felt that [if] she could just be there with her books and Piano [sic] and cigarettes and cold coffee, she would never want to leave it again."[5]

Ernie Pyle therefore purchased two and a third acres "of pinon and juniper bush" in a section called Lovato Heights on the outskirts of New Mexico's capital.[6] He seemed pleased with his purchase for $2,100 when he told Jerry of it in a letter of June 28, 1940.[7] However, he soon abandoned the idea of actually building on this land because the cost of constructing even a "mud [adobe] house" appeared far beyond his means.[8] He may have also decided against Santa Fe because the Santa Fe Holding Company, which had sold him his land, soon began using his name to promote land sales in the area. The company's newspaper ads announced that

Ernie Pyle has just bought a homesite in Lovato Heights. Out of all the 48 states, America's most famous traveling columnist chose New Mexico as his very own. And out of all New Mexico, he and Mrs. Pyle chose Lovato Heights, Santa Fe's finest residential area.[9]

Pyle was probably disturbed not only by the commercial use of his name, but also by the public announcement of his land's specific location. As Jerry wrote in a letter to Pyle's family in Dana, the couple had hoped to build a house in New Mexico "with one idea: that we could come here and rest and be by ourselves away from [all] the people."[10] Their goal would be seriously compromised if the location of their secluded haven was known long before its first adobe brick was laid. Rather than selling their newly acquired land, Pyle decided to keep it "merely as an investment."[11]

Discouraged in Santa Fe, Ernie Pyle traveled on to Albuquerque where he had heard that building prices were more reasonable. He was shown land in a newly developed area about three miles from downtown and about half way between the Shaffers' home (near the University of New Mexico) and the municipal airport. As Pyle described it to Jerry, the land was "fairly high on the Mesa [sic], and is really a nice spot." Clearly interested, Pyle wrote Jerry that he "talked and talked" with the developers, and "that night I studied house books and magazines, and drew out just what I think we'd want as a minimum." Fearing that he'd become "kind of house-crazy" and was acting rashly, he decided to simply deposit twenty-five dollars to hold two adjoining lots for forty-five days.[12] Always frugal, Pyle wrote to Cavanaugh of his disgust with building prices. Contractors were said to be "[not] a bit embarrassed about asking $3,500 for a chicken house, or $6,000 for a stupid, boxy little suburban love nest."[13]

Despite his initial trepidation, Ernie Pyle decided to proceed with the construction of a 1,145 square foot house on the land he had admired in Albuquerque. Although he privately described it as "a regular little boxed-up mass production shack in a cheap new suburb," he quickly added that "it's really as big as we will ever need" and had a "swell" corner lot with a terrific view.[14] Pyle wanted a small house that would be easy to maintain, especially while he was away and Jerry was left behind.[15] A larger dwelling might also appear pretentious. According to architect Charles Edman, Pyle chose a standard floor plan and only insisted that his home face west.[16] With the addition of a real fireplace rather than a false one and "horizontal planking" instead of stucco on its exterior walls, the house cost $3,848, land included. Pyle paid $1,000 as a down payment and the balance soon thereafter.[17]

Construction began in the fall of 1940. Busy as ever, the Pyles were not present to witness most of the work. In their absence, Shafe oversaw each phase of the project, visiting the site frequently, sending the Pyles books of samples, and mailing them photos as the house went up. The house was completed so quickly that Jerry suspected that Shafe didn't give construction workers "time to smoke a cigarette between one board and the next." Pyle worried that with the Shaffers there so often "when they tear [the house] down 30 years from now, they'll find a Shaffer kid buried in the concrete."[18] The contractors, Arthur McCollum and Earl Mount, added "a score of little things they weren't obliged to do," and, in the process, built a "minor gem," in Pyle's words.[19] "The firm of Mount and McCollum are a constant source of joy to Jerry," Pyle wrote, "and I don't know what she would have done without them."[20]

Pyle was, in fact, so pleased with the progress of construction that he let McCollum and Mount know that he had no objection to their running "an ad about the house, if it would help any." All he asked was that they post no sign "sticking up day and night" advertising the Pyles' presence.[21] Pyle's recent experience with the Santa Fe Holding Company was undoubtedly still fresh in his memory. There is no record of McCollum and Mount taking Pyle up on his offer, either because they built most of the homes in this part of Albuquerque and hardly needed the endorsement or because they placed the Pyles' need for privacy above their own desire for profit.[22] In fact, the only newspaper advertisement that Mount and McCollum ran from mid November (when Pyle made his offer) to December 31, 1940, stressed their homes' location near a grade school and a park, rather than near Ernie Pyle's new house.[23] For this and other reasons, Mount and McCollum won Pyle's deep respect. They soon became close friends to the newcomers to New Mexico.[24]

Jerry Pyle arrived in Albuquerque in November 1940. She stayed with the Shaffers while finishing touches were put on her house and while the Pyles' many books and meager furniture arrived from Washington, D.C., where they'd been stored. Jerry's piano (a gift from Ernie early in their marriage) also arrived, to be placed in its designated spot, the dining alcove.[25] Grateful to the Shaffers for all their help, Jerry wrote to Ernie's family in Dana that Shafe and his family were "faithful friends .... always ready to do anything for us ... and doing much more than they should."[26] Once moved into their new home, Jerry spent the winter of 1940-41 fixing the place up for Pyle's anticipated return. Her mother came from Minnesota to help the novice housekeeper for several months.[27]

Given their susceptibility to dramatic mood swings, it was perhaps inevitable that both Ernie and Jerry Pyle experienced ambivalent feelings about their new home. Although he initially wrote of "itch[ing] to be out there [to] putter around" the place, by February 1941 Pyle wrote to Jerry about a fear that new houses might someday block their western view, causing them to grow disillusioned with New Mexico; as he put it, "I'd hate to have my favorite state turn to gall."[28] Jerry's attitude was predictably worse. As early as October 1940 Pyle told Paige Cavanaugh that Jerry had already "lost all interest in the house" and was "merely going out [to help move in] because somebody has to."[29]

Days later Jerry revealed the depths of her mental depression and the impact it had on her feelings regarding the first house she and Ernie had ever owned. According to Jerry,

to pretend that I give one solitary good god damn about a shack or a palace or any other material consideration in this world, [sic] would be to foise upon everybody at all interested, [sic] the greatest gold-brick insult a low mind could conceive. I've no doubt I'll go thru all the motions of doing what must be done. I'll probably even double-hem, and french-seam the window curtains .... and Oh and Ah about every small and thoughtful detail to the complete satisfaction of Messrs. M[ount] & M[cCollum]. And if I live through that, I'll Know [sic] I'm good. For the truth is that the situation seems to me as diabolically ironical as any ever devised.[30]

Jerry's emotional condition only worsened in the fall of 1940 as Pyle made plans to travel to Europe for his first look at the war. Bored with "writing silly dull columns" by September 1939, he wrote to Cavanaugh that he wanted "to get over there as a war correspondent or something so bad [sic]" that he was "about to burst."[31] Always disappointed that he had not fought in the First World War, Pyle was determined to participate in the current conflict in one way or another. This was hardly because he harbored a romantic view of war. He dreaded being drafted and was "saturated with horror" long before he ever crossed the Atlantic to witness the bloodshed first-hand;[32] as early as September 1939 he predicted an even "longer and more terrible war than the [First] World War."[33] Shortly before his departure for England in November 1940 he confessed that he was "scared half to death," yet insisted to the Shaffers that "something inside tells me I've just got to go."[34]

Jerry Pyle also dreaded her husband's involvement in the war. She greeted his early interest with silence that Pyle described as an "unspoken stalemate."[35] Pyle wrote that Jerry was so "terribly upset about the war" that "she says she will jump out of a high window if I go."[36] But soon, "out of clear sky," Jerry announced that she had accepted the inevitable.[37] Overtly "mighty brave" about his departure, she was internally "badly upset and really grieving."[38] Pyle had hoped that the couple's new house might distract her, especially in his absence. But this therapy only worked for short intervals as Jerry grew increasingly isolated in spirit and mind.

Distressed, Ernie Pyle sailed for Europe on the *S.S. Exeter* in late November 1940. Just prior to his departure, he wrote to Shafe to disclose his financial condition "in case anything should happen." He listed his limited assets, including three life insurance policies, and proudly added, "We don't owe a cent to anybody in the world." He cautioned his friend "[not] to show this to Jerry, for it would make her feel badly."[39]

Ernie Pyle survived his first sojourn to the war zones of Europe, remaining in Great Britain from December 1940 until March 1941. While far from actual ground fighting, he experienced the terror caused by German bombings over London in the Battle of Britain.[40] Typically, his columns focused on human interest stories, although no one could accuse him of writing "trivial travelogues" any longer. Instead, Pyle wrote of English rationing, wrecked houses, burned factories, long black-outs, and frightening bomb shelters. In a particularly memorable column, he described one such underground shelter filled with

poor, opportunityless people lying in weird positions against cold steel, with their clothes on, hunched up in blankets, lights shining in their eyes, breathing fetid air—lying there far underground like rabbits, not fighting, not even mad, just helpless, scourged, weakly waiting for the release of another dawn.[41]

The reporter's personal descriptions of war-torn London were so well received back home that his readership skyrocketed by fifty percent. Admirers, led by Roy Howard and Eleanor Roosevelt, thanked him for "doing a grand job," and many of his best columns were published as a book entitled *Ernie Pyle in England*.[42] Pyle dedicated the book to "That Girl Who Waited" and donated a third of his royalties to a British war relief fund. *Ernie Pyle in England* was nearly sold out the first day it went on sale in Albuquerque. By November 1941, 500 books had been purchased in the city. Early sales were equally impressive across the United States.[43]

But Pyle grew weary after only a few months abroad. He "almost froze in ... hotels with no heat" and complained to Cavanaugh of being so "lonesome, homesick, ... and generally crotchety" that he resorted to drinking more, referring to liquor his "wartime stimulant" on his lists of expenses.[44] Exhausted from the constant bombings and hard work, he wrote to Jerry that "All I want to do is sit in Albuquerque about two weeks and not write anything."[45] He looked forward to seeing their "new little mansion" and only feared that the United States would enter the war while he was in London, cutting off trans-Atlantic travel and forcing him to "be here for the duration."[46] Fortunately, the United States did not enter the war for several months. Unfortunately, tragic personal news arrived in a telegram from Jerry: Ernie's mother had died of cancer in Dana.[47] Pyle flew home to Indiana to pay his respects. From there he left for Albuquerque to see Jerry and their new house in New Mexico.

Ernie Pyle wrote a series of columns about his return to Albuquerque and his first impressions of his recently completed home on Girard Avenue. He wrote of flying in at night, "rush[ing] the dark tops of the Sandias and drop[ping] down over the fantastic lights of the valley." He wrote of a friend, undoubtedly Shafe, who met him at the airport and drove him the short distance to the knoll Pyle had picked out months before. He wrote of finding "a little white house" on that knoll, a house with a light on the porch and a bell on the door. He rang the bell and "thought crazily to myself, 'I own that damn bell, what do you think of that?'"[48]

> The lady of the house came to the door, and bade me enter and divest myself of travel dust, ... while she prepared a potion of encouragement for my weary spirits and a spot of sedative for my confused brain. And as the clouds of bewilderment began to clear away, I saw that I was home ... and the lady in residence was that once familiar Girl Who Now Has Not Ridden With Me for Six Months.[49]

Pyle described how "That Girl" had spent a winter in which she had "experimented and moved and shoved things about ... and pounded and bought and created" so that "When at last I came, I entered a house warm with being lived in." Pyle gradually felt less like an intruder and more at home on that first night in their first house together.[50]

Pyle wrote a second column to describe the eclectic artifacts Jerry had used to decorate the interior of their "little white house." The couple had not accumulated many material goods over the years, but they had acquired various personal souvenirs in the course of their many travels. Pyle wrote that until then they "could do nothing with possessions except send them to storage." Now, "for the first time, ... we have all our gadgets from [everywhere] around us." A black and white *serape* from southern Mexico covered their bed, while a *machete* from the jungles of Central America hung on a wall. A spotted seal-skin from Alaska adorned another wall, and a "brightly painted, monster-faced wooden mask" from Guatemala "stare[d] down from the bookshelves." The "saucy bust of a bush Negro girl," sculptured by a convict in French Guinea, sat atop Jerry's piano. Fragments of German bombs, the "latest tokens of distant places," rested on their living room mantle. All were considered "small treasures." Pyle called his wife's thoughtful efforts "practically miraculous"; everywhere he turned he found a memorable artifact, a comfortable chair, a "footstool to drop onto, ... a book to read, or a window that frames a masterpiece of nature."[51]

Ernie Pyle truly enjoyed his life in Albuquerque in the spring and early summer of 1941. Although he complained about New Mexico's cold spring winds and about a terrible sandstorm that damaged his new Pontiac, he soon fixed his car and praised the state's warm summer climate.[52] Referring to Albuquerque as a place "where you can do what you please," Pyle told his readers that he "pleased to stay dirty" for days on end. He announced that he wore overalls for an entire three-week stretch, including on Sundays and to parties, of which there were only two. He also wore a ten-gallon Stetson hat, noting that he defiantly refused to take it off even while in the house. Never claiming to be a gardener, he said that the only thing he ever grew successfully in Albuquerque was a sparse new mustache on his upper lip.[53]

Ernie Pyle had planned to read many books in his leisure time, and he consumed his share, but other activities occupied most of his days and nights.[54] Having befriended Earl Mount of the construction company that built his house, Pyle joined Mount on short excursions; on a drive to the Jemez Mountains they encountered a rattlesnake which they shot with Earl's .22 pistol, although Pyle needed fifteen shots to finally kill the slithering target. Back in Albuquerque, the Pyles enjoyed a small circle of friends, including the Shaffers, who lived less than a mile to the north, and the Mounts, who lived less than half a mile to the south. Pyle became especially close to Earl Mount (who bet—and consistently lost—wagers on croquette matches), Mount's daughter, Shirley (who played soothing music on her piano), and Mount's wife, Eva (who good-naturedly cooked him ham and eggs when he came by in the early morning).[55]

Other new friends included Dan Burrows, George Baldwin, James Toulouse, and Diego Abeita of the *Tribune* staff plus "Barney" Livingston of the Associated Press.[56] Artist Carl von Hassler was also important. Thirteen years Pyle's senior, von Hassler had been born in Germany where he received his early training as an artist. At 22 the painter immigrated to New York's art colony in Greenwich Village. After serving in the U.S. Army during the First World War, von Hassler moved to Albuquerque in the early 1920's, opening one of Old Town's first art studios and establishing a name for himself by painting many well-received works. Specializing in Indian scenes and adobe villages, his murals and paintings were prominently displayed in the Franciscan Hotel, the Alvarado Hotel, the KiMo Theatre, and the First National Bank. Long a familiar figure in Albuquerque, he was easily recognized by his black beret, heavy German accent, Old World manners, and "genial but ... outspoken" nature.[57] Von Hassler was especially outspoken when it came to the Santa Fe art colony, a clique that never accepted the German painter as an equal. Dismayed by the poor location his paintings were assigned at a Santa Fe exhibit, von Hassler reportedly gathered up his work and left rather than tolerate such rude treatment in the state capital.[58]

By the time Ernie Pyle arrived in Albuquerque, von Hassler was known as the "dean of the Albuquerque art colony."[59] But the artist's popularity was of little interest to Pyle who liked Carl von Hassler less for his fame than for his shared taste for hard liquor and distaste for pretenders of the art world. More esthetically, Pyle also admired von Hassler's realistic landscapes of New Mexico, the only style of painting the reporter seemed to appreciate, if not actually buy.[60]

Unfortunately, Pyle did more than his share of social drinking "and raising hell" with several companions.[61] Years later, Earl Mount recalled Pyle coming "down to our house at any old time, [including as early as] 4 o'clock in the morning. And then we'd have a couple of drinks."[62] The pair continued to drink while playing croquet on Mount's front lawn.[63] Wisely, when Pyle drank with Ed Shaffer he and Shafe often recruited Shafe's oldest son to chauffeur them from tavern to tavern in and around Albuquerque.[64] By April, Pyle could contentedly report to Cavanaugh that "Geraldine's [liquor] cellar is well-stocked, I'm in overalls, ... and everything seems pretty nice."[65]

Pyle stayed busy in these various ways, but the activity that occupied the greatest part of his time was building. In his words, he had caught a bad case of "building fever" in 1941.[66] He may have been susceptible to this fever because he had missed out on the actual construction phase of his home. Like several of the New Mexicans he had written about in the 1930s, he fully realized that the process of building was often more meaningful than the product itself. Whatever the explanation, Pyle eagerly built a small terrace in his backyard, "crude" pieces of furniture for his house, and a 280-foot long picket fence around his yard to the south.[67] Ernie Pyle responded to facetious rumors that his fence boards were cut and painted at a cousin's lumberyard and assembled by "a crew of Mexicans" by asserting that he had no such relative in the lumber business and "there was never a Mexican on the place." He had done the work himself, with minor assistance from Shirley Mount and a local carpenter named Troy.[68] Pyle proudly reported that his fence had required 30 postholes, 900 to 1,000 pickets, and over 400 nails. It took two and a half weeks to complete the task, during which time he claimed to have "never hit my thumb once."[69]

When Eleanor Roosevelt made "kind remarks" about Pyle's column and invited him to "drop in ... and sit with her before the Hyde Park fireplace," he suggested that she "drop past Albuquerque some day and help me build fence." The First Lady "wrote back and said that her schedule wouldn't be bringing her west" during Pyle's "allotted days of laziness."[70] Undaunted, Pyle told his readers that the result of his strenuous labor was not only "the finest fence in Albuquerque," but also a small bump on his forearm which, with proper care, had "every indication of turning ... into a real genuine muscle."[71] By July 1941 he announced in his column that he was so "crazy to make things with boards and nails and a hammer" that he was willing to "sell our new house for twice what we paid for it" so he could "buckle right in and build a bigger house upon the hill."[72] Receiving no serious response to this less-than-serious offer, he turned to a new project that fall: overseeing Earl Mount's conversion of his attached garage into a guest bedroom and bath. With typical good humor, Pyle "launched" his completed new addition with a bottle of champagne.[73]

While able to enjoy a much-needed rest from distant travel, Ernie Pyle was still committed to writing his syndicated column six days a week. Many of these columns described his new life in New Mexico, from building fences to buying a new Pontiac because he felt "afflicted with war hysteria and figure cars will cost a lot more pretty soon, and for all I know they might even quit making automobiles and start making buggies again."[74] Pyle also wrote about the war-preparedness boom in Albuquerque. He especially noted the rapid construction of a large new Army air base near the Albuquerque airport not far from his home. Over two thousand men had been hired to build the base, including skilled workers who were "rounded up from all over the state" and cowboys who "came in off the range for a few weeks of good pay."[75] Once the base was completed, troops began arriving in large numbers by train and car; 403 officers and enlisted personnel had appeared by April 10, 1941. Another 2,740 were anticipated as soon as the Army made plans to move "its great bombers away from the [Pacific] coast, where they would be too vulnerable to attack."[76]

Pyle wrote that Albuquerque welcomed the Army "with open arms" because the base's construction spelled "boom times" that promised to end the Great Depression in the city. But boom times did not necessary spell good times in the long run. As a newcomer who had come to Albuquerque to escape larger cities of the East, Pyle suggested that Albuquerque might someday "think back to the days when it didn't have [so many] troops" and such rapid growth. But for now the growth could not be stopped; it was clearly necessary for the country's preparedness. As a result, Pyle saw cars with Michigan license plates parked in front of his local grocery store and cars with California plates parked at his local post office. He seemed particularly amused by the fact that "Tourists used to come to Albuquerque to stare at brightly-garbed Indians on Central Avenue, the main business street. But today the Indians stand and stare at new white men, in brown [military] uniforms." Pyle wistfully concluded that "Everything is changing."[77]

Ernie Pyle was also struck by the vast differences he observed between life in peacetime New Mexico and life as he had seen it in embattled England. As he had written in the epilogue to *Ernie Pyle in England*, Albuquerque seemed "so remote from [the] turmoil" that "the ghostly rustle of a falling bomb can surely be only something you dreamed once in a nightmare."[78] Rather than bombs and sirens and fires, only the sound of his own hammer and saw broke the silence of his otherwise serene neighborhood. Although he was still self-conscious about lighting cigarettes at night (a practice banned during English blackouts), he quickly got more interested in fence-building and domestic life than in the war.[79]

Pyle's interest in the complicated foreign conflict thus faded in peaceful New Mexico. With no radio in his house, Pyle "didn't have to listen to the breathless newscasts" transmitted from Europe; claiming that he read little more than the headlines in Shafe's *Albuquerque Tribune*, he didn't have to engage in discussions "about what was happening and what we should do about it." Pyle kept his war souvenirs stacked on his mantle for guests to inspect, but he had no immediate plans to recross the Atlantic and resume his role as a foreign war correspondent.[80] He was simply content to enjoy his home in Albuquerque.

5

DARK CLOUDS GATHER, 1941-42

Despite months of relative happiness far from war-torn England, dark clouds soon formed over the Pyles' home in Albuquerque. The first of these clouds threatened the couple's coveted privacy. Unlike their eastern friends, those in New Mexico respected their need for solitude. Hundreds told Pyle that they were glad he'd returned from England alive, but were otherwise as considerate of his daily privacy as ever.[1] Jerry had, in any case, turned down all invitations and refused to return all phone calls since the day she moved in so that when "Ernie gets here he won't be bothered."[2] Once home, Pyle requested that his family in Indiana not give his Albuquerque address "to anybody except personal friends."[3] The couple guarded their privacy by going so far as to leave their phone disconnected for incoming calls.[4] Both the *Albuquerque Journal* and the *Albuquerque Tribune* cooperated by not mentioning Pyle's arrivals or departures in the press.[5]

But Pyle's long-sought privacy dwindled as his fame as a journalist soared. Tourists began traveling down Girard Avenue's unpaved surface and arriving at Pyle's door as early as 6:30 a.m. The Pyles soon learned never to answer their door before breakfast. At least one "tourist load" appeared each day, and many insisted on having their pictures taken with the famous reporter.[6] Despite the silence of local newspapers, Pyle complained that "word got around somehow, and the damn place is like a museum. People drive around and around, and park out front and stare, and even come look in the window."[7] Exasperated, Pyle declared that he felt like he'd "practically become a goldfish."[8] When alone, Jerry "practically barricaded herself in the new house" largely because "tourists come by, bring their cameras, want to get into the house and in general carry on like tourists."[9] Ironically, after building a house to escape from crowds and allow him to work in seclusion, Pyle was soon forced to "go downtown to a hotel and hide in order to get my writing done."[10] Jerry had done her best "to fend off the callers," wrote Pyle to a relative, "but I just finally had to leave."[11] He regretted ever having mentioned his new house in his national column.[12] But it was too late. The price of fame proved dear.

Darker, more ominous clouds also appeared for the Pyles and their future. On a summer visit to the Cavanaughs in Los Angeles, Jerry became so distraught and nervous that she flew home to Albuquerque, leaving a note but no reason for her abrupt departure. Returning to Albuquerque from California, Pyle found Jerry drunk in their new house.[13] He wrote Cavanaugh that "from there she went on down," going "completely screwball" and even "tried the gas" one night.[14] Desperate, he drove her to a Denver hospital for a thorough physical examination, although she hated it "ferociously." After ten days of clinical testing, her doctors found nothing physically wrong and, amazingly, considered psychological treatment to "be futile and possibly dangerous." Released in relatively "good shape and good spirits," Jerry flew back to Albuquerque while Pyle renewed his travels, heading east alone.[15] Exhausted, Pyle wrote the Shaffers that he had "to lie down awhile both morning and afternoon. And the columns never came harder, or were any lousier." Referring to a Scripps-Howard editors' meeting Shafe had attended, Pyle "bet [that] all the editors put together aren't half as confused about life in general as I am."[16]

But the worst was yet to come. Seldom hearing from Jerry over a five-week period, Pyle wrote to Liz Shaffer and expressed his growing concern that "she's getting on three- and four-day benders" or had experienced "such a change ... [in] personality that she can't force herself to do anything."[17] "That letter," according to Lee Miller, "saved Jerry's life."[18] Shafe explained that on receiving their friend's letter we went over Saturday [August 30, 1941] and tried to get in but the door was locked and there was no answer to the bell.... Finally I went to her window and got tough, saying "If you don't let us in I'm going to tear this Goddamn house down." That awoke her and she came to the door and let us in. She said she had a terrible headache, [and] didn't want to see us.... But we both had some kind of hunch.[19]

The Shaffers checked on their friend several times that weekend, but by Sunday Jerry "was worse again so we decided that Liz should stay all night with her." About 5:00 a.m. Liz found her hemorrhaging severely and called the doctor. By the time Shafe hurried over "they were taking her away in an ambulance."[20] Hearing this news, Pyle rushed home from Canada, arriving "tired and worried as hell" on September 3.[21] On arrival, he learned that "an ulcer had developed without giving any indication of itself, and it ate into a blood vessel and she lost a good deal of blood."[22] As Pyle told Cavanaugh, "In another hour she would have been gone. If Liz hadn't stayed, they would simply have found her dead next day when they came to the house. The doctor says that he has never seen anyone so nearly dead and come through it."[23] Jerry's serious condition was treated, and she was soon released from the hospital—again.[24]

Ernie Pyle was left to ponder his wife's physical and mental state. Privately, he admitted that Jerry had been "a psychopathic case" for over a decade. In fact,

you might say [she has] a triple personality—one side of utter charm and captivation for people she cares nothing about; one side of cruelty and dishonesty toward the few people she does care about; and another side of almost insane melancholy and futility and cynicism when she is alone, which is her true personality. She is a Jekyll and Hyde; even when not drinking she changes from one mood or personality to another....And without any interest, she frequently gets to wallowing in boredom and melancholy and hopelessness, and that leads to progress from normal drinking to colossal drinking.[25]

With advice from various family members and Albuquerque doctors, including William R. Lovelace ("one of the finest doctors and finest men in the Southwest"), Ernie Pyle attempted to have Jerry committed to a private institution for treatment.[26] Jerry, in the "autocratic way with which she has ruled ever since I've known her," flatly refused to go. Faced with this ongoing domestic crisis, Pyle saw his choices as either abandoning her (which "I couldn't and wouldn't do") or "stick[ing it out] here .... both for her and because I myself am in no mental condition to resume work now." Pyle chose the latter course, taking a three-month unpaid leave from Scripps-Howard and beginning what he called "the toughest battle I'll ever have to face."[27]

Tragically, Ernie Pyle lacked the training to fight this dreaded battle. Staying with Jerry, or having her sister or a nurse stay day and night, made little difference. Urging her to read more or become more involved in the house made no appreciable impact. She entered St. Joseph Hospital in Albuquerque on two occasions, but left in only slightly better condition, despite the strenuous efforts of Mother Superior Margaret Jane Lalor and her fellow Sisters of Charity.[28] By November 1941 Pyle wrote Cavanaugh that the situation had become "so discouraging I don't dare think about it." Jerry was described as "so off balance [that] I have run out of possible ideas for approaching it. Nobody can help her, and she won't, or can't."[29] Discouraged and too weak to serve as a good role model for his wife, Pyle reported that he spent much of his time drinking. In his succinct words, "Everything looks blue."[30]

The only bright spot to appear on the Pyles' dismal horizon arrived in the form of a small pet. In yet another attempt to distract Jerry with a consuming interest, Pyle had brought her a Shetland shepard while on a trip to Washington, D.C., in November 1941.[31] Pyle fondly remembered a shepard he had had as a boy in Indiana, a pet he once eulogized as "kindlier, more understanding, more faithful, [and] more intelligent" than any human he had ever met.[32] Pyle hoped Jerry's new pet might share these same admirable qualities. To his joy, the Shetland did. Pyle described the animal as "sweeter than hell," and Jerry reportedly "took to the dog in ... colossal fashion."[33] When he resumed his columns, he told his readers that the dog (named Cheetah because "Jerry always wanted a real cheetah"[34])

> won't play with her rubber rats and won't lie on her dog-mattress and won't eat her dog biscuits. All she wants to do is either sit on our laps or else get out in the big south lot and scamper and play all day and half the night. Actually the other night That Girl, who should have been snug in her convalescent bed, was out there in the yard in the cold moonlight of 2 a.m. playing catch-the-ball with this beast, just because it woke up and seemed restless in the house.[35]

60

Pleased that Jerry enjoyed her new pet, but concerned because Cheetah showed more affection for him than for Jerry, Pyle went so far as to buy a second dog for his wife in December 1941. In sharp contrast to the toy shepard, this second pet, called Piper, was a Great Dane that was "already waist high and weighed 100 pounds" at seven months.[36] The two dogs got along well, while "That Girl" was said to be "both horrified and riotously delighted with her strange new team."[37] As Pyle told the Shaffers, Jerry seemed "completely wrapped up in the dogs—she writes about almost nothing else."[38]

But even this bit of happiness was short-lived. By the end of December both dogs were sick, and by late January 1942 Piper had died of what Pyle described as a brain infection.[39] For this and other reasons, Jerry wrote of lacking "strength and energy" and soon began drinking heavily again.[40] A registered nurse who stayed with Jerry during the day recalls that her patient was normally "charming," but remained locked in her room most of the time, often refused to eat meals, and had a local store deliver liquor when the nurse was away from the house or off-duty.[41] By March Pyle told Cavanaugh that Jerry was drinking ten quarts of liquor a week and was, of course, in terrible condition.[42] She now spoke of wanting a child as a possible means to recovery, but Pyle disagreed, saying they were too old and too neurotic. He also claimed that it was physically impossible since "the power of sex had gone from me."[43]

Meanwhile, Ernie Pyle had resumed his column and traveled to California where he experienced "a constant[,] almost desperate depression."[44] He drank more, described his column writing as "daily torture," and underwent "agonizing and cruel" treatments in the "faint hope of repairing myself [sexually]."[45] Lonely, he was said to have had a brief platonic affair in San Francisco.[46] He and Jerry were clearly drifting apart. By March 1942 he wrote the Shaffers that "what affection there is left between us is only one that comes in bursts of sentimentalism about old times and long years of wearing the same shoe."[47] Finally, after not hearing from Jerry for three weeks, he wrote her a frank, heartfelt letter which said, in part,

I have waited and waited, but the letters you said were on the way never came.... I can't attempt any longer to know what motivates you in any direction, or what you really want from life. We've done everything as you wished it done, and apparently all in vain. You always said you needed to have me in your background, but now obviously you no longer do. So I'm ready to call the whole thing off if you are. Maybe a drastic change or a fresh start would give you strength and interest. It might send me up or down, I don't know which, but I can't carry on much longer under the present state of turmoil.... [O]ur old companionship is gone—revived only in our thoughts and in waves of sentimentalism—and possibly we might both be less burdened if we ceased to carry the empty carcass.... Actually we have contributed nothing to each other in two years.... There must be some solution soon for both of us, or we'll both collapse completely.[48]

Pyle closed his letter by saying that its words had been written "with a heartbreak."[49] But the message was clear: he wanted a divorce. As he put it in another letter, "I've looked and searched in a million directions, and I can see nothing but that we're trapped. I can't see any way out for us."[50]

Many, including Jerry's doctors, her mother, and sister ("Poe" Jones, a trained nurse), concurred with Pyle's difficult decision. Even Earl Mount, who had been most optimistic about Jerry's recovery, thought that her case was nearly hopeless.[51] In Pyle's view, the divorce was "an experiment on the gamble that it might shock [Jerry] into realization that she had to face life like other people.... It wasn't a divorce of hate and was based on the premise that if Jerry would ... get to work and cure herself, we could some day be remarried."[52]

The Pyles were, therefore, divorced in Judge Albert R. Kool's Albuquerque courtroom in April 1942. Jerry stayed at home while Ernie represented them both, pleading incompatibility. According to Pyle's attorney, Joseph L. Dailey, he had "never saw anybody so distressed" over a divorce as Pyle was that day.[53] The terms of their divorce gave Jerry their house and Ernie their land in Santa Fe, with their savings split evenly. Jerry was also to receive alimony of thirty-five dollars a week over the next year and a half.[54]

But telling Jerry to "get to work and cure herself" was as unrealistic an expectation as thinking that a house or reading or pets could solve Jerry's deep-rooted problems. It would take far more than a strong will or temporary activities to occupy her restless mind and cure her ills. Nor could most doctors help. Indeed, it is unlikely that any amount of care or therapy could assist her, given the limited state of psychiatric knowledge in the 1940s. Predictably, Jerry fell apart again within weeks of the divorce. A friend who had not seen her in two years said that she looked like "she had aged a decade." She was "haggard, terribly tense, and given to tears—though she tried to put up a front."[55]

Notified of Jerry's deteriorating condition, Pyle sought help from friends and relatives. Pyle turned to Earl Mount who, along with Jerry's sister, arranged to have Jerry put under sedation and taken by train to the Woodcroft Sanitarium in Pueblo, Colorado. Pyle declared that "It should have been done long ago, but I never had the heart or the will power over Jerry.... As for me," he told Cavanaugh, "I'm lower than all your gloom periods put together. I abhor the thought of starting to work again, ... of doing anything."[56] Leaving Albuquerque within days after his divorce, Pyle was "so ... emotional that I could only drive quickly out of town, without looking right or left." He stopped in Clovis to write a note to the Shaffers, apologizing for being so upset that he hadn't said good-bye. He closed by saying that he couldn't write more because "I'm feeling low."[57]

By all measures, the Pyles' personal lives seemed in shambles as yet another ominous cloud settled over their future in late 1941. After months of preparedness, the United States finally entered World War II on December 7, 1941. Ironically, Ernie Pyle had scheduled a trip to the Orient as he resumed writing after his three-month hiatus.[58] Finalizing plans for his overseas voyage, he was still in Albuquerque when Japanese planes launched their surprise attack on Pearl Harbor. Pyle wrote Cavanaugh that the residents of Albuquerque were "jittier than hell" when they learned of the attack and finally faced the war they had anticipated, but hardly wanted.[59] It was one thing to prepare for war with the opening of a new air base and the creation of many new jobs that helped end the Great Depression. It was quite another matter to face the dim prospect of war itself, with all the danger and sacrifice it would entail.

New Mexicans were especially anxious because over a thousand of their friends and relatives had recently arrived in the Philippine Islands as members of the 200th Coast Guard Artillery Regiment. News came that the Japanese had attacked American forces in the Philippines within hours after their initial attack on Pearl Harbor.[60] As a result, Pyle reported that "Everybody's chin is a yard long" and "some are scared to death."[61] Others, including Charles Edman, who had designed Pyle's floorplan, volunteered to serve in the new war as early as Monday, December 8.[62]

After sitting "around Albuquerque at loose ends" and "getting jittier and gloomier by the moment," Pyle headed for the West coast to resume his column writing.[63] By January 20, 1942, he wrote to the Shaffers from Portland that he had "terrible periods of depression about the war. Last night I actually dreamed of Jap dive-bombers. If we win at all, it's going to be many years from now. And what all of us will go through between now and then isn't pleasant to think about."[64] His depression regarding Jerry and the war continued into March as he pondered his future plans. He considered quitting his column and going "somewhere as a regular correspondent for S[cripps]-H[oward], radioing back pieces when and if I could." He also thought of joining the Army or just letting "the draft board ... settle the whole thing for me" since he did not intend to seek a draft deferment.[65] He wrote to Jerry about his doing "some kind of defense work" or accepting an offer from a friend in the Roosevelt Administration who had mentioned that he could "dig up something for me to do in Washington."[66] In what seemed like his least appealing alternative, he wrote of continuing "for years just doping around" writing columns as he'd done for years "until sanity gives out completely."[67] Faced with these several poor options, he confessed that "there is nothing but confusion in my mind about everything.... I wish I could go and DO something. Either fight or retire from everything or something."[68]

Interestingly, Pyle did not include work as a war correspondent on his list of serious career options in the spring of 1942. This omission was hardly an oversight. He continued to believe that war correspondents wrote exclusively about troop movements, campaign maneuvers, and similar large-scale military strategy. He apparently thought of his earlier work in London as simply a foreign extension of his regular column, albeit under most unusual circumstances. He was, therefore, willing to return to England in mid 1942 less to don a war correspondent's uniform (in which he always felt rather silly), but because Scripps-Howard hoped that a foreign trip would attract new interest in his syndicated column.[69] Such a trip, with anticipated stops in Africa and either India or China, had been considered earlier, but now he would venture to the Orient by traveling east rather than west.[70]

Such a trip had the added advantage of taking him far from Jerry and the scene of their recent divorce. He truly believed that, having attempted everything else he could think of, it was time to let her fight her illness alone. As he put it in a letter to Jerry,

> there is only one thing left for each of us ... and that's for each of us to buck himself up and do his job and stand on his own feet until we gain a new sense of vitality through each one's own pride of victory over himself, or else just completely go to hell in a hand-basket.[71]

No more realistic than his other efforts to deal with Jerry's tragic problems, Pyle wrote a farewell note from New York which succinctly summarized what impact he hoped his leaving might have on her life. "Be my old Jerry when I come back," he pleaded. "I love you."[72]

Ernie and Jerry Pyle's favorite photo of themselves, taken outside the Lordsburg, New Mexico, Chamber of Commerce building and used on their 1939 Christmas card with the words: "The Rolling Stones wish you lots of Holiday moss." Photograph by Willard E. Holt. Courtesy of the Museum of New Mexico, #138658.

Ernie Pyle sitting on the Four Corners marker where New Mexico, Arizona, Utah, and Colorado meet, 1939. His 1936 Dodge convertible is parked to the left. Courtesy of the Museum of New Mexico,#128927.

The Shaffers and Jerry Pyle
outside the Shaffer family home
on Girard Avenue, Albuquerque.
Left to right, Edward H.
("Shafe") Shaffer, Liz Shaffer,
and Jerry with George and Stella
Mary in front (oldest son,
Edward D., missing). Courtesy
of Edward D. Shaffer.

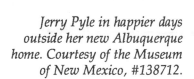

Jerry Pyle in happier days
outside her new Albuquerque
home. Courtesy of the Museum
of New Mexico, #138712.

*Ernie and Jerry Pyle at play
on the lawn of the only
home they ever owned.
Courtesy of the Museum of
New Mexico, #138713.*

*Ernie and Jerry Pyle rolling their own cigarettes outside their home at 700
Girard Avenue. Photograph by Ferenz Fedor. Courtesy of the Museum of
New Mexico, #138783.*

Ernie and Jerry Pyle enjoying their panoramic western view. Courtesy of the Museum of New Mexico, #161825.

Ernie explained that he liked his Albuquerque home in part "because we have a country mailbox instead of a slot in the door". Photograph by Ferenz Fedor. Courtesy of the Museum of New Mexico, #128919.

*Ernie Pyle and his
favorite pet, Cheetah.
Photograph by Bob
Landry of* Life *maga-
zine. Courtesy of the
Museum of New Mexico,
#130793.*

*Ernie and Jerry Pyle
with Cheetah in their
living room, 1944.
Photograph by Bob
Landry. Courtesy of
the Museum of New
Mexico, #161826.*

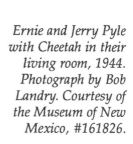

Ernie Pyle at work in his Albuquerque den with Englishman David Low's anti-German political cartoon on desk. Photograph by Ferenz Fedor. Courtesy of the Museum of New Mexico, #161827.

Ernie Pyle working on his south lawn with the fence he built in 1941 in the background. Courtesy of Charles G. Davis.

Ernie Pyle painting the south side of his Albuquerque house. Photograph by Ferenz Fedor. Courtesy of the Museum of New Mexico, #128926.

Ernie Pyle, Earl Mount, and Shirley Mount playing croquet on the Mount family's front lawn in Albuquerque. Photograph by Ferenz Fedor. Courtesy of the Museum of New Mexico, #128923.

Ernie Pyle signing autographs after receiving an honorary doctoral degree from the University of New Mexico, October 25, 1944. Courtesy of the Museum of New Mexico, #138772.

Ernie and Jerry Pyle with New Mexico friends at the Cocina Cantina in Albuquerque's Alvarado Harvey House just prior to Pyle's departure to the Pacific. Left to right, Robert E. Archer, Ella Streger, Liz Shaffer, Stella Mary Shaffer, Shirley Mount, George Shaffer, Pyle, Jerry, Eva Mount, Dan Burrows, and Leonard Oliver. Photograph by Clarence E. Redman. Courtesy of the Museum of New Mexico, #138793.

Ernie and Jerry Pyle at the Santa Fe Railroad depot in Albuquerque. Pyle left for overseas assignments four times during World War II. A field helmet lies among his luggage. Jerry wears a jacket made from sealskins that Ernie brought back from Alaska in 1937. Courtesy of Edward D. Shaffer.

Ernie Pyle examines his famous portable typewriter moments after German bombs fell on his location in Italy, 1944. Courtesy of the Museum of New Mexico, #138764.

Ernie Pyle and Arthur McCollum of the Army Medical Corps in Europe. McCollum and Earl Mount were the contractors who built Pyle's house in Albuquerque. Courtesy of the Museum of New Mexico, #138762.

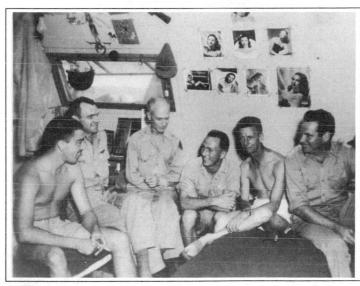

Ernie Pyle drew crowds of admiring G.I.'s wherever he traveled during World War II, including here on Saipan in 1945. Left to right, Russ Cheever, Gerald Robinson (of Albuquerque), Pyle, Bill Clark, Bill Gifford, Andy Meloney. Courtesy of the Museum of New Mexico, #138807.

Ernie Pyle and Bergess Meredith on a stage set in Hollywood. Meredith played Pyle in the hit 1945 movie, The Story of G.I. Joe. *Courtesy of the Museum of New Mexico, #138802.*

The entire world mourned Ernie Pyle's death in the Pacific on April 18, 1945. Albuquerque Tribune, *April 19, 1945.*

Jerry Pyle receiving a posthumous Medal for Merit for Pyle, Washington, D.C., July 3, 1945. Courtesy of the Museum of New Mexico, #138819.

Memorial service for Ernie Pyle at the site of his death on the Pacific island of Ie Shima. Color guard, left to right, Cpl. Herbert N. New, Sgt. Ray L. Wactor, Sgt. Gunther Rathnow, Sgt. Lawrence Eshon, Cpl. Charles Shrope, Sgt. Murray Sweet, Cpl. George Washington. Photograph by Cpl. Edward E. Burris. Courtesy of the Museum of New Mexico, #138824.

6

NEW MEXICANS OVERSEAS, 1942-45

Ernie Pyle had little idea what new direction his life and work would take when he arrived in England in mid 1942 and continued on to North Africa five months later. He could not have realized that he was about to enter the third and final phase of his professional career. Pyle was well prepared for this final phase. After years of honing his journalist skills in the United States, he was ready to take his proven writing style abroad. And, after years of focusing on humble Americans from small towns and large cities at home, he was ready to focus on these same Americans in their new lives as unsung soldiers of the U.S. military.

Living, marching, and barely surviving side-by-side with his subjects, he portrayed the war from the fighting soldier's point of view at the front, rather than from the relative safety of the back lines where most correspondents learned of the war in military briefings by generals and their aides. As a result, Pyle was, at various times, known as the "fox-hole reporter," the "ringside war correspondent," the "G.I.s laureate," the "infantry's Homer," and the "G.I.'s Boswell."[1] John Steinbeck, working as a war correspondent for the *New York Herald Tribune*, declared that Pyle was "the only one of us who has captured the thoughts and the voice of the G.I."[2] Soon, all plans to continue on to India or China evaporated. Instead, the relocated reporter remained with the U.S. Army and the relocated American soldiers who filled its ranks. As a contemporary observer put it, "his farmers, lumberjacks and bartenders had become privates, sergeants and lieutenants" and had marched off to war.[3] It seemed quite fitting that he followed their distant tracks.

Ernie Pyle grew increasingly popular among the soldiers he wrote about overseas. As one G.I. in Italy wrote home to his sister in Albuquerque, "The boys over here went for Ernie Pyle in a big way."[4] G.I.s appreciated his coverage of the war from their perspective not only because he described the misery and dangers of their everyday existence, but also because he put their suffering in perspective and sang their praise in honest, seldom censored terms. American soldiers on every front appreciated his columns, respected his courage, and cared for his safety; the *New York Times* reported that he was "the most prayed for man in the Army."[5] Knowing them as well as he did, Pyle also became the G.I.s' "mouthpiece," lobbying for their special needs like a popular omnibusman as the war progressed.[6]

Most importantly, Pyle's work had a positive effect on troop morale. According to General Omar N. Bradley, he liked having Pyle in his sector because his soldiers' morale always improved, and, as a result, "My men always fought better when Ernie was around."[7] At least one author claimed that "most servicemen would rather had have their names appear in one of Pyle's dispatches than [receive] a medal."[8] Albuquerque's Colonel C.R. Smith recalled a USO show in Africa at which Pyle was introduced to the crowd. Although Pyle's stage fright prevented his climbing on stage, the troops roared "We want Ernie" in such an ovation that "even the stars were jolted."[9] By October 1944 a cartoon in *Yank* magazine showed a weeping soldier whose sorrow was explained because "Ernie Pyle misspelled his name" in a column sent back home.[10]

Ernie Pyle's encounter with a G.I. from Albuquerque was typical. Young Howard met Pyle when the war correspondent visited his Army camp in Europe in April 1944. The soldier reported to his family in New Mexico that he was impressed that Pyle not only ate dinner in the enlisted men's mess, but also served himself on the chow line and sat with the men at Howard's table. Excited, Howard accidently spilled his cup of hot chocolate, making the G.I. feel "small enough to crawl under a snake's belly." But Pyle took the incident in stride, telling his fellow New Mexican not to be embarrassed because such accidents happened to him all the time. "Right then and there ...

I was sold on him," wrote Howard.

Within a few minutes the table was over run [sic] with fellows laughing and having one Hell of a good time. For the short time we were together we forgot Army rules and regulations and had one dam [sic] good bull session. Just like the old times when a bunch of fellows get together.... Ernie Pyle is one great fellow. They don't make them more regular.[11]

Pyle was equally popular among his avid readers back home. Having grown to know and like him from his days as a roving reporter, Americans felt they could trust his frontline observations and heartfelt human stories. As with the average G.I., the average American reader appreciated Pyle's uncanny ability to describe the war in terms that were far more personal and meaningful than newspaper accounts that focused on large battles and mass movements of airplanes, tanks, and men. Careful to note the exact hometown address of each soldier he wrote about, Pyle made his columns read like letters home from an articulate, well-informed relative or friend who'd been sent off to war along with countless other men from hometowns across the nation. Even if they hadn't received a letter from loved ones in many weeks, Americans could always count on a "letter" from Ernie Pyle just by opening the daily newspaper.[12]

Ernie Pyle's columns were often sad and seldom totally upbeat, but they were sometimes humorous and always realistic. His readers appreciated his unique approach through both the brightest and darkest days of the war. Even President Roosevelt "depended on him for information about the realities of the war that he could not get from any other source, [and] certainly not through the regular 'channels.'"[13] Average Americans felt the same way. As Jane Easton wrote to her G.I. husband in Europe, by reading Pyle she had acquired "a close and vivid picture of the infantry .... and I'm glad you are connected with it."[14]

Americans not only read Pyle's columns regularly, they also wrote letters (and even poems) to him, followed his progress from front to front, and phoned their local newspaper offices to inquire about his health and safety. *Time* magazine asserted that Pyle was "well on his way toward becoming a living legend."[15] "Ernie Pyle is as much a part of this war as red points and butter rationing," declared the Reverend Fidelis Rice in a Washington, D.C., speech. "He is a national idol [who] .... rates far ahead of orange juice in the nation's daily diet."[16] Appreciating this praise, Pyle would spend the coming years covering nearly every important military front for newspapers, including the *Albuquerque Tribune*, the *Portales Daily News*, the *Roswell Morning Dispatch*, the *Farmington Times-Hustler*, and the *El Paso Herald-Post*, whose circulation area covered southern New Mexico. By 1943 his columns reached nine million readers. By 1944 his writing appeared in no fewer than 310 weekly and 366 daily newspapers. By 1945 he would write an estimated 700,000 words about the war.[17]

By all outward appearances, Ernie Pyle's hour of lead had turned to an hour of gold by late 1942. Unfortunately, his hour of gold was badly tarnished by homesickness, personal doubts, and ongoing family crises. Despite his sudden fame (or perhaps because of it), Pyle missed New Mexico and those he had left behind in the Southwest. While suffering through a cold autumn in London, he imagined "how warm and lovely it must be" in Albuquerque at that time of year.[18] By October 1942 he wrote to Jerry that

> I suppose that you and our house and the big country out there occupy my mind fifty percent of the time, and yet it all seems to be growing far far away, almost out of my grasp. I wonder if I will ever be a part of it again. Yearning for it has become a phobia for me.[19]

Much like the hundreds of soldiers he would meet and write about, Pyle suffered from a case of homesickness in which the past was refashioned with few memories of pain and exaggerated with vivid memories of joy back home.[20]

A month later, Pyle arrived in North Africa where he was immediately struck by how much that part of the world reminded him of New Mexico. He praised its weather as "warm and bright in daytime and just slightly chilly at night—much like fall in Albuquerque."[21] Its terrain was also similar to New Mexico's. "There are times," he told Jerry, "when, if you could just substitute a Mexican for an Arab in the foreground, you couldn't tell but that you were in the southwest [sic]."[22] Soldiers from New Mexico and Arizona agreed. "In the moonlight ... the rolling treeless hills looked just like home country to them."[23] Arab weavings reminded Pyle of Navajo rugs, although they were no "prettier."[24]

Although intrigued by his surroundings, he still longed to be home. As he put it to Jerry in December 1942, "I'm 'in' our house so much in my mind that sometimes it's hard to believe I'm here."[25] He missed

Cheetah so much that he carved her image in wood before leaving the states and confessed that he thought it "ridiculous for a person to have such affection for a dog."[26] He regularly inquired about friends in Albuquerque, especially Mount, who soon enlisted in the Navy, and Shafe, whose health had begun to deteriorate with various problems.[27] Frequently ill himself, Pyle hated the cold and longed for New Mexico's mild climate. An increasingly typical homeowner, he worried about such mundane matters as the condition of his lawn, keeping enough wood for the fireplace, and having the interior repainted while he was gone. Pyle summarized his feelings in a letter to Cavanaugh in which he declared, "All I ask now is a dog, an easy chair, sunshine and no interruption."[28] Three months later he wrote to Shafe and Liz, "I wish I was there [in New Mexico] doing nothing. I guess Albuquerque has spoiled me for the rest of my life."[29]

And increasingly he missed Jerry. By late 1942 he dreamt the typical soldier's dream of spousal infidelity: he dreamt that Jerry had married someone else. Pyle's nightmare seemed so real that he wrote to Jerry that "for days I couldn't believe you hadn't [married another man]. It was horrible."[30] More than ever, he hoped that her psychological condition had improved to the point that they might remarry, if only by proxy while he was overseas. By October 1942 Pyle went so far as to ask a judge advocate to draw up the legal papers that would allow Shafe to act as Pyle's proxy in a civil ceremony once Jerry was willing and able to take this step in the estimation of Sister Margaret Jane, Mother Superior at St. Joseph Hospital where Jerry still spent much of her time.[31] Sister Margaret Jane eventually discussed Pyle's unorthodox proposal with Jerry, but, as the Mother Superior reported to him by mail, Jerry refused. Pyle reacted by sitting "on a stump all bundled up against the cold [at dusk].... I was so disappointed I almost felt like crying."[32]

Far better news arrived on March 12, 1943, when he learned that Jerry had finally accepted his proposal and had married him with Shafe as his proxy and Liz Shaffer as a witness in Judge Neil McNerney's Albuquerque office.[33] Jerry's wedding day note caught up with Pyle overseas. In it she declared, "Have exercised proxy March 10. Soon [re]settled in house with Cheetah. View still glorious. House dog and gal waiting for their master. All send love."[34] Pyle was overjoyed. He responded by telling Jerry, "I love you very much and am happy for us." Perhaps to justify the divorce he had insisted on a year earlier, he asserted that he had "a feeling we're both better people for what we've been through, and that even this present long and tragic separation will be repaid by smoothness and beauty in our lives someday."[35] About a month after their "wedding," Pyle wrote to Shafe that he had "all the confidence" in Jerry's recovery and truly believed that "the battle she has won with herself is a historic one."[36]

On a lighter note, Pyle accused Shafe of marrying Jerry "the minute a fellow turns his back," leaving "your poor wife and ragged children sitting there at home crying their hearts out."[37] Shafe had his own amusing interpretation of what had transpired. According to him, the Justice of the Peace had gotten confused and married Jerry and him so that now he was a husband with two wives and three perplexed children.[38] Happy and optimistic about his and Jerry's future, Pyle missed his wife and their home in the Southwest more than ever.

Ernie Pyle also missed New Mexico when he encountered soldiers from his adopted state in the course of his wartime travels. While still in North Africa, he met Lieutenant Jack Pogue, a paratrooper from Estancia, New Mexico. Pyle told his readers how he and Pogue spent hours in the Tunisian desert "reminiscing about our own special desert back home."[39] In Algiers, Pyle met another New Mexican, Hoyt Tomlinson. Tomlinson was a Navy cook who was on his ninth round trip across the Atlantic in two years. He told Pyle about the day he discovered a fellow New Mexican in New York and got "so homesick ... that he started to cry." Tomlinson kept the man up til 3:00 a.m. because "he was so delighted at seeing somebody from home."[40] Later, Pyle met Lieutenant Walter Jentzen of Carlsbad in an Army hospital where the officer was recovering from wounds received early in the Italian campaign of 1943. Pyle wrote of how he "tortured" the young man "by telling him what New Mexico sun felt like, how the air smelled, and how beautiful the Sandias were at sunset." Pyle sadly admitted that "The only trouble with torturing a guy that way was that I tortured myself at the same time."[41] A captain from New Mexico gave him a copy of a *New Mexico Magazine* with many "nostalgia-producing pictures" and the same torturous results.[42] Later, when a movie based on his columns was produced and entitled *The Story of G.I. Joe,* a fictional soldier spoke for Pyle and many of his fellow New Mexicans when he said, "I'll sure be glad when I get back to sunny Albuquerque."[43]

Ernie Pyle interviewed many New Mexicans for his syndicated column during World War II. Some were only mentioned in passing, as in the case of Sergeant Cheedle Caviness, U.S. Senator Carl Hatch's nephew.[44] Others were included in columns based on some unusual event or interest. In one instance, Pyle joined Lieutenant Bob Wollard of Clovis and another officer on an "egg orgy" in North Africa after doing without this poultry product for some time. Pyle described how he and his fellow diners "gorged" themselves on twenty-four hard-boiled eggs and twenty tangerines "in half an hour flat."[45] In another column from Africa, Pyle described the importance of G.I.s getting mail, jealously noting that Lieutenant Herbert Desgorges of Gallup received twenty letters at one mail call to Pyle's two.[46] Pyle later met Private Dick Trauth of Albuquerque, a Marine veteran at seventeen. Trauth's hobby was writing to movie stars, including Shirley Temple, who kindly sent an autographed photograph to his company of Marines just as he had requested. Fifty years later, Trauth still treasured this photo as well as fond memories of his brief moments spent with Ernie Pyle.[47]

Pyle also interviewed New Mexicans with unusual assignments in the war. Corporal Thomas Castleman of Albuquerque, for example, "rode his motorcycle over unspeakable roads through punishing weather" to carry the war correspondents' dispatches to a filing point where they could be wired back home from Italy.[48] Captain John Jackson was described as "an unusual fellow" with another unusual job. Because he spoke German, he was "the guy who goes in and brings out German generals who think maybe they would like to surrender." When Pyle interviewed him in 1944, Jackson seemed less concerned about German generals than about his ranch east of Santa Fe which was losing money because there was "nobody left to look after the business" while the war raged overseas.[49]

The New Mexican with probably the most unusual job in the war was Sergeant William H. "Bill" Mauldin, originally of Mountain Park, New Mexico.[50] Pyle described Mauldin as "the finest cartoonist of the war .... not merely because his cartoons are funny, but because they are also terribly grim and real." Mauldin's central cartoon characters were "unshaven, unwashed, unsmiling" combat veterans named Willie and Joe who represented "the tiny percentage of our vast Army who are actually up there doing the dying." Employing methods similar to Pyle's, Mauldin learned about the average G.I.

and his daily plight by spending "about three days out of ten at the front" gathering material to draw in a "large batch of cartoons" once he returned to division headquarters.[51] Given their similar methods and focus, Mauldin could well be called the Ernie Pyle of cartoonists. In fact, the young soldier's black humor became so popular among the troops that when G.I.s were asked how they would suggest making a movie about their lives, many replied, "Make the picture like Bill Mauldin's cartoons."[52]

While Mauldin's work had grown famous as a regular feature in the Army's *Stars and Stripes*, he was far less well known back in the states. That soon changed, partly as a result of Pyle's writing a laudatory column describing Mauldin's fine work. With Pyle's further assistance in the newspaper world, Mauldin's "Up Front" cartoon became nationally syndicated by 1944.[53] Fittingly, Pyle's columns and Mauldin's cartoons often appeared on the same page in many newspapers; Shafe's *Albuquerque Tribune* ran a sample of Mauldin's cartoons when Pyle's column on the young soldier first appeared and regularly when Mauldin's work was syndicated starting April 17, 1944. When Mauldin compiled many of his best cartoons in a new book, entitled *Up Front*, Ernie Pyle gladly wrote its foreword.[54] *Up Front* was soon a best seller, vying with Pyle's latest book at the top of best seller lists in every major American city.[55] The two New Mexicans had begun a warm relationship built on common perception, common purpose, and mutual respect. Mauldin was undoubtedly thinking of Pyle when he praised a "handful of newsmen .... who can find real and honest stuff to write about in a war, regardless of whether or not that particular phase of the war is making headlines."[56]

In contrast to Bill Mauldin, who worked alone, other New Mexicans played key roles on combat teams. Captain Ben Billups of Alamogordo proudly told Pyle of his work with his division's company of engineers:

> Our job is to clear the way for our division of roughly two thousand vehicles to move ahead just as quickly as possible. We are interested only in the division. If we were to build a temporary span across a blown bridge, and that span were to collapse one second after the last division truck had crossed, we would have done the theoretically perfect job. For we would have cleared the division, yet not wasted a minute of time doing more than we needed to do when we passed.[57]

Billups and his fellow engineers built more permanent structures when the need arose during the remainder of the Italian campaign.[58]

Months later and half way around the globe, Pyle discovered probably the only B-29 crew in which three of its eleven officers and men came from New Mexico: Joe McQuade of Gallup, Fauad Smith of Des Moines, and the ship's commander, Major Gerald Robinson of Albuquerque. Pyle described several other characteristics that made this crew unique: Major Robinson's home in Albuquerque was just blocks from Pyle's on Girard Avenue, Robinson filmed their missions on a home movie camera, and the crew had a superstition that they all had to wear blue baseball caps with the number 80 on them if they were to survive each bombing run. So far they'd been lucky: only their bombardier had been wounded. Sergeant Smith told Pyle that with his many missions recorded with marks on the back of his flying jacket, he had room enough for only a few more markings, "and then he'd just have to quit."[59]

Not every New Mexican interviewed by Pyle was fortunate enough to escape injury. Lieutenant Jentzen, whom Pyle had good-naturedly tortured with memories of New Mexico, had been wounded twice in Italy. Hit in his chest by a shell fragment, he insisted that "a notebook which he always carried in his left shirt pocket was all that saved him."[60] Pyle also described Private Joe Gatewood, a Navajo soldier who had attended the Albuquerque Indian School, lived near Pyle in Albuquerque, and received a Purple Heart for wounds sustained during his three years of service in the Pacific.[61]

Gatewood was a Navajo Code Talker, one of a special group of Marines who befuddled the Japanese by sending and receiving a unique code in their unusual native language.[62] Gatewood and his fellow Code Talkers felt confident that their regiment would suffer fewer casualties in the invasion of Okinawa if they performed a ceremonial dance several days ahead of time. Pyle explained that

> The Red Cross furnished some colored cloth and paint to stain their faces and they made up the rest of their Indian costumes from chicken feathers, sea shells, cocounts, empty ration cans, and rifle cartridges. Then they did their own native ceremonail chants and dances out there under the tropical palm trees with several thousand marines as a grave audience. In their chant they asked the great gods in the sky to sap the Japanese of their strength.... [T]hey ended their ceremonial chant by singing the Marine corps song in Navajo.[63]

Gatewood later told Pyle that he was sure that their dance had been effective because he had noticed a rainbow over the convoy of ships that carried his regiment to the invasion site. "I knew then everything would be all right."[64]

Pyle devoted two columns to the 120th Engineers Battalion and a narrow escape involving three of its New Mexican soldiers in Sicily. In fact, most of this battalion's troops had come from Pyle's adopted state; according to the reporter, "It was good to get back to those slow-talking, wise and easy people of the desert" who could talk to him about places like Las Cruces, Socorro, and Santa Rosa. A large number of these men spoke Spanish, and all sorely missed the Mexican food they were accustomed to back home. The more fortunate had their folks send them chili by mail, "and then they had a minor feast."[65]

Pyle did not mention if the men involved in a particularly narrow escape were fortified in this manner. The three New Mexicans in the incident Pyle described were Captain Richard Strong of Albuquerque, Sergeant Martin Quintana of Belen, and Sergeant John W. Trujillo of Socorro. As Quintana recalled years later, they had all volunteered to drive a jeep near an Italian village to observe enemy activity. During their mission, a German shell hit their jeep, causing serious injuries to all three New Mexican soldiers. Quintana remembers that he waited about nine hours before an Italian villager discovered him, gave him cognac to drink, and sent for help. He spent the next forty-two days in an Army hospital, where he was eventually interviewed by Ernie Pyle.[66]

Battle casualties struck even closer to home when Pyle visited Captain Arthur McCollum in England. McCollum, who, with Earl Mount, had built Pyle's home, had joined the Army, just as his business partner had joined the Navy. Like Mount, he had also served in World War I. However, because he had always regretted the fact that he hadn't gone overseas "the other time," he was "very happy that he had made it this time." He was also proud of the fact that his son, Ross, was the lead pilot on a B-17 Flying Fortress. Father and son had been close and had, in fact, planned to open a new business together at war's end. But tragedy struck when Ross and his crew never returned from a mission over Germany. Nearly four months had passed without news by the time Pyle visited Arthur.[67]

Captain McCollum told Pyle how he had initially gone "to the bottom of the barrel over Ross," dropping "so low he felt he couldn't take it." But then one day Arthur reportedly told himself, "Look here, you damn fool. You can't do this. Get yourself together." According to Pyle, McCollum obeyed his own command. He talked a lot about his missing son, "and felt better for the talking," but didn't break down and felt confident that if Ross never came back "he could take it." Pyle admired his friend for his strength of character and suggested that his readers might use him as a model in the face of their own tragedies. Pyle considered McCollum "one of the finest examples I know of what people can and must do when the tragedy of war falls fully upon them."[68] Later, when this column was included in a book by Pyle entitled *Brave Men*, the author noted that word finally came that Ross had definitely died. "And Mac took that final news in the same brave way."[69]

Sometime later Pyle spent several days with McCollum in France. Traveling through the French countryside, they came across two downed English fighter planes. A soldier ran up and breathlessly shouted, "Hey, there's a man alive in one of those planes across the road! He's been trapped there for days!" They all ran to the wreckage, fell to their knees, and peered into the plane. To their amazement, they discovered a still-breathing pilot who'd been trapped for five days.

His left leg was broken.... His back was terribly burned by raw gasoline that had spilled. The foot of his injured leg was pinned rigidly under the rudder bar. His space was so small he couldn't squirm around to relieve his own weight from his paining back.... He couldn't see out of his little prison. He had not had a bite to eat or a drop of water.... Yet when we found him ... his mind was as calm and rational as though he were sitting in a London club. He was in agony, yet in his correct Oxford accent he even apologized for taking up our time to get him out.[70]

Pyle and McCollum worked frantically to rescue Lieutenant Robert Gordon Fallis Lee, but even with the help of others who joined their rescue effort, it took almost an hour to free the brave pilot. Intensely involved, McCollum ripped a board from a nearby fence to use as a brace for the injured man's back. A doctor soon arrived and took the English officer to a hospital where, after several operations, he was told that he would recover.[71] Pyle did not say, but one may suspect that Arthur McCollum's participation in this fortuitous rescue of a young English pilot may have helped him recover from the trauma of losing a young American pilot of his own just months before.[72]

In terms reminiscent of Pop Shaffer in Mountainair, several New Mexicans later recalled their encounters with Ernie Pyle in World War II. As with Shaffer's interview of 1942, Pyle generally began his wartime interviews by putting his subjects at ease and finding common ground, if possible. The latter task was especially easy when dealing with fellow New Mexicans who loved to talk about their home state as much as, if not more than Pyle. Private Dick Trauth of Albuquerque remembers just such a conversation with the itinerant author in April 1945. Trauth says that he was sitting on a log cleaning his rifle when Pyle came by, sat down next to him, and humbly introduced himself. Trauth didn't realize that the small, reticent man beside him was even a reporter until he spotted his war correspondent's patch and made the connection. Pyle asked the private where he came from, which naturally steered their conversation in the direction of various topics relating to Albuquerque and their homes in New Mexico. The two also shared the common bond of having terribly swollen eyes caused by "mosquito trouble." As Pyle had contended in a recent column, he considered himself "the world's choicest morsel for mosquitoes." Trauth opened up to this "quiet, chipper little man," telling him about his hobby of collecting celebrity photographs. Trauth recalls that Pyle never took a note during their brief meeting; the young Marine didn't even realize that Pyle had written about him until he returned home later. Appreciating Trauth's time and information, Pyle gave the soldier a Zippo cigarette lighter as a small gift.[73]

Pyle had developed the habit of giving Zippo lighters to nearly all of the men he interviewed. Starting in the spring of 1944, the Zippo Manufacturing Company of Bradford, Pennsylvania, gladly shipped him fifty free samples a month as a means of promoting their product. According to Pyle, the company hardly needed this publicity because its lighters were prized possessions among most soldiers. As he wrote Zippo founder George B. Blaisdell, "Getting hold of a Zippo is [like] getting hold of a hunk of gold."[74] "There is truly nothing the average soldier would rather have."[75] Durable, the lighters were said to burn in the wind and light at high altitudes. Pyle wrote that he liked his special nickel-plated Zippo lighter so much that he began smoking twice as many cigarettes simply because he enjoyed lighting them so much with the new gadget. He also appreciated the lighter's use in his press work. In Pyle's candid words, "I found myself equipped with a wonderful weapon for winning friends and influencing people." Soldiers like Trauth appreciated the gesture, regardless of the ulterior motive.[76]

Others had similar memories of their moments with Ernie Pyle. Bill Mauldin recalled that "the main reason Ernie Pyle and I hit it off when I knew him during World War II in Italy was we were both involved in New Mexico." Coming from the southern part of the state, the young cartoonist never understood why Pyle favored Albuquerque for his home, since Mauldin thought it a "poor choice, being somewhat dusty and not really balmy enough in wintertime to make up for it." Years later, looking back at the time he spent with Pyle, Mauldin remembered how he had "humored the old boy but kept wondering why a man who had already seen as much of New Mexico as he had wanted more of it." Mauldin only realized the reason once he turned Pyle's age and "stopped working my way out of New Mexico and was working my way back to it."[77]

Lieutenant Victor Coreno of Kirtland Air Base provided additional information regarding Pyle's interviewing style, clearly reinforcing what all others from New Mexico had said. Interviewed about his time with Pyle by the *Albuquerque Journal*, Coreno recalled his initial surprise in meeting the nondescript author. "Instead of facing a battery of ... hungry-looking guys prepared to give them the third degree," Coreno and his B-17 crew encountered "a small man in ridiculous 'G.I.' clothes, with welcome written all over his face." "It was amazing," said the lieutenant. "We were hardly through the door before he had thawed us out, passed the cigarettes, and had us laughing and joking. We might have mistaken him for a [congenial] buck private ... if it hadn't been for his correspondent's arm band." Relaxed, Coreno remembered that the "first thing we knew, we were talking back and forth to bring out every incident" that interested the reporter. "Ernie sat and listened mostly, smoking one cigarette after another, and getting up once in a while to pass some refreshments he had for us. The boys talked freely and boisterously. After all, Ernie didn't have a pencil and didn't seem to give a hoot about taking a note. I don't know how long we stayed that night. None of us gave a thought to time."[78] As with Pop Shaffer and so many others Pyle had interviewed before and during the war, Pyle had skillfully disarmed his subjects in the interest of writing a good column. A naturally shy, unassuming man, he knew no other way.

The New Mexicans Pyle wrote about during World War II shared many of the same characteristics as the men he wrote about from other states in the Union. According to one student of Pyle's work, a goodly number of the men he wrote about derived their strength of purpose from an upbringing close to nature or from the ties of a small community. His fondest profiles would be of men fresh from the country or small towns, unsullied by the fractiousness and wise-guy posturing of the big cities. It wouldn't be that these men were necessarily better soldiers than their city counterparts, or even better human beings; but they would strike him as somehow more *American,* or at least closer to what an American ought to be [in his traditional mind].[79]

The only advantage that New Mexican soldiers may have had in being included in Pyle's columns or books was that most New Mexican G.I.s came from small communities by the very nature of their rural state. However, there is no evidence that Pyle sought out New Mexicans in particular to write about. Although he was always glad to see them, of the 572 soldiers interviewed in columns compiled in his three wartime books, only 23, or about four percent, hailed from New Mexico. Rather than focusing on New Mexicans, Pyle may have consciously avoided favoring them, just as he apparently did while living in the Southwest, for fear of "too much New Mexico," in Shafe's prudent words as a long-time editor and friend.[80]

7

HOMECOMINGS, 1943 & 1944

Of course it was far better to live among New Mexicans in the Southwest than to simply write about those he encountered overseas. Ernie Pyle thus returned to New Mexico on two "furloughs" in 1943 and 1944. On both occasions, he hoped to relax and recapture the serenity he had experienced on most of his first extended visit of 1941. In his words, he thought that "a few months of peace will restore vim to my spirit.... We'll see what a little New Mexico sunshine does along that line."[1]

As before, Ernie Pyle spent much of his time working in and around his house. In addition to the Arab rugs he had sent home from North Africa, he brought such items as an African vase, a Moroccan hassock cover, and an enlarged political cartoon by the famed English cartoonist, David Low.[2] The latter depicted a proud soldier (England) defying a grim figure of death (Germany). The cartoon had been on exhibit in a window at the *London Evening Standard* when a bomb exploded nearby, tearing a gaping hole in the picture. Pyle was given this prized souvenir when he visited the London newspaper; pleased, he showed his gift to Low, who gladly autographed it with the words: "Dear Hitler— Thanks for the criticism. Yours, Low." Carrying the inscribed illustration home to Albuquerque, Pyle gave it a prominent place in his increasingly crowded study.[3] As generous as ever, he also brought home small souvenirs to Earl Mount's daughter and the

Shaffer children. A special ivory Madonna was delivered from Africa to the Sisters of Charity at St. Joseph Hospital.[4]

Pyle's good days were much like his good days of 1941. He wrote of making hot tea in the early morning and drinking it slowly as "the first dawn comes over the Sandias."[5] As before, he played with the "calm and lovable" Cheetah, attempted to catch up on his reading, and, more impossibly, tried to answer his mountains of mail.[6] Although no new construction was begun, he performed typical homeowner tasks like battling the weeds in his lawn and cleaning out the shed in his back yard.[7] In one of his "greatest pleasures," Pyle appreciated having a "real" automobile after many months of uncomfortable travel in Army jeeps and trucks. He took his Pontiac convertible out of storage and drove it for both pleasure and business. Amazed by the relative smoothness of local roads as compared to those of war-torn Europe, he asserted that "you'd think that the country around Albuquerque was all made of velvet."[8]

Although Earl Mount and Arthur McCollum were still overseas, Pyle visited other friends, especially Paige Cavanaugh, who came from California in the fall of 1943, and Shafe, when his failing health allowed. Pyle and Shafe had lunch with Governor Jack Dempsey who, in yet another fit of "civic convulsion," named Pyle an honorary colonel a third time.[9] Pyle accompanied Shafe's son, Edward, and two of his friends to the state fair (known as New Mexico's Victory Fair in deference to the war), staking cash for their small bets at the racetrack.[10] He also accompanied Shirley Mount to the Alvarado Hotel's Cocina Cantina for lunch. Years later, Shirley recalled the arrival of a troop train of hungry soldiers who joined them at the railside restaurant. Quickly recognized, Pyle signed many autographs and kidded with the men, just as he had done so often overseas. True to form, he insisted that young Shirley was really his mother. As was evident by their laughter, Pyle had won over yet another company of soldiers with his easy-going, friendly style.[11]

In addition to frequent troop trains, other reminders of the war surrounded Pyle in New Mexico. The Albuquerque Army Air Base (renamed Kirtland Field in 1942) grew larger and larger; its planes became common sites in the local skies as training crews practiced maneuvers and flew to bombing ranges (with simulated cities, warships, and other military targets) west and southwest of town.[12] Many goods were rationed, although Pyle wrote that rationing didn't seem "so bad, once you get onto it." Indeed, "our little annoying restrictions and shortages" seemed "puny" compared to the hardships Pyle had witnessed overseas.[13] He was fortunate that the local ration board gave him enough coupons for forty gallons of gasoline a week so that he could travel and continue to write his column while home in New Mexico. Pyle had a slightly harder time acquiring other ration stamps, until Office of Price Administration officials cut through red tape for him, though "not at Ernie's request, for he asked no favors."[14] Otherwise, Pyle reported, "there are lots of little things you can't buy, but honestly I don't see that anybody is in much pain from it." In fact, Pyle discovered that his local grocer actually doubled his fruit and vegetables business with rationing as his customers used their coupons for fresh fruit and vegetables most of the month "and then at the last of the coupon period, in order not to let coupons go unused, they come in and buy just as much canned stuff as they used to."[15] Pyle only complained about a shortage of good liquor. When Cavanaugh planned his visit to New Mexico in 1943, Pyle asked his friend to bring plenty of liquor, as "liquor is unobtainable here." Repeating a tragic pattern, he nearly "drank himself to death" whenever liquor became readily accessible.[16]

Ernie Pyle was also reminded of the war by the people he saw —or didn't see—in New Mexico. He clearly missed his "old set" (Mount and McCollum) and grieved for Arthur's son, Ross. Charlie Binkley, head carpenter of the construction crew that built Pyle's house, dropped by and told Pyle he was now working at the new air base. He also said that he had recently lost his only two sons, one in an operation and the other in a crash in New Guinea. Binkley worried for his wife, who was "about to go crazy," and tried to stay busy "to keep from being too lonesome and blank."[17] The Pyles' former butcher also came by to "swap yarns" and report that, like Mount, he had reenlisted in the Navy even though he was fifty, had already served in the First World War, and had a son in the Navy as well.[18] Shafe's son, Edward, was old enough to join the Navy by early 1944; he enlisted on the same day as his close friend, Hugh Cooper, who had previously accompanied Pyle to the state fair with his younger brother, Robert, and Edward. Fortunately, Edward survived the war. Sadly, Hugh Cooper did not.[19] In other disappointing news, Lieutenant Jack Pogue, the paratrooper from Estancia who spent hours reminiscing with Pyle about New Mexico while both were in Tunisia, was listed as a German prisoner of war. "Sobbing violently," Pogue's mother called to tell Pyle her son's fate in 1943.[20]

The largest single group of New Mexicans lost or captured in the war consisted of those soldiers of the 200th Coast Guard Artillery Regiment who fought on the Bataan Peninsula in the Philippines.[21] In a column that appeared in the *Albuquerque Tribune* on November 17, 1943, Pyle wrote about the 1,300 New Mexicans on Bataan, including 400 from Albuquerque alone. Of these, official death notices had been received for 113 men, but about 300 were still listed as missing. Pyle reported that a large percentage of the 1,300 were of "Spanish or Indian blood." Many families, including those of the workers who laid the bricks for Pyle's house and the boy who delivered his groceries, had two or more relatives among the 1,300.[22]

Moved by these terrible circumstances, Pyle attempted to assist his fellow New Mexicans by writing about the Bataan tragedy and the gallant efforts of a new stateside group known as the Bataan Relief Organization (BRO). Pyle informed the millions of Americans who read his syndicated column that the BRO worked tirelessly to collect and send all possible supplies to their friends and relatives held captive in Japanese prison camps. Carefully prepared relief packages included vitamins, salt tablets, candy, chewing gum, underwear, socks, sweaters, shoestrings, pencils, and so many razors that Pyle contended that they had "bought up every razor in Albuquerque." The New Mexico state police cooperated in these efforts by transporting relief packages from throughout the state. Not satisfied with these efforts alone, the BRO helped raise money for its cause by holding dances and conducting a war bond drive in which they doubled their initial goal of $300,000. Finally, the group received military permission to name a Flying Fortress stationed at the Albuquerque air base. The B-17 was fittingly christened "The Spirit of Bataan."[23]

While eager to maintain his privacy and otherwise relax during his short stays in New Mexico, Ernie Pyle contributed to Albuquerque's war effort in other ways as well. On November 20, 1944, he helped kick off the Sixth War Loan drive by agreeing to autograph as many as 250 bonds bought in the lobby of the city's Gas and Electric Building. Shunning publicity, he insisted on signing the bonds in private because, as he wrote to Albuquerque's bond drive chairman, "I just do not make public appearances or radio speeches at all."[24] Helping in the best way he knew how, he also wrote a special article on war bonds that appeared in the *Albuquerque Tribune*; the article never mentioned that he had personally bought $30,000 in war bonds in 1943 alone.[25] Thanks to his help, $652,971 in war bonds were sold in Bernalillo County during the drive's first two days. Inspired by this early success, Pyle agreed to another bond signing session for November 25.[26]

The reporter's new book, *Brave Men*, was released in mid November, becoming an instant success in Albuquerque and across the nation.[27] Book ads appeared in the *Albuquerque Tribune*, as did complimentary reviews in the press and in local discussion groups. Copies of the book were said to be "as scarce as your favorite brand of cigarettes."[28] When 800 copies at the New Mexico Book Store were "sold out quickly," another 500 were "sent to Albuquerque only because this is Ernie Pyle's home town. Otherwise, they would have gone to ... one of dozens of bigger cities clamoring for more books."[29] As a prized possession, an autographed copy of *Brave Men* was auctioned off during a war bond auction held at the Sunshine Theater on December 7, the third anniversary of the bombing of Pearl Harbor. Anton R. Hebenstreit, a local business executive, purchased the book, which normally sold for $3.00, for $10,000. The *Tribune* reported that Hebenstreit liked the book so much when it was delivered that he paid an additional $5,000 for a total of $15,000 in war bonds.[30] Less than a week later, a portrait of Ernie Pyle by local artist Terence M. Clark, Jr., was auctioned off at another war bond auction in Albuquerque. A "Texas man" reportedly paid over a million dollars in bonds for this small painting of the famous author.[31] In May of the following year, the *Albuquerque Tribune* awarded a copy of *Brave Men* and two copies of *Ernie Pyle in England* to the local 4-H Club that sold the most war bonds.[32] On June 21, 1945, young Mayme Cimino won an original Ernie Pyle manuscript when her bond number was drawn in Albuquerque on a special Ernie Pyle Bond Day.[33]

Far beyond his local efforts in Albuquerque, Pyle contributed to the national war effort through his influential columns and books. Indeed, Pyle and thousands of Americans considered his typewriter the most powerful weapon he could shoulder in the Allies' struggle against the fascist enemy; as early as 1942 he "had come to equate writing with service" to his country.[34] Millions would agree that he served his country well in this role. He also contributed by helping in the production of a Hollywood movie that attempted to depict the life of the average American soldier, based on the unique perspective reflected in Pyle's columns. Leery of Hollywood, Pyle agreed to be of assistance in the project, but insisted on several stipulations: that the movie must not be made to glorify him, that his character must not have a "love interest," that his character must not be shown taking notes or writing his column in longhand, that other war correspondents must be included in the script, and, most importantly, that the central focus must be on the American fighting soldiers themselves.[35] Appropriately, the movie was to be called *The Story of G.I. Joe*. Its producer went so far as to poll G.I.s to see what they would like to see in such a film about their lives.[36] About a hundred G.I.s "just being themselves" appeared in the final cast.[37] Arthur Miller, who helped write the film's script, was sent to Albuquerque to help alleviate Pyle's apprehension about working with the movie industry at a time "when the very word 'Hollywood' meant fraud to him."[38] Miller's description of the several days he spent with Pyle provides an intimate view of the reporter's life in Albuquerque at this juncture of the Second World War.

After a rough trip from California on a C-47, Miller was met by a taxi (sent by Pyle) and transported to a hotel in downtown Albuquerque. He soon met his noted host and, like most people, liked him immediately. The two authors spent a great deal of time together over the next week, walking downtown, drinking, and reflecting on their respective lives. Miller was quite impressed with the view from Pyle's front lawn, describing "the endless scope of New Mexico spread out in all its marvelous ... colors, always changing, always new." He was not at all as impressed with Albuquerque's downtown. Ironically echoing Pyle's earlier comments about Taos, Miller found "the main street ... empty by sundown, an occasional passing car only emphasizing the amazing silence of this small city."[39] A particular scene stayed etched in his memory:

One evening we saw a lone Indian man standing on [an Albuquerque] corner with a bundle under his arm, staring straight ahead toward the setting sun. I thought he was waiting for the traffic light to change, but when it did he remained motionless.[40]

Years later, Miller wrote "this symbol of the American displaced person" into a screenplay directed by John Huston, but Huston impatiently "swept the camera past him without really registering him." Miller concluded that the Indian's "symbolism was too personal to mean much to others."[41]

Arthur Miller also made several observations regarding Ernie Pyle's perception of himself as a displaced, or at least misplaced, person. Miller found that, "as is so often the case with American heroes, Pyle was a tortured man, uncertain of himself and ridden with guilt." One night Miller told Pyle of a play he was working on called "The Man Who Had All the Luck." According to the playwright, "The Man Who Had All the Luck" "wrestled with the unanswerable ... question of the justice of fate, how it was that one man failed and another, no more or less capable, achieved some glory in life." After acting out the plot for his host, Miller "discovered a look of amazement and baffled awe forming on [Pyle's] face." Pyle insisted on knowing where Miller had gotten his story because, he declared, "That's the story of my life." "Luck had been his lifelong companion," he told Miller, "and he had never understood why his professional life had been so successful. Despite all the praise he had received before and during the war, Pyle still suffered grave doubts about his ability. In the back of his mind disaster waited for the moment when it was least expected."[42]

Pyle and Miller shared other personal stories and ideas as they sat in Pyle's living room. Years later, Miller remembered Pyle as "slight of build, with sandy hair thinning to baldness, gentle and self-effacing ... [seemingly] the last man in the world to bring himself willingly into battle." After only a short stay in Pyle's home, Miller perceptively noted that the "place seemed somehow airless and unhappy," especially in comparison to the "endless scope" and beauty that surrounded it.[43] Arthur Miller had sensed dark problems, problems that were destined to appear in much the same forms as they had taken earlier in the war.

8

DARK CLOUDS
REAPPEAR, 1943-45

As before, the first ominous cloud to appear on Ernie Pyle's horizon endangered the reporter's great thirst for privacy and solitude. Unlike his earlier experience, the problem was less local than national in scope. Indeed, gasoline rationing effectively reduced the stream of troublesome tourists, and most of Pyle's neighbors in Albuquerque continued to respect his desire to be left alone. "People out here are swell," he told a friend back East. "Downtown they gather around ... and shake hands and say nice things, ... and then go right on, not hounding you with requests.... [T]hey are glad I'm here, but they [still] have a certain Western dignity which keeps them from badgering you."[1]

There were, of course, exceptions. Cavanaugh recalled that during his 1943 visit to Pyle's home, "a zealot campaigning for peace" drove up on a bicycle "and started haranguing" the famous war correspondent. Pyle reportedly replied by saying, "I'm sorry, ... I've come 8,000 miles to get some rest, and I just can't talk to you. I'm sick of war." The stranger then asked, "Are you sick of peace too?" to which Pyle declared, "Yes I am."[2]

But while few local residents intruded on Pyle's private life, many national demands did. In his words, his national fame brought so many new demands and "a thousand and one details" that "he hadn't had two hours to himself since he got back [from Europe] and actually wasn't rested at all" by late 1944.[3] He politely refused most public appearances, including requests to speak to the Albuquerque Kiwanis Club, attend a parade and mass rally planned by the University of New Mexico, and appear at a 500-guest welcome home dinner planned by Clyde Tingley in 1944. But he could not ignore all obligations.[4] Lincoln Barnett and a *Life* magazine photographer thus came to prepare an article on Pyle's work and home, the second such article to be featured in *Life* during the war;[5] Pyle's picture had already appeared on the cover of *Time* magazine on July 17, 1944.

Constant telephoning, telegraphing, and writing were also required to complete his war books, *Here Is Your War* (1943) and *Brave Men* (1944).[6] Once published, Pyle autographed as many as a hundred copies of *Here Is Your War* at an Albuquerque bookstore in a single day; the book was so popular that it was read in a radio dramatization on Albuquerque's KOB station and climbed to number two on the national best seller list.[7] *The Story of G.I. Joe* required additional hours of labor both in Hollywood and in Albuquerque.[8] Many involved in the project came to New Mexico to discuss its progress. Film tests were sent to Pyle who viewed them in a private audience, thanks to a cooperative local movie theater manager.[9] Exhausted by these many efforts, Pyle was said to have yawned no fewer than fourteen times in 45 minutes on the movie's Hollywood set in early 1945.[10]

A procession of other guests arrived in Albuquerque, demanding room and attention from their quickly tiring host. Although some, like Miller, stayed in downtown hotels, many did not. Reflecting back on his time in New Mexico in late 1944, Pyle told his readers that he had had "so much company ... that one night I slept on a canvas cot in the woodshed, and one night on the living room floor in my new sleeping bag."[11] He was even faced with the task of often preparing meals for his house guests. It was as if the Pyles' "big-city problem" of too many friends and associates finally caught up with them in far smaller, more remote Albuquerque. Their hope for a secluded "home base" where they could rest and be themselves seemed compromised beyond recognition. In a particularly upsetting moment, Pyle complained to Cavanaugh of "calls, visitors, opportunists, pricks, nice people, doctors, soldiers, sailors — ... never a moment of peace."[12]

Faced with this onslaught of attention, Pyle and Jerry began considering a new home with more land "and breathing space" as early as January 1944.[13] By April he insisted that "it would be utterly impossible for us even to live on a street or be accessible."[14] By January of the following year Pyle was even more insistent that Jerry go to the west mesa to look for more secluded, spacious ranch or house sites.[15] There was even talk of moving to southern California where they "could have the mountains and the desert and isolation, and still be close to things."[16]

Ernie Pyle was also kept busy with the sheer volume of gifts and awards he received during the war. Pyle merely had to refer to the need for a particular item before readers or firms (like the Zippo Lighter Company) would inundate him with great numbers of the mentioned article. Having mentioned that he needed a cookstove, he soon received more than forty. The Coleman stove company even sent a special model with his name engraved on its chrome-plated side, although he wrote that "it's so damned pretty I can hardly bear to use it."[17] In jest, Pyle mentioned that he was glad he'd never expressed a desire for a Baldwin locomotive. A representative of the Baldwin locomotive company thereafter wrote to Pyle that "the publicity afforded Baldwin was so good that [Pyle] had earned a locomotive, and where did he want it sent?" A reply from Pyle's Washington office said that he "certainly appreciated the offer and would the [company] please send him a fresh big engine to Albuquerque, New Mexico." As an afterthought, it was asked if about 800 miles of track could be sent as well.[18]

Other unsolicited gifts arrived all the time. Kind readers mailed him paintings, apples, pecan nuts, homemade hunting knives, a Texas cowboy belt, foxhole shovels, helmets, sun glasses, scarfs, neckties, socks, home remedies, and countless cigarettes.[19] Closer to home, Clyde Tingley, in his usually generous manner, gave Pyle a $500 wrist watch, "which so overwhelms me [and scares me to wear] that I left it in a safety deposit box" for safe keeping, preferring to wear a more practical watch given to him by Amelia Earhart years earlier.[20] Maurice M. Maisel, owner of Maisel's Indian Trading Post, gave Pyle a specially designed turquoise ring, which Ernie wore the rest of his life.

As many as 5,000 letters a year also appeared, including many from mothers (by an almost two to one ratio) and many from readers who "want me to find out the details of how [their] sons or husbands got killed," a clearly impossible task in most cases.[21] Each gift and letter had to be acknowledged and dealt with, a time-consuming task that took so much of each day that he required the assistance of Shirley Mount, a part-time secretary in Albuquerque, and another secretary,

Rosamond "Roz" Goodman, in Washington, D.C.[22] "I certainly have ceased to have any life or time of my own," he reported in an exasperated tone.[23]

Gaining attention on a higher level, Ernie Pyle was honored with several coveted awards for his wartime reporting. Foremost of these was the Pulitzer Prize for journalism, which he received in the spring of 1944.[24] (In typical fashion, he wrote home that "the nicest thing [about winning the Pulitzer] is that all the other correspondents seem glad about it too, and I don't think anybody is jealous."[25]) Among other honors, he received the Raymond Clapper Award from the national journalism fraternity in both 1944 and 1945.[26] In November 1944 he received the first honorary Doctorate of Humane Letters awarded by Indiana University.[27] A month earlier, New Mexico presented him with an honorary doctorate of its own. The proposal to honor Pyle in this way had been suggested by a group of students and professors at the University of New Mexico. The school's Graduate Committee approved the idea with unanimous support.[28]

On October 25, 1944, a delegation of professors accompanied Pyle from his home to the commencement exercises held at Carlisle Gymnasium on the UNM campus. A "considerable crowd" witnessed the graduation of 108 students and the presentation made to Pyle by Graduate Dean George P. Hammond.[29] Judge Sam G. Bratton, president of the UNM Board of Regents and Justice of the U.S. Circuit Court of Appeals, described Pyle to the crowd as a

writer, journalist, war correspondent, world traveler, and interpreter of the American way of life, sympathetic and understanding friend of our soldiers on the fields of battle, friend and comforter of thousands of relatives whose loved ones have fallen in the service of their country.[30]

Honored by these words, Pyle was nevertheless glad that he was not asked to make a speech, a request he would have undoubtedly turned down, given his deep aversion to stage appearances. (Asked to say a few words at a similar Indiana University ceremony, the "acutely shy" reporter had managed to "force out two words in a kind of stage whisper: 'Thank you.'"[31]) Kidding Shirley Mount that he looked like a sparrow in academic regalia, Pyle stayed after to patiently sign autographs and pose for photographs in his cap and gown.[32] One such photo featured Pyle and Mary Elena Davis of Gallup, the only enlisted woman to receive a Bachelor's degree that day.[33] Having received his honorary degree, Pyle confided that he'd have to "start policing ... my grammar, now that I'm ... a doctor of letters." He added that he hoped not to hear any "cracks about it taking me 25 years to get a degree when other people make it in four." Despite these feigned concerns, he affirmed that "I am pleased, you bet."[34] Already named an honorary colonel by three New Mexico governors, Pyle was further honored when the New Mexico state legislature declared his birthday "Ernie Pyle Day" in 1945.[35]

While many of these honors had been bestowed while Pyle was overseas, many others were given during the precious few months he had had to rest. In receiving his honorary degree from the University of New Mexico, for example, Pyle had had to travel back to Albuquerque from California, taking the Santa Fe Railroad's overnight *El Capitan*. Sitting up all night in a coach car, he engaged in a "bibulous conversation" with two Marines and had only a few hours of sleep before reaching his destination and accompanying the distinguished group of professors who brought him to the graduation ceremonies at UNM. Photos of a "haggard 'Doctor' Pyle" tell the story all too clearly.[36] Exhausted, he returned home to get some sleep at last, but, as so often happened, an old friend phoned to say that she had just arrived by plane in Albuquerque. Pyle insisted that she come right over.[37] The circumstances were typical: some event or individual had interrupted nearly every chance Pyle had had to relax while at home. In a real sense, it was as if Pyle had retreated to his small house on Girard Avenue only to have the world rush in behind him.

The death or poor health of several relatives and friends represented the second recurring cloud on Ernie Pyle's horizon during World War II. His mother had, of course, died in early 1941. Shafe remained ill during much of the following three years. In and out of St. Joseph Hospital, he rallied at times, but slowly deteriorated, despite treatment by Dr. Lovelace and care by the hospital's capable nuns. Shafe was able to serve as Pyle's proxy on March 10, 1943, but suffered a relapse and lost all but ten of his teeth by October of that year.[38] Emotionally distressed as well as physically ill, Shafe felt that World War II had only proven that World War I, in which he and others had suffered so much, had been fought in vain.[39] As early as 1938, with war threatening Europe, he had written a special Armistice Day editorial in the *Tribune*, saying that "The Unknown Soldier ... honored today at Arlington died in vain to make this a warless world safe for democracy."[40] A year later, when war had broken out overseas, his November 11 editorial declared that "The 'war to end wars' [had] turned out to be just another war to sow the seed for new ones."[41] One can only imagine the agony he felt when the next generation of young men, including his oldest son, marched off to another costly foreign war. Finally, after showing some signs of improvement in March 1944, Shafe died of cirrhosis of the liver on April 3 while Pyle was away in London.[42] Many tributes followed, although Pyle undoubtedly agreed most with a tribute that appeared in a *Tribune* editorial entitled "Shafe." Among other things, this editorial recalled that "friendship to him was a sacred word. No man was ever more staunchly loyal to his friends."[43]

Jerry Pyle's health followed a similar pattern of peaks and valleys in the years following her remarriage to Pyle in 1943. Unfortunately, her physical and emotional valleys were far deeper and more numerous than her relatively few peaks. For years, Jerry had consciously or subconsciously defined herself in relation to her husband's life and career. Maintaining such a relationship was difficult enough while Pyle pursued his career as a domestic reporter. Maintaining their relationship became nearly impossible when Pyle left for extended periods of time during World War II and essentially "married" his work overseas. Pyle constantly urged Jerry to define her life in new ways and with new interests, starting with their new house in Albuquerque. At various times, she also attempted to learn Spanish, attended business school, and worked as a file clerk at Albuquerque's military base.[44] More often, she remained isolated at home, often putting a sign on her front door which read, "Am resting. Please do not ring bell."[45] Unable to drive and unwilling to face intrusive strangers, she saw few people other than Liz Shaffer. Neighbors recall that she often played "weird" piano music into the night, read obscure poetry, burned candles throughout the house, and insisted on not having any clocks. She also gardened in her yard and read; a photo of Jerry, Pyle, and Cheetah in their living room shows Jerry "drawing sustenance" from Joseph Wood Krutch's 1944 biography of Samuel Johnson while Pyle and his dog sat patiently by.[46]

Tragically, Jerry also filled much of her life with the same liquor and drugs that had brought her to the brink of disaster in 1942. As a result, she was in and out of St. Joseph Hospital at least five times from 1942 to 1945, often living in a former TB patient's cottage on the hospital's grounds. Jerry was, in fact, admitted to St. Joseph so often that Pyle could seldom keep track of her from abroad and had to rely on Sisters Margaret Jane and Mary Isidore to report on her whereabouts and relative condition.[47] Doctors dealt with their recalcitrant patient the best they could, resorting to such extremes as shock treatment by 1944 and 1945. Discouraged, some physicians, including William Lovelace, referred her elsewhere, while other doctors and nurses were simply dismissed by the patient herself.[48]

Jerry's vacillating condition had a profound impact on Ernie Pyle, both while he was away and while he was at home. Overseas, his not knowing of her whereabouts or condition added to his periodic depressions and, ironically, drove him to drink more often than he might otherwise have done. Optimistic one moment, as when they remarried in 1943, he was filled with despair the next. At one point, the couple even resorted to renting their house on Girard to an officer from the air base while Jerry stayed on at St. Joseph.[49] By mid 1943 a staff sergeant who knew Pyle in Italy described him as

a lonely, unhappy man. Often in the dead of night he liked to talk—of his wife, her illness, their life together before the war, the friends they knew, and the little humorous incidents that brightened their nomadic path. His voice was tired and .... he liked to drink.[50]

But there was no more talk of separation or divorce. In fact, when a married Arthur Miller visited in 1943 and spoke of his attraction to a young war widow, Miller recalled that Pyle "was ahead of me and cut me off. 'Don't, don't do anything like that ever.... Your wife sounds like a wonderful woman.... The marriage is everything.'"[51]

The greatest test of Pyle's commitment to his marriage came about a month after his final return home, on October 30, 1944. Jerry had been experiencing a manic depression for several days. "She would get up early each morning," Pyle later wrote, "and bathe and dress, and then sit bolt upright on the edge of her bed all day long, just staring. It was pretty horrible."[52] Her doctor predicted that her condition would grow far worse and eventually reach crisis proportions. Pyle prepared for the coming storm by scheduling extra nurses and stocking up on necessary medication. Jerry rallied on Sunday, October 29, but was in bad shape again the following morning when her nurse, Ella Streger, arrived and Pyle left for a dentist appointment. When he returned two hours later

Mrs. Streger was out in the yard, crying and wringing her hands and calling, "Oh, Ernie, she's stabbed herself all over and now has locked herself in the bathroom." I'd broken that bathroom door open once before about three years ago. So I took two lunges at it, and on the second one down it went. Jerry was standing there at the washbowl, looking into the mirror. She turned and looked at me with that awful stare and never said a word or changed expression. She was blood from head to foot. She had dressed all up that morning in a linen suit. Everything was blood.[53]

Pyle explained that it was the loyal Cheetah who had sounded the alarm by dashing around and jumping in the air to get Mrs. Streger's attention. When the doctor arrived, they counted at least twenty self-inflicted wounds in Jerry's neck, wrists, and chest. Fortunately, Jerry had "missed every vital point." A surgeon came "and began sewing her up," although she "never uttered a sound ... but just stared at us."[54] An ambulance took them to Nazareth Sanatorium north of Albuquerque where she simply stared into space, asked for a cigarette, and inquired, "Are you Ernie Pyle?"[55] Later, she told her doctor that the only thing she remembered "was when the surgeon was sewing up her neck, and she wondered how it happened."[56] The doctor prescribed a series of shock treatments (one a day for thirty days) followed by a period of convalescence at another sanatorium.[57]

Numbed by one crisis after another, Pyle described Jerry's attempted suicide and subsequent condition in almost clinical terms, in sharp contrast to the "moral sensibility" that characterized his description of even the bloodiest scenes in the world conflict.[58] Pyle was not to see Jerry during her thirty days of treatment; she was in fact still undergoing her "drastic" cure on the day he received his honorary degree at UNM. Perplexed, Pyle wrote that he'd "long ago given up hope for Jerry, yet there's nothing to do but hope."[59] Sadly, little had changed in the four years since he uttered a similar phrase to Cavanaugh: "There's no sense to the struggle, and there's no choice but to struggle."[60] The notion seemed to have become Pyle's maxim in an increasingly tragic life.

As in 1941, war was the third great cloud that darkened Ernie Pyle's horizon in New Mexico. After covering many military fronts in North Africa and Europe from 1942 to 1944, Pyle was now asked to cover the war in the Pacific. Recognizing the impact that his presence and his writing had had on the average G.I. and the Army overall, the Navy was particularly eager to have Pyle report on its progress in the war against Japan.[61] Eleanor Roosevelt had mentioned this need as early as November 1943, telling Pyle that "he should do for the men in the Pacific what he had done for the men of the African and European areas."[62] It was not that Pyle really wanted to be a war correspondent again. On the contrary, after reporting the Normandy invasion and the liberation of Paris in 1944, he wrote that "it seemed to me that if I heard one more shot or saw one more dead man, I would go off my nut."[63] He had hoped that some time off would help, but after several months at home in the fall of 1944, he was as "wrung and drained" as he had described himself to be at the start of his state-side respite.[64] He was clearly in no condition to return to the front and report from the Pacific as he had done for so long in Europe and Africa.

He nevertheless felt obligated to go because he considered it his duty to the nation as a whole and, especially, to the average soldier he wrote of and admired so much. In Pyle's words, "I'm going simply because there's a war on and I'm part of it.... I'm going simply because I've got to, and I hate it."[65] As he had written to Jerry shortly before D-Day, he couldn't leave his post because he would feel like he was deserting.[66] He could never feel at ease if he stayed behind while so many others still sacrificed their comfort and risked their safety in the war. Well aware of the potential danger, he vowed that he would try not to do anything "foolish ... but there's just no way to play it completely safe and still do your job."[67] "You just have to take your chances if you're going to cover a war."[68]

Ernie Pyle had had his share of close brushes with death. As early as his first trip to London, he described the "savage" German fire-bombing of December 29, 1940, and estimated that "if chance had shifted us six blocks in either direction, I would have been [in mortal danger]."[69] In North Africa, "the danger of bombing was so acute that it was forbidden to expose white laundry;"[70] Pyle declared that he learned "to hate absolutely flat country where there are no ditches to jump into or humps to hide behind."[71] On one occasion, he was "caught in an air raid with no helmet and used his shovel to protect his head."[72] In Italy, he was staying on an upper floor of a house that was bombarded early one morning. Putting his helmet on, he had gone "to the window for a look at the shooting" when

a terrible blast swirled me around and threw me into the middle of the room.... The half of the window that was shut was ripped out and .... blown into thousands of little pieces. Why the splinters or the window frame itself didn't hit me I don't know.... There was

107

debris flying back and forth all over the room. One gigantic explosion came after another. The concussion was terrific. It was like a great blast of air in which your body felt as light and as helpless as a leaf tossed in a whirlwind. I jumped into one corner of the room and squatted down and just cowered there. I definitely thought it was the end.[73]

Ernie Pyle's next brush with death came during the Allied invasion of France in mid 1944. Of the nearly 500 American reporters who had gathered in England to cover the invasion, only 28 were chosen to accompany the first assault. Rather than being pleased, Pyle wrote that he and other veteran correspondents "felt our chances were not very good. And we were not happy about it." Those "who had been through the mill so long and so boldly, began to get nerves. And frankly I was the worse of the lot."[74] Pyle watched the D-Day invasion of June 6 from a U.S. ship off the coast of Normandy and landed "on the morning of D plus 1, while the beach was still getting a liberal sprinkling of shell and mortar fire."[75] Nine days later, he wrote to a friend that "I haven't had too bad a time, and yet the thing is about to get me down. Last night I was just abnormally terrified when the bombers were right over us all night.... I'm so sick of living in misery and fright."[76]

Ernie Pyle was most terrified on July 24, 1944, when some 400 American bombers mistakenly bombed his location with the U.S. First Army in a terrible instance of amicicide (or "friendly fire") caused by a combination of bad weather and human error. Two hours of heavy bombing, meant to proceed American tank and infantry attacks on Saint-Lo, were tragically dropped on American forces, killing or wounding over 800 G.I.s and barely missing Pyle.[77]

An indescribable kind of panic comes over you at such times. We stood tensed in muscle and frozen in intellect, watching each flight approach and pass over us, feeling trapped and completely helpless. And then all of an instant the universe became filled with a gigantic rattling.... It was bombs by the hundred, hurtling through the air above us.... There is no description of the sound and fury of those bombs except to say it was chaos, and a waiting for darkness.... At last the sound died down and we looked at each other in disbelief.[78]

Pyle later wrote that "he could never go through another such experience and retain his sanity."[79]

Ernie Pyle remembered such harrowing moments with consternation as he prepared to join American fighting forces in the Pacific. As General Bradley had reminded him after the fall of Paris, the odds of his survival decreased with every additional day he spent in a combat zone.[80] Pyle wrote to a fellow correspondent that he knew that "the longer we stay [out here] the smaller our chances are of getting out."[81] By mid 1944 he told of "feeling I've used up all the chances a man is endowed with.... I'm quite depressed, and hang on only by the feeling that it can't be too long now."[82] While he had known correspondents who were wounded in action, Pyle's fragile mortality was never more evident than when a fellow reporter was killed. This was especially true in the case of Raymond Clapper, whom Pyle admired greatly and whose columns often appeared side-by-side with his in newspapers like the *Albuquerque Tribune*.[83]

Ernie Pyle expressed his trepidation to several New Mexicans in the weeks before his departure for the Pacific.[84] Jerry of course opposed his leaving; her doctor in fact suggested that for psychological reasons it would be best for Jerry to leave for a trip before Pyle ever attempted another traumatic departure from her. But this was not to be. Instead, Pyle prepared to leave and, as urged by Dr. Lovelace, made arrangements for Jerry to enter a private hospital in Pasadena, California, for the next phase of her recovery while he was gone; she was to stay through April 1945, or until Albuquerque's dreaded spring winds died down.[85]

On the afternoon of their departure from Albuquerque, Pyle and Jerry visited with those who remained of their shrinking social circle. Liz and two of the "Shaffer kids" (George and Stella Mary) were present at the Alvarado Hotel, as were Eva and Shirley Mount, Dan Burrows (the new editor of the *Tribune*), and two friends, Leonard Oliver and Robert E. Archer. A surviving photo shows the group seated at a long table with Pyle at its head.[86] Military service and death had clearly taken their toll. Shafe, his oldest son Edward, Mount, and McCollum were conspicuously absent. Pyle may well have considered his precarious fate at this telling moment. Prudently, he had written his will shortly before this picture was taken; he left a trust to provide Jerry with one hundred dollars a week for the rest of her life. Lesser amounts were designated for his father, an aunt, his mother-in-law, and "Roz," his secretary in Washington, D.C. The First National Bank of Albuquerque was listed as the will's executor.[87] Ernie Pyle had prepared for the worst.

9

DEATH IN THE PACIFIC, 1945

Ernie Pyle left New Mexico for the last time on Wednesday afternoon, December 20, 1944. A widely-circulated photo showed a distracted Ernie and Jerry Pyle standing among their luggage at the Santa Fe Railroad depot in Albuquerque.[1] In a poignant moment, both appeared morose and uncertain. The famous couple undoubtedly realized that everything was about to change in their separate and married lives. Foreboding clouds had darkened their path before, but never as menacingly as on this late December day.

Once on board, the Pyles and Jerry's nurse, Mrs. Streger, traveled to Pasadena, only to be frustrated in their efforts to have Jerry admitted to Las Encinas, the private hospital Pyle had contacted from Albuquerque. With no rooms available, Pyle complained that the doctors expected them "to sit in a hotel and wait," not knowing "whether it might be two days or two months."[2] After weighing their limited options, he and Jerry decided that Jerry would return to Albuquerque with Mrs. Streger to seek medical help there. In a letter to Dr. Lovelace, Pyle wrote that he thought it best that Jerry be at home with Mrs. Streger in the day where she could "be induced to get out just as much as possible," but "always, without exception, be at [a] hospital during the night." Pyle asked Lovelace if he could work on Jerry's "numb and lifeless" hands and back ("a result, she feels, of the electrical shock treatments"), while cutting back on her sleeping pills, controlling her use of benzadrine, and seeing that she ate more. With Mrs. Streger serving as a "sort of ... sentry watching for trouble" and Dr. Lovelace attending to Jerry's medical needs, Pyle vowed to return home soon so he could "from then on devote my own time to her."[3]

The couple's parting at the Los Angeles railway station was described as tearful and "tremulous."[4] Neither knew when or where they would be together again. In a note written in longhand, Pyle told his wife that "leaving is brutal for us both, but there'll be a better day."[5]

Meanwhile, Pyle remained in California, staying with Cavanaugh, drinking heavily, and visiting the set where *The Story of G.I. Joe* was being shot.[6] He telephoned Jerry frequently, wrote often, and, in response to her request, sent a wedding ring, the first she had ever worn.[7] When Jerry asked Pyle what he wanted most, he replied that "I want your mind to be calm and clear, and for you to enjoy being alive, and be interested in things."[8] Referring to their future, Pyle expressed his hope that, "We'll live simply when I get back—and we'll have time for ourselves, or else. I couldn't go on forever leading this frenzied goldfish life.... We'll just have to drift out of the limelight and let it die its natural death, that's all."[9]

After traveling up the California coast to San Francisco, Ernie Pyle flew to Hawaii in a Navy plane, arriving on the morning of January 15, 1945. From Hawaii, he sailed with the Navy to Guam, but soon suffered a "dual nostalgia" for the land war in Europe and his home in far-off Albuquerque.[10] Unlike North Africa in 1942, there was little in the Pacific or its scattered islands to remind him of New Mexico. This "other war" seemed strange and impersonal compared to his experiences with the Army in Africa and Europe. Given the very-important-person treatment he now received from Navy brass, Pyle wondered if he ever would be able to work as he had worked so successfully from 1942 to 1944. He wrote to Jerry that

Things over here are so different—the distances, the climate, and the whole psychological approach—that I still haven't got the feel of it. Also censorship is much different, due to the different type of security necessity, and I'm afraid I may be frustrated quite a bit in trying to give the average guy's picture of the war.[11]

Despite his concerns, Pyle was eventually able to escape his VIP treatment and "give the average guy's picture of the war" in the Pacific by conducting informal interviews and writing as he had done before. Of those he interviewed in the first three-and-a-half months of 1945, at least seven were from his adopted state, including four New Mexicans in the Marines, a military branch he had never written about before. It was during this brief period that Pyle interviewed New Mexicans Gerald Robinson, Fauad Smith, and Joe McQuade of a B-29 crew; Joe Gatewood and Joe Kelliwood of the Navajo Code Talkers; and Dick Trauth of Shirley Temple picture fame.[12] In fact, three of the last five columns Pyle wrote and published were about New Mexicans.[13] As in Africa and Europe, Pyle reminisced with these men about New Mexico, asking those on their second tour of duty if they "hated to come back overseas as badly as I did." "Twice as bad," Fauad Smith told him. "You couldn't" was Pyle's heartfelt reply.[14]

Ernie Pyle accompanied several New Mexicans on the invasion of Okinawa scheduled for Easter Sunday, April 1, 1945. In fact, although Pyle never knew it, Shafe's son, Edward, was aboard one of the over 2,400 naval vessels poised for the invasion.[15] The reporter continued to brood about his safety. To Jerry, he wrote that he'd "like so much to be home, and not ... ever see any more war."[16] To Cavanaugh he candidly wagered that "I wouldn't give you two cents for the likelihood of me being alive a year from now."[17] To another friend, he confessed that "sometimes I get so mad and despairing I can hardly keep from crying."[18] Finally, to a colleague who said they'd see each other soon, Pyle pessimistically shook his head and said, "I am not coming back from this one."[19] When reminded that he had said the same about the invasions of Sicily and Normandy, Pyle replied he had always felt this way, but never as strongly as now.[20] And, as he had promised her before every other combat landing, he told Jerry that "if I come through this one I will never go on another."[21]

Much to Ernie Pyle's surprise, his landing in the seventh invasion wave at Okinawa was relatively easy. Although this invasion represented the last great land battle of the Pacific and cost the United States 49,999 casualties over an 83-day period, Pyle's landing went so smoothly that he reported that he had "never before ... seen an invasion beach like Okinawa.... There wasn't a dead or wounded man in our sector. Medical corpsmen were sitting among their sacks of bandages and plasma and stretchers with nothing to do."[22] The worst, for the American forces as a whole and for Pyle in particular, was yet to come. For now, all Pyle could complain about was a cold, uncomfortable night and a swollen eye caused by insect bites.[23]

Pleased by his relative good fortune, Pyle wrote to his family in Dana that "outside of an accident of some kind, I feel now that at last I have a pretty good chance of coming through the war alive."[24] On April 8 he told Jerry by mail that "everything is fine with me now. You can't know the relief I felt, for I had dreaded this [invasion] terribly. Now it is behind me, and I will never make another landing."[25] Relieved and thinking of New Mexico in what was probably his last letter to Jerry, Pyle anticipated that "in another couple of weeks your wonderful spring weather should start. I can visualize you planting your flowers and vines and wish I could be there to putter around and help."[26]

Released from St. Joseph's and home with Mrs. Streger and Cheetah, Jerry responded to Pyle in optimistic terms regarding the future. Referring to the New Mexico state legislature's action to make August 3 Ernie Pyle Day,[27] Jerry told her husband of her desire to plant shrubs and trees and get "the house and grounds in order" not because it made any "real difference so far as the factual aspect goes," but because she wanted "the house to fit in with the honor ... to better justify [it] being yours." She looked forward to the day she'd enter their house and find him there. She also looked forward to the day when she'd recovered sufficiently "to be able to really help you" as she had done in the pre-war past. Jerry wrote of "a bright morning" in Albuquerque as she closed one of her last letters to her husband half-way around the world.[28]

But the Pyles' optimism was premature. On April 17 Pyle accompanied several other correspondents to the ten square mile island of Ie Shima, just west of Okinawa. Ironically, he told a fellow correspondent that the island's landscape reminded him of the area surrounding his home in Albuquerque, although he was quick to assert that he "liked New Mexico better than any place."[29] Ie Shima had been identified as strategically important because the Japanese had built three valuable airfields there. The initial American invasion of the tiny island was described as "rapid ... with slight casualties."[30] Except for scattered resistance, including land mines and sniper fire, the area was considered relatively secure. But land mines and sniper fire were not to be taken lightly. Having seen a soldier step on a live mine shortly after their arrival on Ie Shima, Pyle told a companion that, "I wish I was in Albuquerque!"[31]

Snipers were equally as dangerous, as Pyle had stressed in several of his columns from 1942 to 1944. In North Africa, a well-camouflaged German sniper had fired at his position so frequently while he had tried to type a column that he had had to move four times in a single day; he finally resorted to working in a foxhole to meet his impending deadline.[32] Later, following the invasion of Normandy in June 1944, Pyle wrote of German snipers being everywhere and "pick[ing] off our soldiers one by one as they walk down the roads or across the fields." While he realized that sniping "is recognized as a legitimate means of warfare ....[,] there is something sneaking about it that outrages the American sense of fairness.... The average American soldier has little feeling against the average German soldier who has fought an open fight and lost. But his feelings about the sneaking snipes can't very well be put into print."[33] On the very day he landed in Okinawa, he noted that "there are still a few snipers hiding around. An officer was brought in just before dark, shot through the arm. So we were on our toes." Pyle heard "spooky" spurts of firing all through that first night on shore.[34]

Ernie Pyle may well have been thinking of his previous encounters with enemy snipers as he traveled down a rural road on Ie Shima with four G.I.s in a jeep at about 10:15 a.m. on April 18, 1945. When sniper machine gun fire broke out suddenly, Pyle's driver quickly stopped his jeep, allowing Pyle and the others to dive into roadside ditches in search of cover. Pyle and his companions were said to have been "fairly safe ... as long as they hugged the ground, for the [enemy sniper] had a clear field of fire from his elevated nest."[35] But Ernie Pyle didn't hug the ground. Instead, in "a characteristic gesture of compassion," he looked up to locate a comrade, smiled and asked, "Are you all right?"[36] These would be his last words. The sniper opened fire, hitting Pyle with a fatal shot to the left temple.[37] The diminutive reporter, who had traveled so far afield from his native Indiana and adopted New Mexico, was dead at 44. According to one news magazine, Pyle had shared the average soldier's lot "even to death in a roadside ditch."[38] As the *Albuquerque Tribune* put it, he was "one of them now, these infantrymen."[39]

Word of Ernie Pyle's death spread quickly around the world. The American people were stunned by the terrible news, especially since it came just six days after President Roosevelt's sudden death in Warm Springs, Georgia.[40] In the midst of mourning a statesman who had led them through the darkest days of war, Americans now faced the agony of mourning a journalist who was their greatest interpreter of that long, terrible conflict. Tragically, while both men were closely identified with the war and its progress, neither would live to see the end of the bloodshed in Europe on May 8, 1945, or in the Pacific on September 2, 1945.[41]

Words of tribute and sorrow were uttered by political leaders, average citizens, and distant soldiers alike.[42] President Harry S Truman expressed the nation's sentiment best when he said that

The nation is quickly saddened again by the death of Ernie Pyle. No man in this war has so well told the story of the American fighting man as American fighting men wanted it told. He deserves the gratitude of all his countrymen.[43]

State legislatures passed resolutions in Pyle's honor. Despite her own grief, Eleanor Roosevelt noted the passing of "this frail and modest man" in "My Day," her daily newspaper column.[44] The Navy's Admiral Chester W. Nimitz described Pyle as "one of the greatest heroes of this war."[45] Army commanders, including generals George C. Marshall, Mark W. Clark, Omar N. Bradley, and Dwight D. Eisenhower, all agreed.[46]

News of Pyle's tragic death shocked New Mexicans as well. Banner headlines in the *Albuquerque Tribune* and other state newspapers announced the terrible loss.[47] Editorials, letters to the editor, political cartoons, and photos of Pyle's life appeared in the *Tribune* and elsewhere.[48] An "Up Front" cartoon by Bill Mauldin showed a G.I.'s helmet beside a typewriter where someone had typed the number thirty, journalistic shorthand for "the end."[49] State and local leaders, including Senator Dennis Chavez, Senator Carl Hatch, Judge Bratton, Dean Hammond, UNM President Tom Popejoy, and Kirtland Air Base commander Colonel Frank Kurtz, issued statements of extreme regret.[50] Senators Chavez and Hatch supported a Senate resolution that Pyle be awarded nothing less than a Congressional Medal of Honor.[51] Oscar Love of the First National Bank declared that Albuquerque had "lost its No. 1 citizen."[52] Rising from three weeks in a sickbed, Clyde Tingley asserted that Ernie Pyle "was Albuquerque's adopted son, and all of us sorely grieve his passing."[53]

Scores of average New Mexicans also mourned Pyle's death. Many called the *Tribune's* office to ask if the news was really true. Those "who had made Pyle's 'acquittance' through his columns and felt that he was their neighbor were too shocked to comment."[54] A young *Tribune* reporter wept; "there wasn't a dry eye in this city," a charter member of the BRO said of Albuquerque.[55] Surgeons at St. Joseph Hospital were said to have mourned Pyle even more than they had mourned FDR. TB patients at the Methodist sanatorium spoke of Pyle's death as a great loss among those who were not able "to contribute physically to the war" and had relied on Pyle as their best source about the conflict. A scientist's wife in isolated Los Alamos noted in her journal that "we lost a well-loved correspondent who hated war but never shirked his duty."[56] New Mexican soldiers, especially those Pyle had met and interviewed, were distressed by the news. According to Bill Mauldin, "The only difference between Ernie's death and the death of any other good guy is that the other guy is mourned by his company. Ernie is mourned by the Army."[57]

Ernie Pyle was the thirtieth American war correspondent killed in World War II.[58] Two thousand, two hundred and sixty-three New Mexicans died in the war,[59] and, while Pyle never officially enlisted in the military, most New Mexicans counted him as a casualty of combat as surely as if he had carried a rifle rather than a typewriter.[60] Caught up on his writing prior to his death, Pyle's columns continued to appear in the press for a week or more after his death. His final column appeared as late as April 28 for dailies like the *Tribune* and June 1 in weeklies like the *Farmington Times-Hustler*. Ironically, his last column was a tribute to another fallen correspondent, Fred Painton, who had died of natural causes on Guam. Like Pyle, Painton was described as having "gone on many invasions .... [and] was certainly living on borrowed time." Like Pyle, "he had grown pretty weary of war. He was anxious to get home to have some time with his family."[61] Unable to get home to New Mexico and be with his family, Pyle could not "sign off" after his final column. That task was left to Jerry, who wrote:

> To all of you who have tried to find words to express the grief in your hearts for the deeply personal loss you feel because Ernie has gone from us, I want to say I am one of you. Our loss is a common loss. Your letters and messages made me feel you had come to me for comfort—the comfort that Ernie had given you each day. That he will live in your hearts forever will be his reward—his monument.[62]

Jerry Pyle had first learned of her husband's death from a

small delegation of friends. The Navy had contacted Dr. Lovelace who brought the news to Jerry with Liz Shaffer and her younger son, George.[63] A telegram from Secretary of the Navy James Forrestal also arrived, along with messages of condolence from local groups, national figures, and many of Pyle's millions of readers.[64] Cavanaugh quickly flew from California to be at her side.[65] Responding to a call from a *New York Times* reporter, Jerry answered the phone "in a calm but very low voice," saying that she had not yet learned all the details regarding Pyle's last moments.[66] Jerry reportedly dealt with the situation "bravely."[67]

Jerry was especially brave on Sunday, May 13, 1945, when a memorial service for Pyle was held at Carlisle Gymnasium on the University of New Mexico campus, the same place Pyle had received his honorary degree less than seven months before. An estimated crowd of 3,000 attended, making this one of the largest memorials held in Albuquerque since the death of Senator Bronson Cutting.[68] According to press reports and the service's 5,000 printed programs, Naval ROTC students served as ushers and a cadre of soldiers from the nearby air base served as a color guard. The stage was draped in blue velour with U.S. and New Mexican flags on either side.[69] Jerry sat quietly in the second row, wearing a hat, although she admitted that "Ernie would have laughed ... to see me in a hat" because she seldom wore one in their twenty years together.[70] Although Pyle was hardly religious, the air base's chaplain gave the invocation, a local rabbi said a prayer, and a priest gave the benediction. Tributes were presented by a G.I., Sergeant William E. Teets (who had known Pyle in North Africa) and two of Pyle's Albuquerque friends, lawyers William A. Keleher and Joesph L. Dailey. Three of Pyle's favorite songs (as identified by Jerry) were sung by military choruses, including "On the Banks of the Wabash," "If I Had My Way," and finally, "Farewell to Thee."[71]

Composed through most of the hour-long ceremony, Jerry only wept during this last song. Perhaps she remembered the moment when residents of a Hawaiian leper colony sang the same farewell song to Pyle on his trip to the islands in 1937.[72] She may well have recalled Pyle's words in a column describing that moving experience:

The night was dark, and even the nervous palm fronds were still. I stood while they sang. Aloha oe ... farewell to thee ... farewell to thee forever.... And any man, going away, who can stand and hear the last fragile notes fade from the throats of the leper singers of Kalaupapa without tears in his eyes—well, he would be better off dead.[73]

In another dramatic moment, four P-63 fighter planes and three B-29 bombers circled over Carlisle Gym, dipping their wings to salute the fallen correspondent who had praised these air ships and their crews in columns published from coast to coast.[74] The small squadron of planes flew so low that Jerry's hat blew off in a sudden gust of wind. Taps were played to end the day's solemn service.[75]

Jerry was equally brave in early July when she and her sister "Poe" flew to Washington, D.C., to receive a posthumous Medal for Merit for Pyle and to view an advanced showing of *The Story of G.I. Joe* at the National Press Club. With Burgess Meredith (who played Pyle in the movie) serving as master of ceremonies, speakers uttered words of tribute to Pyle before an audience of war correspondents, Supreme Court justices, members of Congress, the British Ambassador, and top-ranking officers from the Army, Navy, and Marines.[76] But seeing Washington on this occasion "undoubtedly increased Jerry's pain."[77] A photo of her receiving the Medal for Merit on July 3, 1945, shows an emaciated woman with eyes lowered and a terribly sad expression. Saying a few words, Jerry told the crowd of dignitaries that "Ernie should be here. He wouldn't quite understand how he'd earned this, but he would be humbly grateful."[78]

Returning to Albuquerque, she accepted a bust of Ernie Pyle sculptured by Jo Davidson and presented by the Scripps-Howard newspaper chain on July 15, 1945. The presentation was broadcast from the Pyles' home on KGGM and the Columbia radio network. Friends, including Shirley Mount, Liz Shaffer, and Dan Burrows, attended the ceremony to lend support, although Jerry appeared uncomfortable at this and every ceremony she attended.[79] As she was heard to say during these terrible months, "I've never had a right to bask in Ernie's reflected glory."[80]

All this attention in the wake of her husband's violent death seemed too much for a thoroughly private woman like Jerry Pyle. Her health deteriorated in the fall of 1945. She spent three weeks in St. Joseph Hospital, leaving only relatively well on October 15.[81] By mid-November she had contracted influenza. Soon her kidneys failed. On Wednesday, November 21, she was rushed back to St. Joseph's in serious condition. Despite her failing condition, she thought to ask that Cheetah be taken to the kennel and, seeing a familiar nun, told her of a photo of Ernie she wanted her to have as a memento.[82] Jerry lapsed into a comma within two hours of her arrival at the hospital. She never regained consciousness. On Friday morning, November 23, Jerry Pyle died of uremic poisoning with her sister "Poe" and her brother, Captain Fred Siebolds, at her side.[83] As Dan Burrows editorialized in the *Albuquerque Tribune*, Jerry's last few years had been marred by "loneliness, illness, [and] pain," while her last few months had been marred by "shock and heartache." Burrows and her Albuquerque friends mourned Jerry's "once gay spirit."[84]

Like so many couples, the Pyles had died within months of each other.[85] Jerry's chronic depression had adversely affected her already poor will to live and worsened her already serious medical condition. After a viewing in Albuquerque on November 24, Jerry's body was buried in her native Minnesota, while Pyle (still wearing his Southwestern turquoise ring) was eventually buried in the National Memorial Cemetery of the Pacific in Hawaii.[86] An astute observer has noted that their burials 4,500 miles apart "befits the physical and emotional distance at which they lived in the last decade of their lives."[87] Only Cheetah, who had provided so much of the limited joy the couple had known in their final years, was buried in Albuquerque, in the yard behind the only house the Pyles had ever owned.[88]

Short of burying Ernie Pyle in Albuquerque, as some hoped might happen, many New Mexicans sought to honor Pyle's memory with a permanent memorial of one kind or another.[89] Now chairman of the Albuquerque city commission, Clyde Tingley appointed an eight-person committee to consider various proposals for such a memorial.[90] Chaired by author Erma Fergusson, the new group solicited ideas from the public, urging New Mexicans to mail their suggestions in care of the *Albuquerque Tribune*.[91] A great variety of proposals arrived for consideration. Some urged that Girard Avenue's name be changed to Pyle or Ernie Pyle Avenue. Others thought it right that a proposed national cemetery in Albuquerque be named after him. An Ernie Pyle concert bowl, auditorium, or library gained support from various quarters. A statue of Pyle in his typical G.I. attire seemed appropriate to some; Roosevelt Park was suggested as the best location for such a fitting monument. Clyde Tingley favored naming a park near Pyle's home after him. Thinking of future generations, at least one person liked the idea of funding a scholarship in Pyle's name.[92] The *Carlsbad Daily Current-Argus* even proposed that Ie Shima be renamed Ernie Pyle Island, although it is doubtful that anyone could have imposed such a name on an island half way around the world.[93]

None of these suggestions resulted in immediate action. Jerry had a role in this initial impasse because she had been given the opportunity to approve or disapprove whatever project was finally proposed.[94] Understandably, she had set ideas about which plans were or were not appropriate, given her knowledge of Pyle's values and great aversion to pretension. Jerry thus reacted vehemently to the creation of an elaborate memorial park in Dana when it was planned by a New York public relations firm in mid 1945. It was, according to Jerry, "entirely out of keeping with everything that Ernie ever did, or said, or thought, or was."[95] In her words, Pyle would have been "horrified and indignant" by such plans.[96] While no such scheme was ever considered in New Mexico, Jerry remained leery of any notion that seemed counter to her late husband's humble character and style.

But the desire to honor Ernie Pyle in Albuquerque was hardly extinguished. As a result, many places in town were soon named or renamed in his memory. Indeed, so many places were named or renamed in his honor that at least one local resident complained to the *Albuquerque Tribune* that they should simply "change the name of Albuquerque, New Mexico, to Ernie Pyle, New Mexico."[97] A popular beach on the Rio Grande, developed by the Middle Rio Grande Conservancy District, was thus renamed Ernie Pyle Beach for a while; it remained open until a polio scare closed it for a period, after which it was (and still is) popularly known as Tingley Beach.[98] In 1948 a new junior high school in Albuquerque's southwest valley was also named after Ernie Pyle, becoming the first and only junior high school in the city to be named after someone other than a U.S. President.[99] In October 1950 a 44 mm single barreled anti-aircraft gun that Pyle had inscribed while in the Pacific was put on display at the Naval Reserve Training Center not far from the reporter's former home. Appropriately, Earl Mount was one of the three men who unveiled the World War II naval weapon.[100] Commercially, a movie theatre in the northwest valley was named after the reporter, although it is doubtful that Pyle's *Story of G.I. Joe* ever showed on its large screen while it remained open for business from 1947 to 1955.[101]

120

The Story of G.I. Joe had premiered in Albuquerque with great fanfare on July 12, 1945. Its world premiere had occurred on Okinawa on June 9, fulfilling producer Les Cowan's promise to show it first "wherever Ernie Pyle happens to be."[102] It seemed appropriate that Pyle's G.I.s see this film about them first, even if Pyle's presence was only symbolic. Following its private showing to Jerry and the elite audience that gathered in Washington on July 3, the movie's first public showing took place as part of ceremonies for Pyle in Indianapolis three days later.[103]

Albuquerque's turn was next. Audiences were so eager to see the film that it was booked at two of the city's largest theatres simultaneously. Its director, William A. Wellman, arrived for the gala event on July 12, as did several stars from the movie, several movie executives, and Paige Cavanaugh, who was identified by the press as a "technical advisor."[104] An *Albuquerque Journal* photograph showed Wellman and others outside Pyle's "little white house," having paid their respects to Jerry, who was not up to attending the New Mexico premiere.[105] A dinner in Pyle's honor was also held at the Albuquerque Hilton Hotel that evening. Invited guests included not only Wellman and his California entourage, but also Governor Dempsey, Clyde Tingley, and, most importantly, the relatives of all the local servicemen mentioned in *Brave Men*, Pyle's popular book about combat in Sicily, Italy, and France.[106]

Long lines of movie goers greeted the out-of-town celebrities at both the KiMo and Sunshine Theatres when they arrived at 8:30 p.m. Military equipment from Kirtland Air Base lined the streets, thanks to the efforts of base commander, Colonel Kuntz. A half hour of introductions prior to the viewing was broadcast on local radio station KOB; Jerry was said to have listened from her home. Both theatres were described as "packed" when their curtains finally rose and the show began.[107] Those in attendance gave the film excellent reviews, as did the *Albuquerque Tribune's* assigned critic, Cordell Hicks. According to Hicks, Burgess Meredith played Pyle well, depicting the reporter as the "mild, kind, tenacious and salty" character he was remembered as. Impressed by the overall production, Hicks concluded that "every person should see" *The Story of G.I. Joe* because it will "always be remembered."[108]

Based on this review, promotional photographs, newspaper ads, and word-of-mouth advertising, record crowds appeared while the movie played for a week at the KiMo and for five days at the Sunshine. Theatre management reported that more than 30,000 New Mexicans crowded in to see *The Story of G.I. Joe*, a total that surpassed all previous records in Albuquerque, including those set by such award winning films as *Gone With the Wind* and *Mrs. Minever*.[109] The movie enjoyed similar success throughout New Mexico, appearing for two- to four-day showings in at least nine major cities or towns from July to late November 1945.[110] *The Story of G.I. Joe* was equally well received nationwide. Outstanding reviews appeared in leading newspapers and magazines, led by the *New York Times*, the *New Republic*, and the *Nation*.[111] Nearly half a century later, it is still praised as the "most realistic and moving film" of World War II.[112]

Ernie Pyle was more permanently honored when his former home was made into the first branch library in the Albuquerque Public Library system. Jerry had indicated her preference for such a project as early as May 1945 when Clyde Tingley's appointed committee first met at city hall.[113] But complications held up plans for several years. First, Jerry had stipulated that in addition to converting their home into a library, the city would also have to convert a tract of land directly west of the house into a park, as Pyle had hoped might happen as early as 1941.[114] Pyle's widow clearly hoped to preserve the panoramic view that her husband enjoyed (and worried over) so much. According to committee member William Keleher, scarcity of money prevented action and "the contemplated project was abandoned."[115]

Later complications arose when it was discovered that Jerry had changed her will sometime prior to her death in November 1945. Family members challenged these changes until attorneys Keleher and Irwin Moise negotiated a satisfactory settlement, which was signed by no fewer than 26 heirs on May 10, 1946. With Paige Cavanaugh's further assistance, the heirs were convinced to donate the Pyles' small house to the city so it might become a memorial library to honor its famous first occupants.[116] Although some remodeling was necessary, the humble structure had been well maintained and was soon converted to become Albuquerque's first branch library.[117] Reflecting his deep respect for Pyle, Clyde Tingley donated one hundred dollars for the purchase of the library's first books.[118] Given the Pyles' love of books, it was fitting that their home be used for this purpose; when asked why he had built the house in 1940, Pyle only half factiously replied that he and Jerry simply needed a place to store their many books.[119]

The tiny Ernie Pyle Memorial Library has served its dual function as library and memorial well over the years. Opened on October 11, 1948, its intimate setting made it a favorite for many neighborhood residents, especially children. As one of its librarians put it, it's "the kind of library you grow up in."[120] By its first anniversary in 1949 it boasted 5,629 volumes and 1,056 registered borrowers.[121] Books filled every knock and cranny, with many in converted closets and 300 in the bathroom alone. By 1994 an Albuquerque public library official estimated that a million books had been borrowed from the branch in its 46 years.[122] Jerry's wish that a park be built to the west was never realized, but the house remains in excellent condition despite its obstructed view in all directions.

The building also became a veritable shrine for those who knew Pyle or who greatly appreciated his many contributions in World War II. Adding to the feeling of a shrine, a glass case in the library's front room displays Ernie Pyle memorabilia (or icons), including seven war correspondent patches, a portable typewriter (like the one Pyle used in World War II), a July 17, 1944, *Time* magazine cover featuring Pyle's picture, a replica of the Southwest ring Maurice Maisel had designed for him, a pair of his sun goggles, Pyle's Stetsen hat, his pewter cup, and a bust by artist John Gilleland.[123] More than 200 visitors from fourteen different states appeared at the site in the first week it was open. By 1949 2,728 visitors had signed the library's guest book.[124] A neighbor recalled frequent inquiries about the house's location whenever she gardened in her front yard. "They gaze to where I point," wrote Isabel Wiley Grear,

> then they thank me and drive on.... There are polished cars and muddy cars, baggage-laden cars and cars with trailers. Some are crammed with adults and children; others hold just a man and his wife. But their eyes all carry the same message—"He was our friend."[125]

By 1950, Pyle's former home was considered "one of Albuquerque's outstanding tourist attractions."[126] An average of fifteen to twenty tourists dropped by each day, with a record 114 on a single summer day in 1950.[127]

Visitors still arrive from all parts of the United States and around the world. They look at the house, walk reverently through its small rooms, and sign the guest book, sometimes with short comments reflecting their connection to Pyle and his memory. A Massachusetts veteran of the 45th Infantry Division thus noted on a visit in 1991 that, like so many in the military, "We loved him."[128] Another veteran wrote that, like Pyle, he had landed on Ie Shira in April 1945.[129] Others proudly commented that Pyle had written of them in one of his wartime columns or books. Meanwhile, so many people still asked why Pyle had chosen Albuquerque as his home that 100,000 reprints of Pyle's 1942 article-answer were issued by 1949; the original manuscript remains on display in the library.[130] In fact, so many visitors requested souvenirs at the library that thousands of picture postcards of the Pyles' "little white house" were printed for distribution to eager tourists.[131] One librarian went so far as to distribute Pyle's signature (cut from canceled checks found in the house) as small souvenirs.[132] Much like Ernie Pyle himself, this small, humble dwelling seems eager to serve its literary function, but rather bewildered by all the inquiries and constant attention it still receives from neighborhood friends and countless total strangers.

10

NEW MEXICO'S ERNIE PYLE & ERNIE PYLE'S NEW MEXICO

New Mexico had a great impact on the last ten years of Ernie Pyle's professional career and personal life.

Professionally, Pyle discovered many intriguing New Mexican subjects to describe in his nationally syndicated column. Prior to World War II, these subjects included at least 29 individuals, ranging from a semi-hermit priest to a colorful Depression-era governor. Pyle was likewise intrigued with certain places in the state, including such natural formations as Carlsbad Caverns and White Sands. On the other hand, Pyle wrote of people and places he appreciated far less, including Pueblo Indians in Taos and the often-pretentious artists of Santa Fe. Despite his aversion to certain groups and locations, Pyle consciously or subconsciously found exceptions: for all the snobbish artists he had no use for in Santa Fe, he described a Carl von Hassler; for all the "loafing" or "sinister" Indians he encountered in the Southwest, he described a Pablo Abeita. Clearly, the respect Pyle had for the Carl von Hasslers and Pablo Abeitas of New Mexico outweighed the criticism he had for a handful of less-admired individuals he encountered elsewhere in the state.

Ernie Pyle also discovered many interesting New Mexicans to write about during World War II. Meeting these fellow New Mexicans on nearly every front, Pyle regularly tormented them (and himself) with memories of their beloved home state. Using their common interest in New Mexico as a means to establish rapport, the famous war correspondent aptly described the combat experiences of New Mexicans ranging from cattle ranchers and railroad men to home builders and cartoonists. As he had done with hundreds of G.I.s from across the country, Pyle described these soldiers' plight in apt terms never equaled by other correspondents in the war. Though hardly intentional, it was fitting that Ernie Pyle's last published columns featured some of the very subjects he knew best and thought of most: New Mexicans and a fellow war correspondent.

New Mexico had an even greater impact on Pyle's personal life from 1935 to 1945. Prior to 1940, New Mexico represented a safe harbor in which the Pyles could "drop anchor" and rest in the course of their exhausting journeys. Inspired by the region's wide-open spaces, they swore that they could kiss the Southwest's "old empty desert" whenever the rest of the country closed in too closely around them.[1] Healed by the region's climate, Pyle suffered far fewer debilitating colds in New Mexico; he was no longer as cold as he'd been in places where sometimes "my mind would hardly work and my fingers would actually get so still I couldn't hit the keys."[2] At ease with the state's residents, the Pyles returned to New Mexico to visit the Shaffers and other close friends whenever possible. Pushed from elsewhere and pulled to the state by these and other attractions, the couple's natural choice for a "home base" was New Mexico, especially when Jerry's health deteriorated and the world conflict escalated by 1940.

Once relocated in Albuquerque, the Pyles enjoyed at least brief moments of happiness. They certainly enjoyed their small home, their spectacular view, their small circle of friends, their pet dogs, and the informality of a city that is said to never comb its hair before noon. Ernie Pyle was, in fact, so moved by his reception and treatment in Albuquerque that he went so far as to write a public letter to the editor of the *Tribune* (Shafe) to express his deep appreciation. Pyle wrote that his neighbors had made his time in New Mexico "pleasant by saying nice things to me about the column when we'd meet on the streets or in the stores; by doing so many extra little things for me; and, above all, by being understanding enough to let my time be largely my own."[3]

But the Pyles had pinned their hopes too high. Sadly, the couple's favorite state had begun to "turn to gall," as Pyle had feared it might, for reasons beyond anyone's control during World War II. Shafe and other friends had died or left, Kirtland Air Base (and the changes it brought) continued to expand, and Pyle's jealously guarded view to the west (symbolizing Albuquerque's semi-rural setting) was increasingly endangered by 1945.[4] Pyle's wistful comment that everything was changing at the beginning of the war was far more accurate, and upsetting, by the final year of the great conflict. Rapid change continued in the post-war era. The population of Bernalillo County (dominated by the city of Albuquerque) skyrocketed 110 percent in the decade 1940 to 1950 alone. As Marc Simmons concluded his general history of Albuquerque, "In size and physical appearance, [Albuquerque soon] bore scant resemblance to the lean town Ernie Pyle knew and loved in the mid 1940s."[5] Ironically, two of Pyle's closest friends, Earl Mount and Arthur McCollum, were among the largest builders of the post-war era. Adding to this irony, Pyle's own "Why Albuquerque?" undoubtedly helped draw newcomers to the growing city. An ad urging readers to "Make Your Home in ALBUQUERQUE" appeared on the same pages with Pyle's famous article in the *New Mexico Magazine*.[6]

Given this considerable urban growth, there can be little doubt that Ernie and Jerry Pyle would have left their "little white house" had they survived World War II; Pyle had begun to discuss this possibility by early 1944.[7] The question remains if Ernie Pyle could have been happy at any place or in any job of the post-war era. "Torn up inside and maladjusted" by war,[8] he may have constantly moved from place to place in search of his coveted peace and privacy; still revered by the public, it was unlikely that his readers would have let him "drift out of the limelight" any time soon.[9] Professionally, Pyle was no more attracted to returning to the exhausting life of a roving reporter in 1945 than he had been attracted to a desk job earlier in his career. Perhaps mercifully for Ernie Pyle, the question of just how well he could have adjusted to post-war life, in the ranks of Bill Mauldin and other New Mexican veterans, will never be answered.

If New Mexico's impact on Ernie Pyle was profound, it is well to ask what impact Ernie Pyle had on New Mexico and New Mexicans. Clearly, Pyle had a great impact on a number of New Mexicans, starting with those who read his column regularly and those he interviewed and wrote about both before and during World War II. With the exception of the few he bluntly criticized, every New Mexican interviewed by Pyle recalled his time with the reporter vividly and fondly. Indeed, given Pyle's pleasant nature, easy interviewing style, and subsequent fame, each interviewee proudly recalled his encounter with Pyle and appearance in his columns or books as a high point of their lives. Some, like Pop Shaffer and Ross Calvin, wrote about the experience; after spending much of a day and two hours at dinner with Pyle, Calvin enthusiastically noted in his diary that it had been a "Notable day!"[10] Others, like Dick Trauth, saved small mementos or showed their undying respect by visiting the Ernie Pyle Library and signing the guest book at this secular shrine. All realized that they had played a small part in the larger history of their times. All realized that in meeting Ernie Pyle, they had known a hero and brushed with history.

Some New Mexicans were fortunate to know Ernie Pyle for longer than a passing moment; his impact on their lives was proportionately larger and deeper. This was certainly the case with several younger New Mexicans of the era, led by Ed Shaffer's children. It was especially true of a handful of Southwesterners he mentored in one way or another. Based on Pyle's admiration for Bill Mauldin, for example, Pyle enthusiastically praised the young cartoonist in his syndicated column and in his second book of World War II, *Brave Men*.[11] While there is little doubt that a New Mexican with Mauldin's remarkable talent would have succeeded on his own, Pyle's kind assistance smoothed the road to success by helping to introduce Mauldin to readers on the home front following his immense popularity among readers in the military.

Shirley Mount benefited from Ernie Pyle's mentorship as well. As a family friend who recognized Shirley's intelligence and great potential, Pyle encouraged her to enter a professional career at a time when most young women were still urged to consider only traditional roles.[12] In addition to wise words of advice, Pyle gave Shirley a $500 gift when she graduated from the University of New Mexico at the age of nineteen. Earl Mount's daughter helped Pyle with his correspondence during World War II and later worked as Burgess Meredith's secretary in California, having been introduced to the actor by Pyle during the making of *The Story of G.I. Joe*. By 1949 she had graduated with a law degree from Stanford. After practicing law through the 1950's, she received her first appointment as a California state superior court judge in 1961. Other appointments quickly followed, culminating in her becoming only the second woman appointed to the U.S. Court of Appeals by 1968. As the highest ranking woman jurist in the nation, there was talk of her becoming the first woman justice on the Supreme Court. At the height of her successful career, President Jimmy Carter named her the first U.S. Secretary of Education when the Department of Health, Education and Welfare split in 1979.[13] Like Bill Mauldin, Shirley Mount would have undoubtedly succeeded on her own, but Ernie Pyle's early encouragement and assistance did much to ease her way and define her future direction in life.

Ernie Pyle also had a great impact on New Mexicans of his own generation who were close enough to call him friend. Despite his quiet nature, Pyle made friends easily in his adopted community. As one newspaper friend put it, "Ernie was all man, but there was something about him that made you want to take care of him, to lend him a hand whenever possible."[14] While Pyle clearly benefited from the kindness of friends like Shafe and Mount, these men and their families also benefited from as much support and understanding as Pyle could provide from overseas or, for short intervals, at home in New Mexico during the war.[15] Remembering Pyle fondly the rest of their lives, Mount and McCollum cherished their autographed copies of his books. In typical fashion, Pyle inscribed McCollum's copy of *Ernie Pyle in England* with the words: "For Arthur, God's chosen housebuilder— our affection. Ernie."[16]

Ernie Pyle had a similar impact on the Catholic nuns at St. Joseph Hospital. Sister Margaret Jane and her fellow nuns could not have been kinder to Jerry during her many illnesses, visiting her at the Woodcroft Sanitarium in Colorado, caring for her when she arrived at St. Joseph's in emergencies, keeping Pyle aware of her condition by mail, allowing her to stay in the relative seclusion of a "lunger's" cottage on hospital grounds, including Jerry as a regular guest on holidays like Thanksgiving (when she was most vulnerable to drinking), and accompanying her to meet Pyle at the Albuquerque Airport as early as 3:00 a.m.[17] Pyle reciprocated with many thoughtful gestures of his own, sending gifts and cards from overseas, showering the nuns with praise in his column, and providing special intervention on at least one occasion.[18] In this instance, a valued male employee at the hospital was about to be drafted into the military when Pyle stepped in and wrote to Governor John J. Dempsey to see if the man could be deferred. Two months later, Pyle reported that the governor had made arrangements with the draft board so that the employee could continue his work at the hospital undisturbed.[19] Such action was a true measure of Pyle's friendship and support. Given his aversion to politics, he rarely used his influence to pull political strings.[20] As a final token of her and Ernie's appreciation, Jerry gave the nuns at St. Joseph's a golden chalice, engraved with her and Pyle's names, within weeks of her death in November 1945.[21] Ernie Pyle would have approved of this special gift of thanks.

In addition to his indelible impact on individual New Mexicans, Ernie Pyle made a lasting impression on New Mexico as a whole in several ways. First, this astute observer left a written "mural" of New Mexican life in the era 1935 to 1945. In writing his many columns about the state, Pyle provided insightful, albeit brief and biased, views of New Mexico's New Deal politics, Native American population, art colonies, health care industry, tourist trade, wartime economic success, and varied military service. If journalism is the first draft of history, then Ernie Pyle left an excellent first draft of New Mexico history just prior to and during World War II.

Ernie Pyle also left a lasting impression on his adopted state by casting New Mexico and New Mexicans in a highly favorable light in the vast majority of his columns on the region. This was especially true when Pyle described why he and Jerry chose New Mexico as their "home base" in 1940. It was likewise true when he described unique persons and places. In Clyde Tingley's grateful, somewhat exaggerated terms, Ernie Pyle "never failed to speak and write a good word for his adopted city and state."[22]

Pyle's "good words" about New Mexico benefited the state in direct and indirect ways, ranging from drawing tourists to the region during his lifetime to attracting new funding for the University of New Mexico after his death. When Pyle visited Carlsbad Caverns in early April 1938, for example, the caverns had just suffered their worst attendance in five years. After Pyle's column featured the caverns in newspapers across the country in mid April, attendance shot from an average of about 195 visitors a day up to 464 on May 19, 1938, alone.[23] Years later, the Scripps-Howard Newspaper Alliance created the Ernie Pyle Memorial Fund which not only awarded prizes to top journalists, but also helped support various academic departments of journalism, starting with UNM's in 1953. The Journalism Department used its $4,000 grant to purchase as many as 900 journalism books for its own student library.[24] That same year, several wealthy New Mexicans contributed one hundred dollars each to purchase a portrait of Ernie Pyle. The painting was permanently hung in the Journalism Department's newsroom after having been displayed in the National Museum in Washington, D.C., among other locations across the United States.[25]

But as valuable as these several contributions were to New Mexico and its citizens, they pale in comparison to Pyle's contributions to the state during World War II. Like millions of readers across the United States and around the world, New Mexicans at home and abroad were informed, amused, and inspired by the simple prose found in Pyle's popular columns and books. Over two dozen New Mexicans were directly honored by their inclusion in the journalist's wartime writings. Others appreciated Pyle's efforts in behalf of the Bataan Relief Organization and war bond campaigns. Having seen this slight, unassuming man risk so much and serve so well, New Mexicans were better prepared to work harder and sacrifice more for the war. The creation of an Ernie Pyle Day and UNM's honorary degree were simply the most public expressions of New Mexico's gratitude for Pyle and his services beyond the call of duty.

Finally, Ernie Pyle contributed to New Mexico's collective memory of World War II long after V-E Day and V-J Day had passed. In a state whose memories of its wartime contributions are an enduring source of unifying patriotism and pride, Pyle's status as a prominent folk hero is firmly secure. Like other war heroes, including the Navajo Code Talkers, the soldiers of Bataan, and the atomic scientists of Los Alamos, Ernie Pyle is frequently remembered in large and small ways. A special Ernie Pyle edition of the *New Mexico Magazine* and an eight-minute film depicting his life in New Mexico were produced as early as the summer of 1945.[26] The anniversary of his death is often noted in the local press, as on its first anniversary in 1946, its fifth in 1950, its tenth in 1955, its twentieth in 1965 (when fourteen of his previously unpublished columns appeared in the *Tribune*), and its twenty-fifth in 1970.[27] Calling Pyle "the greatest human-interest journalist that America has ever produced," the *Santa Fe Reporter* reprinted many of his pre-war columns as a weekly special from April 1980 to January

1983.[28] The *Tribune* followed suit by reprinting "The Best of Ernie Pyle" as part of the newspaper's remembrance of World War II from 1992 to 1995. The series' last installment (a reprint of Pyle's last column of 1945) appeared on the 50th anniversary of the journalist's death.[29]

Ernie Pyle Day is celebrated often, as in 1946 when Maynard Meuli, a Bataan survivor, spoke at Highland Park; in 1948 when speakers remembered him in radio presentations on four local stations; in 1976 during the bicentennial celebration; and at recent annual observances by the Scottish-American Military Society on the south lawn of his former home.[30] The *Tribune's* Howard Bryan wrote a column entitled "Adopted Hometown Treasures Journalist's Memory" on what would have been Pyle's 83rd birthday. The Albuquerque city commission declared an entire Ernie Pyle Week in August 1960.[31]

In May 1971 a commemorative Ernie Pyle stamp was issued by the U.S. Post Office with the enthusiastic support of New Mexico's Senator Clinton P. Anderson, Senator Joseph A. Montoya, and Congressman Manual Lujan, Jr. Headlines in the *Albuquerque Tribune* announced "Our Ernie Pyle to Get His Stamp!"[32] Twelve years later the Albuquerque public television station, WNME-TV, produced an exceptional documentary entitled "Remembering Ernie Pyle."[33] The City of Albuquerque also honored the correspondent by constructing a concrete memorial at the Ernie Pyle Library in 1984; the memorial was engraved with phrases from Pyle's most famous war column, about a fallen young officer, Captain Henry T. Waskow, killed on the Italian front.[34] In yet another effort to honor Pyle and his perception of the world, a dramatic reading entitled "Through Ernie's Eyes" was performed in Albuquerque in June 1992 and again in August 1994.[35] A special chapter on Pyle appeared in a volume entitled *Victory in World War II: The New Mexico Story*.[36] As Governor Thomas J. Manby put it at the unveiling of the anti-aircraft gun with Pyle's engraved signature in 1950, "All ... New Mexicans have a great fondness for Ernie Pyle. His memory will be in the hearts of all forever."[37]

Both Dana, Indiana, and Albuquerque, New Mexico, have celebrated their memories of Ernie Pyle, albeit in different ways. Reflecting the familiarity and ease of the small town's relationship to its respected native son, celebrations in Dana have included parades, a big band dance, a fish fry, and an Ernie Pyle look-alike contest.[38] A more formal event, attended by Shirley Mount, Bill Mauldin, George

Shaffer, and students from Albuquerque's Ernie Pyle Middle School, was held in Dana to commemorate the fiftieth anniversary of Pyle's death.[39] In contrast, events to honor Pyle in his adopted city of Albuquerque have generally been smaller, if no less respectful, reflecting the awe New Mexicans still feel for this affable writer and his enduring memory. Citizens of the city and state have thus continued to display their deep affection for New Mexico's Ernie Pyle, just as the famous journalist had displayed his deep appreciation for what friends, relatives, and countless readers clearly recognized as Ernie Pyle's New Mexico.

NOTES

INTRODUCTION

1   Ernie Pyle's Column, *Albuquerque Tribune*, April 26, 1941; Ernie Pyle's column hereafter cited as EPC. Pyle's column never had a continuous title like other syndicated columns of his era, although many newspapers carried his column under the headline "Hoosier Vagabond" in deference to his Indiana roots.

2   EPC's (dated February 18, 1937, & November 16, 1940) in David Nichols, ed., *Ernie's America: The Best of Ernie Pyle's 1930s Travel Dispatches* (New York: Vintage Books, 1989), 366, 391-92; Ernie Pyle to Ed & Liz Shaffer, Santa Rosa, California, December 26, 1942, Edward H. Shaffer Collection, Albuquerque, New Mexico; hereafter sited as the Shaffer Collection.

3   Ernie Pyle, "Why Albuquerque?" *New Mexico Magazine*, vol. 20 (January 1942), 17; later reprinted in a Special Ernie Pyle Number, *New Mexico Magazine*, vol. 23 (June 1945).

4   EPC, *Albuquerque Tribune*, April 17, 1941.

5   Lee G. Miller, *The Story of Ernie Pyle* (New York: Viking Press, 1950); Lee G. Miller, *An Ernie Pyle Album: Indiana to Ie Shima* (New York: William Sloane Associates, 1946). David Nichols wrote biographical sketches of Pyle in his *Ernie's America*, xvii-l, and *Ernie's War: The Best of Ernie Pyle's World War II Dispatches* (New York: Random House, 1986), 3-37.

6   With urban growth, the Pyle's original address at 700 Girard Avenue SE later became 900 Girard Boulevard SE.

CHAPTER 1

1   Quoted in Nichols, *Ernie's America*, 11.

2   Miller, *Pyle*, 25-26; Steve Sanders, "Hoosier Vagabond: Ernie Pyle," *Indiana [University] Alumni*, vol. 47 (July/August 1985), 17-19; Maurice Trimmer, "Ernie Pyle Called Albuquerque 'Home'," *New Mexico Magazine*, vol. 38 (October 1960), 34. Trimmer's article later appeared as a chapter in George Fitzpatrick, ed., *This Is New Mexico* (Albuquerque: Horn & Wallace, 1962), 307-312. The anecdote regarding Pyle's milking ability was attributed to his aunt, Mary Bales. Undated newspaper clipping, Box 2, Ernie Pyle Collection, Special Collections Department, Albuquerque Public Library, Albuquerque, New Mexico; hereafter sited as the E. Pyle Collection.

3   Miller, *Pyle*, 50; Miller, *Album*, 20-21. Pyle had written a successful column on modern aviation from 1928 to 1932. See Mike Harden & Evelyn Hobson, eds., *On A Wing and A Prayer: The Aviation Columns of Ernie Pyle* (Dana, Indiana: The Friends of Ernie Pyle, 1995).

4   Pyle, "Why Albuquerque?" 274; Miller, *Pyle*, 36 & 51; Nichols, *Ernie's War*, 3; Pyle interview in the *[New Mexico State Teachers College] Mustang*, November 16, 1939. Pyle visited New Mexico at least once between 1926 and 1935 when he landed in Clovis, New Mexico, as one of the first passengers on Transcontinental Air Transport's new New York-Los Angeles air-rail line in August 1929. EPC (dated August 1, 1929) in Harden & Hobson, *A Wing and A Prayer*, 24-25.

5   Miller, *Pyle*, 51. The Pyles made similar courtesy calls to various Scripps-Howard editors. For a description of such a visit, see Ernie Pyle to Pyle Family, El Paso, Texas, November 12, 1939, Ernie Pyle Collection, Indiana University, Bloomington, Indiana; hereafter sited as the Pyle Collection. Pyle wrote family letters to his Aunt Mary, his father, Will, and his mother, Maria (until her death in March 1941).

6   *Washington Daily News*, April 2, 3, 8, & 13, 1935.

7   *Washington Daily News*, April 4 & 11, 1935. Harvey Fergusson, *Rio Grande* (New York: Alfred A. Knopf, 1933); Ross Calvin, *Sky Determines* (New York: Macmillan, 1934); Mary Austin, *Land of Little Rain* (Boston: Houghton, Mifflin, 1903).

8   *Washington Daily News*, April 4 & 5, 1935.

9   *Washington Daily News*, April 12, 1935.

10   *Ibid.*

11   EPC, *Albuquerque Tribune*, June 21, 1939.

12   Quoted in Miller, *Pyle*, 53.

13   Quoted in *ibid.*

14   EPC, *Albuquerque Tribune*, November 22, 1943.

15   Miller, *Album*, 32; Lila Noll Liggett, "'That Girl' of Ernie Pyle's," *The Woman With Woman's Digest* (July 1945), 9. While accurate in general, this article was marred by misinformation regarding several specifics about Jerry Pyle's life, especially her health.

16   Miller, *Pyle*, 33-34; Miller, *Album*, 23; *Albuquerque Tribune*, November 23, 1945; Pyle to Pyle Family, Hollywood, California, February 14, 1938, & Pyle to Pyle Family, Santiago, Chile, October 26, 1938, Pyle Collection.

17   Quoted in Liggett, "That Girl," 9.

18   *Ibid.*; Liz Shaffer quoted in "We the People" radio script, KGGM, July 15, 1945, Box 4, E. Pyle Collection.

19   Miller, *Album*, 50. George Baldwin of the *Albuquerque Tribune* recalled that he and other reporters at the newspaper gave story tips to Pyle whenever he was in town. *Albuquerque Tribune*, April 17, 1995.

20   Black notebook, Box 6, E. Pyle Collection.

21   Pyle to Shaffers, Washington, D.C., February 23, 1937, Shaffer Collection.

22   Wade Jones, "Just a Small, Shy Guy We Remember," *Santa Fe Reporter*, January 5, 1983.

23   Don Freeman, "Point of View," *San Diego Union*, December 11, 1984.

24   Walter Morrow (*Rocky Mountain News* editor) to Pyle, Denver, Colorado, May 31, 1938, Pyle Collection. For other examples see E.T. Leach (*Pittsburgh Press* editor) to Pyle, June 3, 1938; Edward M. Pooley (*El Paso Herald-Post* editor) to Pyle, El Paso, Texas, May 31, 1938; J.B. Stephens (*San Diego Sun* editor) to Pyle, San Diego, California, June 1, 1938, Pyle Collection. Fellow columnist Drew Pearson praised Pyle's work in Pearson to Pyle, Washington, D.C., September 9, 1936, Box 2, E. Pyle Collection.

25   E.H. Shaffer to Pyle, Albuquerque, May 31, 1938, Pyle Collection; "Ride With Ernie" editorial (by E.H. Shaffer), *Albuquerque Tribune*, May 12, 1939.

26   Pyle to E.H. Shaffer, Afton, Minnesota, July 24, 1936, Shaffer Collection.

27   O.J. Miller to the Editor, *Albuquerque Tribune*, July 12, 1939. A similar letter was written in Alice J. Harrison to the Editor, *Washington Daily News*, Washington, D.C., January 9, 1937, Box 2, E. Pyle Collection.

28   *New York Times*, April 19, 1945.

29   Exceptions to this rule appeared in columns on the Dust Bowl and on a Hooverville (or Depression shantytown). Nichols, *Ernie's America*, 112-26, 147-49.

30   For striking examples of the latter photographs, see Marta Weigle, ed., *New Mexicans in Cameo and Camera: New Deal Documentation of Twentieth-Century Lives* (Albuquerque: University of New Mexico Press, 1985). Also see Milton Meltzer, *Dorothea Lange: A Photojournalist's Life* (New York: Farrar, Straus, Giroux, 1978); Werner J. Severin, "Cameras with a Purpose: The Photojournalists of [the] F.S.A.," *Journalism Quarterly*, vol. 41 (1964), 191-200.

31   "Ernie Pyle's War," *Time*, vol. 44 (July 17, 1944), 72.

32   Quoted in the *Albuquerque Tribune*, May 8, 1939.

33   Pyle to Shaffers, Portland, Oregon, August 27, 1937; Pyle to Shaffers, Seattle, Washington, May 15 (no year), Shaffer Collection. Pyle sequestered himself to write columns in various hotels, including the Nickson Hotel in Roswell, New Mexico. Pyle to Pyle Family, Roswell, April 3, 1938, Pyle Collection.

CHAPTER 2

1   Pyle to Paige Cavanaugh, Indianapolis, Indiana, April 23, 1937, & Pyle to Pyle Family, Hawaii, November 25 & 28, 1937, Pyle Collection; Pyle to Shaffers, Hawaii, December 2, 1937, Shaffer Collection. In contrast, Pyle disliked certain regions of the nation and the world, including the Southern states and most of South America. Pyle to Shaffers, Houston, Texas, March 7 (no year) & Pyle to Shaffers, Cayenne, French Guyana, December 7, 1938, Shaffer Collection. A fellow Hoosier who met Pyle at Indiana University, Paige Cavanaugh was Pyle's closest lifelong friend.

2   Pyle to Pyle Family, Roswell, April 7, 1938, Pyle Collection.

3   EPC, Albuquerque Tribune, April 19, 1938. The best description of the caves was provided by explorer/photographer Robert Nymeyer in his Carlsbad, Caves, and a Camera (Teaneck, New Jersey: Zephyrus Press, 1978).

4   EPC, Albuquerque Tribune, April 19, 1938. This column later appeared in Nichols, Ernie's America, 243-45.

5   Unpublished EPC, November 1, 1940, Box 6, E. Pyle Collection. Also see EPC, Albuquerque Tribune, February 21, 1939.

6   EPC, Albuquerque Tribune, December 12, 1939. This column later appeared in Ed Ainsworth, ed., Ernie Pyle's Southwest (Palm Desert, California: Desert-Southwest, 1965), 64-65. For the history of White Sands, see Dietmar Schneider-Hector, White Sands: The History of a National Monument (Albuquerque: University of New Mexico Press, 1993).

7   EPC, Albuquerque Tribune, April 21, 1938. This column later appeared as a chapter in Ernie Pyle, Home Country (New York: William Sloane Associates, 1947), 287-88. On Billy the Kid's daring escape from the Lincoln County courthouse, see Robert M. Utley, Billy the Kid: A Short and Violent Life (Lincoln: University of Nebraska, 1989), 176-85.

8   Pyle to Shaffers, Santa Fe, (April) 1938, Shaffer Collection.

9   "Ernie Is Right" editorial (by E.H. Shaffer), Albuquerque Tribune, April 13, 1938.

10   EPC, Albuquerque Tribune, July 25, 1939. This column later appeared in Ainsworth, Ernie Pyle's Southwest, 23-25.

11   EPC, Albuquerque Tribune, July 26, 1939.

12   Pyle to Pyle Family, Flagstaff, Arizona, June 23, 1939, Pyle Collection.

13   EPC, Albuquerque Tribune, July 26, 1939. This column later appeared in Ainsworth, Ernie Pyle's Southwest, 26-27. Shafe described his trip with Pyle in the Albuquerque Tribune, June 26 & July 21, 1939.

14   EPC, Albuquerque Tribune, April 28, 1941.

15   EPC (dated June 23, 1936) in Nichols, Ernie's America, 356. Pyle also described driving conditions in New Mexico in two series he wrote about traveling with truckers through the Southwest. EPC's, Albuquerque Tribune, May 11, 15, 16, 17, 1939, & July 13, 1939.

16   EPC, Albuquerque Tribune, May 4, 1938.

17   Ibid. Poor roads had prevented Pyle from visiting Mabel Dodge Luhan on another visit to northern New Mexico. Jerry Pyle to Shaffers, Oklahoma City, Oklahoma, n.d., Shaffer Collection.

18   EPC, Albuquerque Tribune, May 3, 1938.

19   Ibid. This column later appeared in Pyle, Home Country, 288-90; Nichols, Ernie's America, 247-49. Abeita's story also appeared in Marc Simmons, Ranchers, Ramblers and Renegades: True Tales of Territorial New Mexico (Santa Fe: Ancient City Press, 1984), 107-109.

20   Pyle, Home Country, 413.

21   EPC (dated July 22, 1939) in Nichols, Ernie's America, 267.

22   EPC, Albuquerque Tribune, January 18, 1937. This column also appeared in Pyle, Home Country, 80.

23   EPC, Albuquerque Tribune, May 2, 1938.

24   EPC, Albuquerque Tribune, May 3, 1938.

25   Pyle to Pyle Family, Flagstaff, Arizona, June 23, 1939, Pyle Collection.

26   Taos Review, June 30, 1938.

27   On Mabel Dodge Luhan's far more favorable first impression of Taos Pueblo, see her Edge of Taos Desert (Albuquerque: University of New Mexico Press, 1987), 92-101. J.B. Priestley shared this favorable impression of Taos Pueblo when he toured the Southwest in the era, although his observations

about profit-minded Acoma Pueblo sounded much like Pyle's views of Taos and its many curio shops. J.B. Priestley, *Rain Upon Godshill: A Further Chapter of Autobiography* (New York: Harper & Brothers, 1939), 154.

28 Pyle to Shaffers, Albany, New York, September 10, 1938, Shaffer Collection. No record of the Taos "ultimatum" has been located in Pyle's papers or in Taos.

29 Pyle to Liz Shaffer, Amarillo, Texas, January 3, 1936; Pyle to Shaffers, Santa Fe, December 27, 1936, Shaffer Collection. EPC, *Albuquerque Tribune*, January 19, 1937.

30 *Ibid.*

31 EPC, *Albuquerque Tribune*, January 20, 1937.

32 *Ibid.*

33 EPC, *Albuquerque Tribune*, April 29, 1938.

34 *Ibid.*

35 See Edna Robertson & Sarah Nestor, *Artists of the Canyons and Caminos: Santa Fe, The Early Years* (Salt Lake City: Gibbs M. Smith, 1982); Arrell Morgan Gibson, *The Santa Fe and Taos Colonies: Age of the Muses, 1900-1942* (Norman: University of Oklahoma Press, 1983).

36 Pyle to Shaffers, Santa Fe, (April) 1938, Shaffer Collection.

37 *Ibid.* Many issues of the *Santa Fe Examiner* are missing in the New Mexico State Library, the only place where this newspaper is housed; the issue that accused Pyle of having a "vitriolic pen" appears to be among the missing.

38 *Santa Fe New Mexican*, January 18, 1937.

39 EPC's, *Albuquerque Tribune*, April 15, 1938, & December 2, 1939.

40 EPC's, *Albuquerque Tribune*, January 18, 1937, & December 7, 1939. Fisher referred to her box car home (a condemned refrigerator car bought from the Santa Fe Railroad for $40) in her semi-autobiographical books, *Bathtubs and Silver Bullets* (Albuquerque: Albuquerque Historical Society, 1976) and *More Bathtubs, Fewer Bullets* (Albuquerque: Albuquerque Historical Society, 1977). Whitehill's dwelling was also described in Mildred Jordan, "Description of An Underground Home," July 7, 1936, WPA research, Cornelious Cosgrove Whitehill File, Silver City Museum, Silver City, New Mexico. Also see the *Silver City Enterprise*, April 8, 1982.

41 EPC's, *Albuquerque Tribune*, May 5, 1938, & July 24, 1939. Pyle's young cowgirl was Unabelle Pitt.

42 EPC, *Albuquerque Tribune*, April 27, 1938.

43 EPC, *Albuquerque Tribune*, April 28, 1938. On Tingley's relationship with Franklin Roosevelt, see Erna Fergusson, "The Tingleys of New Mexico," Unpublished Manuscript, 237-40, Box 13, Folder 45, Erna Fergusson Papers, Special Collections, Zimmerman Library, University of New Mexico, Albuquerque, New Mexico. As governor, Tingley took a total of 23 trips to Washington, D.C. William A. Keleher, *New Mexicans I Knew: Memoirs, 1892-1969* (Albuquerque: University of New Mexico Press, 1983), 140. Tingley was Roosevelt's special guest on a train trip through seven western states in 1936. Marc Simmons, *Albuquerque: A Narrative History* (Albuquerque: University of New Mexico Press, 1982), 365.

44 EPC's, *Albuquerque Tribune*, April 27 & 28, 1938. On Tingley's political career, see Ferguson, "The Tingleys of New Mexico"; Keleher, *New Mexicans I Knew*, 119-22 & 130-48. On Carrie Tingley, see Eunice Kalloch & Ruth K. Hall, *The First Ladies of New Mexico* (Santa Fe: The Lightning Tree Press, 1982), 85-89. The Pyles apparently contributed to the Carrie Tingley Hospital fund in 1945. Miller, *Pyle*, 390.

45 EPC, *Albuquerque Tribune*, April 26, 1938. Pyle's health seeker hostess may well have worked for the Albuquerque Civic Council, which not only recruited health seekers to the city, but also welcomed them to the area by providing a "sympathetic guide" whose "whole desire" was to make sure "comfortable lodgings" were found and that "all the little details" were taken care of so they were "left with a feeling that [they were] amongst friends who [took] an active interest in [their] welfare." *Health City Sun*, August 23, 1935.

46 EPC, *Albuquerque Tribune*, April 26, 1938.

47 *Ibid.* For an autobiographical look at life in Albuquerque's sanatoriums, see Anne Ellis, *Sunshine Preferred* (Lincoln: University of Nebraska Press, 1984). Also see Jake W. Spidle, Jr., *Doctors of Medicine in New Mexico: A History of Health and Medical Practice, 1886-1986* (Albuquerque: University of New Mexico Press, 1986), 87-170. At least one other TB haven, in Saranac Lake, New York, had a similar hostess to meet new arrivals. Sheila M. Rothman, *Living in the Shadow of Death: Tuberculosis and the*

Social Experience of Illness in American History (New York: Basic Books, 1994), 220-21.

48 EPC, *Albuquerque Tribune*, December 5, 1939.

49 Ross Calvin, "Man Determines," *New Mexico Quarterly*, vol. 35 (Autumn 1965), 287.

50 Ross Calvin Diary, November 7, 1939, entry, Box 4, Ross Calvin Collection, Special Collections, Zimmerman Library; hereafter cited as the Calvin Collection.

51 EPC, *Albuquerque Tribune*, December 5, 1939.

52 Lawrence Clark Powell, Introduction, Ross Calvin, *Sky Determines* (Silver City: High-Lonesome Press, 1993). Also see Lawrence Clark Powell, "Southwest Classics Reread: *Sky Determines* by Ross Calvin," *Westways*, vol. 63 (September 1971), 18-21 & 64.

53 EPC, *Albuquerque Tribune*, December 5, 1939.

54 *Ibid.*

55 Back cover, 1993 High-Lonesome Press edition.

56 EPC, *Albuquerque Tribune*, December 8, 1939. Also see Anthony Caporaso, *The Miracle of Father Aull* (New York: Pageant Press, 1958), 30-31.

57 EPC, *Albuquerque Tribune*, December 8, 1939.

58 EPC's, *Albuquerque Tribune*, December 8 & 9, 1939. Also see Audrey H. Hartshorne, "Father Roger Aull: Saint, Sinner or Scientist?" Unpublished manuscript; George Blackwell, "I Remember Father Aull," *Hatch Courier* (n.d.), Father Aull File, Silver City Museum.

59 Pyle, *Home Country*, 80-82. A short biography of Abeita's colorful life is included in Joe S. Sando, *The Pueblo Indians* (San Francisco: Indian Historian Press, 1976), 141-49.

60 EPC, *Albuquerque Tribune*, April 13, 1942.

61 *Ibid.*

62 "'Pops' [sic] Handwritten Record," displayed in the lobby of the Shaffer Hotel, Mountainair, New Mexico.

63 *Ibid.* For a description of Rancho Bonito, see the *Albuquerque Journal*, June 5, 1984.

64 "'Pops' [sic] Handwritten Record."

65 *Ibid.*

66 *Mountainair Progressive*, April 17, 1942.

67 Keleher, *New Mexicans I Knew*, 147.

68 Sando, *Pueblo Indians*, 148-49; Glen O. Ream, *Out of New Mexico's Past* (Santa Fe: Sundial Press, 1980), 149; Marta Weigle & Peter White, *The Lore of New Mexico* (Albuquerque: University of New Mexico Press, 1988), 429.

69 Keleher, *New Mexicans I Knew*, 119-22.

70 Quoted in EPC, *Albuquerque Tribune*, December 9, 1939. Sadly, Father Aull was soon forced to leave his house because owners of the land it occupied objected to so much traffic moving to and from the priest's complex. Friends acquired new land for him, and he built his house all over again. Hartshorne, "Saint, Sinner or Scientist?" Father Aull was later known for inventing a controversial health restoring machine known as the halox therapeutic generator. *Ibid.*; Caporaso, *Miracle*.

71 EPC's, *Albuquerque Tribune*, April 22, 1938; May 16, 1939; December 11, 1939.

72 EPC's, *Albuquerque Tribune*, April 27, 1938; December 8, 1939.

73 EPC, *Albuquerque Tribune*, January 25, 1937.

74 These health chasers (or their relatives) included Clyde and Carrie Tingley, Ross Calvin, Pop Shaffer, Father Aull, Carlos Vierra (EPC, *Albuquerque Tribune*, January 21, 1937), McHarg Davenport (EPC, *Albuquerque Tribune*, January 26, 1937), Jim Terry (EPC, *Albuquerque Tribune*, April 22, 1938), Willard E. Holt (EPC, *Albuquerque Tribune*, December 4, 1939), & Wayne Wilson (EPC, *Albuquerque Tribune*, April 11, 1942).

75 EPC, *Albuquerque Tribune*, April 25, 1938. A biographical sketch of Oliver LaGrone appeared in Kathryn A. Flynn, ed., *Treasures of New Mexico Trails: New Deal Art and Architecture* (Santa Fe: Sunstone Press, 1995), 237-38.

76 EPC, *Albuquerque Tribune*, April 21, 1938. This column was later included in Pyle, *Home Country*, 287-88; Nichols, *Ernie's America*, 241-43.

77 Lincoln Barnett, "Ernie Pyle," *Life*, vol. 15 (November 15, 1943), 97. Pyle was said to have so few suits that he wore a coat with holes in its sleeves when he visited Eleanor Roosevelt in the White

House. Eleanor Roosevelt, *This I Remember* (New York: Harper & Brothers, 1949), 314. This same coat is displayed at the Ernie Pyle State Historic Site, Dana, Indiana. Pyle bought his first pair of shoes in seven years while visiting Albuquerque in 1939. EPC, *Albuquerque Tribune*, July 3, 1939.

78 Barnett, "Pyle," 97.

79 EPC, *Albuquerque Tribune*, January 7, 1942.

80 Miller, *Pyle*, 87 & 175.

81 Pyle, "Why Albuquerque?" 17.

CHAPTER 3

1 Richard A. Van Orman, *A Room for the Night: Hotels of the Old West* (New York: Bonanza Books, 1966), 11.

2 Miller, *Pyle*, 157. Fitzpatrick later included "Why Albuquerque?" in the 1948 edition of his edited volume, *This Is New Mexico* (Santa Fe: Rydal Press, 1948), 273-78.

3 Pyle, "Why Albuquerque?" 16.

4 Interview, Edward D. Shaffer (E.H. Shaffer's youngest son), Albuquerque, July 22, 1993; telephone interview, Stella Mary Jordon (E.H. Shaffer's daughter), Olympia, Washington, September 9, 1993; interview, George R. Shaffer (E.H. Shaffer's oldest son), Albuquerque, December 28, 1993; Edward H. Shaffer entry in Michael D. Abousleman, ed., *Who's Who in New Mexico: Biographical Sketches of Contemporary New Mexicans* (Albuquerque: The Abousleman Company, 1937); *Albuquerque Tribune*, April 4, 1944.

5 *Ibid.*

6 *Ibid.*

7 "The Governor Sends Troops to Gallup" editorial, *Albuquerque Tribune*, August 31, 1933.

8 Stella Mary Jordon interview. Despite their differences, Shaffer was called "one of Tingley's strongest adherents." Ferguson, "The Tingleys of New Mexico," 268. Tingley praised Shaffer in the *Albuquerque Tribune*, April 4, 1944.

9 Telephone interview, Shirley (Mount) Hufstedler, Los Angeles, California, September 12, 1993. Pyle's parents had insisted that he finish high school before entering the military. Short of enlisting in the regular service, Pyle joined the Naval Reserve on October 1, 1918. He was discharged on September 21, 1921. *Albuquerque Tribune*, April 17, 1945; Nichols, *Ernie's America*, xxviii.

10 *Albuquerque Tribune*, April 4, 1944.

11 *Ibid.*; Edward D. Shaffer interview; telephone interview, James R. Toulouse, Albuquerque, October 31, 1994; Pyle to Pyle Family, Albuquerque, April 7, 1938, Pyle Collection. James Toulouse worked as a reporter for the *Albuquerque Tribune* before later becoming a local attorney.

12 See, for example, Elizabeth Dickens, "Please Omit Flowers," *The New Yorker*, 15 (March 18, 1939), 52-53. Liz Shaffer used Dickens, her maiden name, as her pen name. Letters of support for Liz's writing included Pyle to Shaffers, Washington, D.C., February 25, 1937, & Jerry Pyle to Liz Shaffer, Springfield, Illinois, May 7, 1938, Shaffer Papers.

13 Stella Mary (Shaffer) Jordon interview. See, for example, Pyle to Shaffers, Boise, Idaho, August 4, 1939, & Jerry Pyle to Shaffers (postcard), San Francisco, California, August 13, 1940, Shaffer Collection.

14 Pyle to Pyle Family, Albuquerque, April 7, 1938, Pyle Collection.

15 Stella Mary (Shaffer) Jordon interview; Pyle to Cavanaugh, London, England, November 3, 1942, Pyle Collection.

16 See, for example, Pyle to Shaffers, Albany, New York, September 10, 1938, & Pyle to Shaffers, Miami, Florida, December 31, 1938, Shaffer Collection.

17 Pyle to Shaffers, Santa Fe, December 27, 1936, Shaffer Collection.

18 Jerry Pyle to Shaffers, Santa Fe, December 29, 1936, Shaffer Collection.

19 EPC (dated October 11, 1938) in Nichols, *Ernie's America*, 283.

20 Pyle, "Why Albuquerque?" 56. Although they were never close, Pyle had three cousins who lived elsewhere in New Mexico. Pyle to Pyle Family, Beaumont, Texas, March 4, 1939, Pyle Collection.

Pyle, "Why Albuquerque?" 56.

22 Pyle to Pyle Family, Evansville, Indiana, September 17, 1940, Pyle Collection.

23 Pyle to Shaffers, Phoenix, Arizona (October 1939), Shaffer Collection.

24 Pyle to Cavanaugh, n.p., October 26, 1939, Pyle Collection.

25 Quoted in Miller, *Pyle*, 120. The Pyles' arrival at the Murray Hotel in Silver City was publicly announced on the front page of the *Silver City Daily Press*, November 7, 1939.

26 EPC, *Albuquerque Tribune*, December 6, 1939. Also see Pyle to Pyle Family, El Paso, Texas, November 12, 1939, Pyle Collection; *[New Mexico State Teachers College] Mustang*, November 16, 1939.

27 One of these Christmas cards is found in the Willard E. Holt File, Box 2, E. Pyle Collection. The photo alone appeared in the *El Paso Herald*, December 4, 1939, and, later, in Miller, *Album*, 48.

28 Pyle to Willard E. Holt, San Antonio, Texas, November 28, 1939, Willard E. Holt File, Box 2, E. Pyle Collection. Pyle wrote a column about Holt and fellow Chamber of Commerce manager John O'Leary (of Deming) in EPC, *Albuquerque Tribune*, December 4, 1939.

29 Miller, *Pyle*, 95 & 108; Pyle to Pyle Family, Washington, D.C., May 22, 1938, & October 29, 1940, Pyle Collection.

30 Pyle's heavy drinking began during his days as a cub reporter when "sobriety did not prevail" on most social occasions. Miller, *Pyle*, 29 & 31. Pyle was heard to say that he didn't trust anyone who didn't drink. Nichols, *Ernie's America*, 79n. In 1938 he wrote that he was convinced that "booze is good for a man." Pyle to Shaffers, Cayenne, French Guyane, December 7, 1938, Shaffer Collection. His words would haunt him during countless hangovers and, later, during Jerry's serious bouts with alcoholism.

31 Pyle to Pyle Family, Hollywood, California, February 22, 1938, Pyle Collection.

32 Pyle to Cavanaugh, Evansville, Indiana, September 17, 1940, Pyle Collection.

33 Pyle to Pyle Family, New York, New York, June 3, 1940, Pyle Collection.

34 EPC (dated August 14, 1935) in Nichols, *Ernie's America*, 35.

35 Pyle to Pyle Family, New York, New York, September 1, 1940, Pyle Collection.

36 EPC (dated October 11, 1938) in Nichols, *Ernie's America*, 281.

37 Quoted in Nichols, *Ernie's America*, 129. Also see Pyle to Cavanaugh, Seattle, Washington, May 14, 1937, Pyle Collection; Pyle to Shaffers, Seattle, Washington, May 15, 1937, Shaffer Collection.

38 Pyle to Pyle Family, Taunton, Massachusetts, August 21, 1938, Pyle Collection.

39 Pyle, "Why Albuquerque?" 17.

40 Pyle to Shaffers, Phoenix, Arizona, October 30, 1939, Shaffer Collection.

41 Unpublished, undated column, Ernie Pyle File, Main Branch, Albuquerque Public Library, Albuquerque, New Mexico.

42 Pyle, "Why Albuquerque?" 17, 56, 58. Also see EPC's, *Albuquerque Tribune*, April 17, 1941, & November 22, 1943.

43 EPC (dated May 30, 1936) in Nichols, *Ernie's America*, 249; Pyle, "Why Albuquerque?" 56 & 58.

44 *Ibid.*

45 See, for example, Pyle to Shaffers, San Jose, Costa Rica, January 8, 1939, Shaffer Collection; Pyle to Cavanaugh, Lincoln, Maine, September 5, 1938, & Pyle to Cavanaugh, O'Hara, Canada, August 28, 1941, Pyle Collection.

46 Pyle to Shaffers, Cayenne, French Guyane, December 7, 1938, Shaffer Collection.

47 Pyle to Cavanaugh, Indianapolis, Indiana, April 23, 1937, Pyle Collection.

48 "Ernie Pyle's War," *Time*, vol. 44 (July 17, 1944), 68.

49 Pyle to Pyle Family, Lima, Peru, October 19, 1938, Pyle Collection.

50 Pyle to Cavanaugh, Rio de Janero, Brazil, November 12, 1938, Pyle Collection.

51 Quoted in Miller, *Pyle*, 76.

52 Pyle to Cavanaugh, Evansville, Indiana, September 17, 1940, Pyle Collection.

53 Quoted in Miller, *Pyle*, 80.

54 See, for example, Carl D. Groat (*Cincinnati Post* editor) to Pyle, Cincinnati, Ohio, June 1, 1938, Pyle Collection; P.R. Atterberry to Pyle, Washington, D.C., March 17, 1937, E. Pyle Collection.

141

55 Westbrook Pegler Column, *Albuquerque Tribune*, May 10, 1939. Pyle had privately expressed his low regard for Pegler two years earlier in Pyle to Shaffers, Portland, Oregon, August 27, 1937, Shaffer Collection.

56 Quoted in Nichols, *Ernie's War*, 10.

57 Miller, *Pyle*, 80.

58 Liz Shaffer quoted in "We the People" radio script, KGGM, July 15, 1945, Box 4, E. Pyle Collection.

59 Pyle to Cavanaugh, San Francisco, California, May 1, 1939, Pyle Collection.

60 Nichols, *Ernie's War*, 9.

61 See, for example, Pyle to Jerry Pyle, London, England, February 9, 1941, Pyle Collection.

62 Jerry Pyle to Shaffers, Toledo, Ohio, April 20, 1937, Shaffer Collection.

63 Miller, *Pyle*, 70.

64 Pyle to Cavanaugh, Seattle, Washington, August 18, 1937, Pyle Collection.

65 Pyle to Cavanaugh, Columbus, Ohio, June 27, 1938, Pyle Collection.

66 Quoted in Miller, *Pyle*, 137.

67 *Ibid.*, 69-70.

68 Pyle to Cavanaugh, Evansville, Indiana, September 17, 1940, Pyle Collection.

69 Pyle to Jerry Pyle, Indianapolis, Indiana, June 28, 1940, Pyle Collection.

70 Pyle to Shaffers, Biloxi, Mississippi, May 19, 1940, Shaffer Collection.

71 *Ibid.*

72 *Ibid.*

73 EPC (dated November 16, 1940) in Nichols, *Ernie's America*, 391.

74 EPC, *Albuquerque Tribune*, October 17, 1938.

75 EPC (dated February 18, 1937) in Nichols, *Ernie's America*, 366.

76 EPC (dated October 11, 1938) in Nichols, *Ernie's America*, 283.

77 EPC, *Albuquerque Tribune*, April 16, 1941.

78 Quoted in Hal Boyle column, newspaper clipping, June 25, 1952, Box 2, E. Pyle Collection.

CHAPTER 4

1 EPC, *Albuquerque Tribune*, May 15, 1939.

2 EPC, *Albuquerque Tribune*, January 21, 1937.

3 EPC, *Albuquerque Tribune*, January 22 & 23, 1937. Also see Jerry Pyle to Shaffers, Santa Fe, December 29, 1936, Shaffer Collection.

4 EPC's, *Albuquerque Tribune*, May 2, 1938, & April 16, 1941.

5 Pyle to Cavanaugh, Evansville, Indiana, September 17, 1940, Pyle Collection.

6 Pyle to Cavanaugh, Indianapolis, Indiana, July 20, 1940, Pyle Collection.

7 Pyle to Jerry Pyle, Indianapolis, Indiana, June 28, 1940, Pyle Collection.

8 *Ibid.*; Pyle to Cavanaugh, New York, New York, September 4, 1940, Pyle Collection.

9 *Santa Fe Capital Examiner*, June 29, 1940.

10 Jerry Pyle to Pyle Family, Albuquerque, February 1941, Pyle Collection.

11 Pyle to Cavanaugh, Indianapolis, Indiana, June 29, 1940, Pyle Collection.

12 Pyle to Jerry Pyle, Indianapolis, Indiana, June 28, 1940, Pyle Collection.

13 Pyle to Cavanaugh, Indianapolis, Indiana, June 29, 1940, Pyle Collection.

14 Pyle to Cavanaugh, Winchester, Virginia, October 29, 1940, Pyle Collection.

15 Shirley (Mount) Hufstedler interview.

16 Telephone interview, Charles Edman, Phoenix, Arizona, September 4, 1994.

17 Pyle to Cavanaugh, Winchester, Virginia, October 29, 1940, Pyle Collection. Also see Earl Mount interview in *Albuquerque Tribune*, July 15, 1965, & Arthur McCollum interview in *Albuquerque Journal*, July 29, 1965.

18 Pyle to Shaffers, Williamsburg, Virginia, October 20, 1940, Shaffer Collection. Also see Pyle to Shaffers, Pittsburgh, Pennsylvania, November 11, 1940, & Pyle to Shaffers, Washington, D.C., November 11, 1940, Shaffer Collection.

19 EPC, *Albuquerque Tribune*, April 16, 1941. In 1965, McCollum and Mount clarified that McCollum built Pyle's house on his land with plans developed by Mount. *Albuquerque Journal*, July 29, 1965. Charles Edman, in Mount's employ, drew the actual plans. Charles Edman interview.

20 Pyle to Cavanaugh, Albuquerque, April 1, 1941, Pyle Collection.

21 Pyle to Shaffers, Washington, D.C., November 11, 1940, Shaffer Collection.

22 Charles Edman interview.

23 *Albuquerque Tribune*, December 7, 1940; *Albuquerque Journal*, December 8, 1940.

24 EPC, *Albuquerque Tribune*, April 16, 1941.

25 Pyle to Cavanaugh, Winchester, Virginia, October 29, 1940, Pyle Collection; Miller, *Pyle*, 140; Liggett, "That Girl," 11.

26 Jerry Pyle to Pyle Family, Albuquerque, February 1941, Pyle Collection.

27 *Ibid.*; Pyle to Pyle Family, London, England, February 10, 1941, Pyle Collection; EPC, *Albuquerque Tribune*, April 16, 1941.

28 Pyle to Jerry Pyle, London, England, February 9, 1941, Pyle Collection.

29 Pyle to Cavanaugh, Winchester, Virginia, October 29, 1940, Pyle Collection. Also see Pyle to Shaffers, Winchester, Virginia, October 29, 1940, Shaffer Collection.

30 Jerry Pyle to Shaffers, n.p., November 5, 1940, Shaffer Collection.

31 Pyle to Cavanaugh, Gold Beach, Oregon, September 11, 1939, Pyle Collection.

32 Pyle to Shaffers, Biloxi, Mississippi, May 19, 1940, Shaffer Collection. Pyle's experience with the draft is covered in Miller, *Pyle*, 195, 197-99, 209-210. He eventually avoided the draft when the maximum draft age was set at 38. *Ibid.*, 210.

33 Pyle to Pyle Family, Portland, Oregon, September 4, 1939, Pyle Collection.

34 Pyle to Shaffers, Winchester, Virginia, October 29, 1940, Shaffer Collection.

35 Pyle to Cavanaugh, Gold Beach, Oregon, September 11, 1939, Pyle Collection.

36 Pyle to Cavanaugh, San Francisco, California, September 20, 1939, Pyle Collection.

37 Pyle to Cavanaugh, San Francisco, California, September 28, 1939, Pyle Collection.

38 Pyle to Shaffers, Pittsburgh, Pennsylvania, November 11, 1940, Shaffer Collection.

39 Pyle to E. Shaffer, On Board the *S.S. Exter*, November 22, 1940, Shaffer Collection.

40 Pyle's first column on his trip to Europe appeared in the *Albuquerque Tribune*, December 12, 1940. Also see Richard Hough & Denis Richards, *The Battle of Britain: The Greatest Air Battle of World War II* (New York: W.W. Norton, 1989).

41 EPC (dated January 29, 1941) included in Nichols, *Ernie's War*, 54.

42 Roy Howard telegram to Pyle, New York, New York, December 10, 1940, & Roy Howard telegram to Jerry Pyle, New York, New York, January 10, 1941, Pyle Collection; Eleanor Roosevelt to Pyle, Washington, D.C., February 14, 1941, Ernie Pyle File, Albuquerque Public Library, Main Branch; Barnett, "Ernie Pyle," 100; Ernie Pyle, *Ernie Pyle in England* (New York: Robert M. McBride & Company, 1941). Roy Howard headed the Scripps-Howard newspaper chain.

43 Miller, *Pyle*, 161-62; Pyle Expense Account Book, 1940-41, Pyle Collection. *Ernie Pyle in England* was favorably reviewed in the *New York Times*, August 31, 1941. While in London, Pyle also wrote about another famous American correspondent on the scene, radio journalist Edward R. Murrow. A.M. Sperber, *Murrow: His Life and Times* (New York: Freundlich Books, 1986), 189. Murrow wrote of his experiences during the bombing of London in *This Is London* (New York: Simon & Schuster, 1941). Murrow later urged Pyle to broadcast a weekly radio show about the war for CBS, but Pyle turned the offer down. Miller, *Pyle*, 211-12.

44 Quoted in Miller, *Pyle*, 152.

45 Quoted in *ibid.*, 151.

46 Pyle to Jerry Pyle, London, England, January 12, 1941, Pyle Collection.

47 Jerry Pyle telegram to Pyle, Albuquerque, n.d., Box 2, E. Pyle Collection; Miller, *Pyle*, 153. Pyle's moving column (dated April 10, 1941) on his mother's death was included in Nichols, *Ernie's America*, 396-98.

48 EPC, *Albuquerque Tribune*, April 17, 1941.

49 *Ibid.*

50 EPC, *Albuquerque Tribune*, April 16, 1941.

51 EPC's, *Albuquerque Tribune*, April 16 & 17, July 10, 1941.

52 Pyle to Cavanaugh, Albuquerque, April 1, 1941; Pyle to Pyle Family, Albuquerque, April 6 & 21, 1941, Pyle Collection. Pyle disliked Southwestern sandstorms so much that he was heard to say that he "might have to run for the [New Mexico] State Legislature and get a bill passed against sandstorms." Quoted in the *El Paso Herald Post*, April 18, 1945.

53 EPC, *Albuquerque Tribune*, July 7, 1941.

54 *Ibid.* Pyle reported that he had read Ben Fobertson's *I Saw England* ("a serenely beautiful book"), Max Miller's *Reno* ("a dandy book"), H. Allen Smith's *Low Man on a Totem Pole* (which "everybody wants to read"), some Mark Twain stories, and Lin Yutang's *With Love and Irony* (a "disappointment" which he never finished). EPC, *Albuquerque Tribune*, July 9, 1941. Also see Pyle to Cavanaugh, Albuquerque, June 5, 1941, Pyle Collection.

55 *Ibid.*; EPC, *Albuquerque Tribune*, July 7, 1941; Pyle to Cavanaugh, Albuquerque, June 5, 1941, Pyle Collection; Shirley (Mount) Hufstedler interview; Earl Mount interview in the *Albuquerque Tribune*, July 15, 1965. Shirley Mount also humored Pyle with high school jokes, including several he retold in EPC, *Albuquerque Tribune*, April 16, 1942.

56 Telephone interview, George Baldwin, Albuquerque, January 18, 1994; James R. Toulouse interview; telephone interview, Louise (Abeita) Chewiwi, Bosque Farms, New Mexico, November 5, 1994; Miller, *Pyle*, 161. Louise Chewiwi is the late Diego Abeita's daughter.

57 Interview, Betty Sabo, Albuquerque, August 26, 1994. Sabo, a well-known New Mexico artist, studied with von Hassler at his Albuquerque studio. *Albuquerque Tribune*, April 3, 1961; *Albuquerque Journal*, November 26, 1961, & December 2, 1969.

58 Betty Sabo interview.

59 *Albuquerque Journal*, December 2, 1969.

60 Shirley (Mount) Hufstedler interview; Edward D. Shaffer interview; George R. Shaffer interview; James R. Toulouse interview.

61 EPC, *Albuquerque Tribune*, November 17, 1943; Earl Mount interview in the *Albuquerque Journal*, July 15, 1965.

62 *Ibid.*; Pyle to Cavanaugh, Albuquerque, October 11, 1941, Pyle Collection.

63 Charles Edman interview.

64 Edward D. Shaffer interview.

65 Pyle to Cavanaugh, Albuquerque, April 1, 1941, Pyle Collection.

66 EPC's, *Albuquerque Tribune*, July 7 & 10, 1941.

67 Pyle to Cavanaugh, Albuquerque, June 5 & October 11, 1941, Pyle Collection; Pyle, "Why Albuquerque?" 56. Years later, Ed Pigeon of Albuquerque bought a small end table for 75 cents at a local junk yard. An inscription on its underside read: "To who it may concern, Ernie Pyle made this table. His wife colored it." *Albuquerque Tribune*, March 9, 1972.

68 Pyle to the Editor of the *Denver Star*, Albuquerque, June or July 21, 1941, Pyle Collection; Shirley (Mount) Hufstedler interview; "We the People" radio script, KGGM, July 15, 1945, Box 4, E. Pyle Collection; EPC, *Albuquerque Tribune*, July 8, 1941. Photos of Pyle and Shirley Mount by their fence project appeared in *ibid.* & Miller, *Album*, 63.

69 EPC, *Albuquerque Tribune*, July 8, 1941. Also see Pyle to Pyle Family, June 1941, Pyle Collection.

70 EPC, *Albuquerque Tribune*, July 10, 1941. Pyle eventually enjoyed tea at the White House with the First Lady, as described in E. Roosevelt, *This I Remember*, 314.

71 EPC, *Albuquerque Tribune*, July 7, 1941.

72 EPC, *Albuquerque Tribune*, July 10, 1941.

73 Charles Edman interview; Earl Mount interview in the *Albuquerque Journal*, July 15, 1965; Pyle to Pyle Family, Albuquerque, October 28, 1941, & Pyle to Cavanaugh, Albuquerque, October 11 & November 8, 1941, Pyle Collection. According to his expense records, Pyle paid Mount $962.30 for this addition. Expense Account Book, 1940-41, Pyle Collection.

74 EPC, *Albuquerque Tribune*, April 26, 1941. The assistant manager of Albuquerque's Hilton Hotel apparently agreed with Pyle. After installing hitching posts by two of the hotel's entrances, Billy

Salter said, "We're looking ahead back to horse and buggy days." *Albuquerque Journal*, February 12, 1942.

75 EPC, *Albuquerque Tribune*, April 25, 1941.

76 EPC, *Albuquerque Tribune*, April 24, 1941. Also see EPC, *Albuquerque Tribune*, April 10, 1941. On wartime aviation developments, see Don E. Alberts, *Balloons to Bombers: Aviation in Albuquerque, 1882-1945* (Albuquerque: Museum, 1987), 59-63.

77 EPC, *Albuquerque Tribune*, April 24, 1941.

78 Pyle, *Ernie Pyle in England*, 228.

79 EPC's, *Albuquerque Tribune*, July 8 & 10, 1941.

80 EPC, *Albuquerque Tribune*, July 10, 1941.

CHAPTER 5

1 EPC, *Albuquerque Tribune*, April 22, 1941.

2 Jerry Pyle to Pyle Family, Albuquerque, n.d., Pyle Collection.

3 Pyle to Pyle Family, Albuquerque, April 21, 1941, Pyle Collection.

4 Pyle to Pyle Family, Albuquerque, May or June, 1941, Pyle Collection.

5 Pyle to Pyle Family, Albuquerque, April 6, 1941, Pyle Collection.

6 Pyle to Cavanaugh, Albuquerque, June 5, 1941, & Pyle to Pyle Family, Albuquerque, May or June, 1941, Pyle Collection.

7 Pyle to Pyle Family, Albuquerque, April 6, 1941, Pyle Collection.

8 Quoted in Miller, *Pyle*, 161.

9 E.H. Shaffer to Walker Stone, Albuquerque, (September 3, 1941), Shaffer Collection.

10 Pyle to Pyle Family, Albuquerque, April 6, 1941, Pyle Collection.

11 *Ibid.*

12 Pyle to Pyle Family, Albuquerque, (May or June) 1941, Pyle Collection. Janie Meuli, a neighbor on Girard Avenue, recalls the many tourists who came down their still-unpaved road. Interview, Janie Meuli, Albuquerque, December 12, 1994. Pyle's name appeared in the *Albuquerque City Directory* (El Paso: Hudspeth Directory Company) in each of its editions from 1941 to 1944.

13 Pyle to Jerry Pyle, Los Angeles, California, November 12, 1941, Pyle Collection; Miller, *Pyle*, 163-64.

14 Pyle to Cavanaugh, Denver, Colorado, June 25, 1941, Pyle Collection.

15 Pyle to Cavanaugh, Denver, Colorado, July 10, 1941, Pyle Collection; Pyle to Shaffers, Denver, Colorado, September 27, 1941, Shaffer Collection; Miller, *Pyle*, 164-65.

16 Pyle to Shaffers, Denver, Colorado, September 27, 1941, Shaffer Collection.

17 Pyle to Liz Shaffer, Ottawa, Canada, August 28, 1941, Shaffer Collection.

18 Miller, *Pyle*, 167.

19 E.H. Shaffer to Walker Stone, Albuquerque, (September 3, 1941), Shaffer Collection.

20 *Ibid.*

21 *Ibid.*

22 Quoted in Miller, *Pyle*, 167.

23 Pyle to Cavanaugh, Albuquerque, September 4, 1941, Pyle Collection.

24 E.H. Shaffer to Walker Stone, Albuquerque, (September 3, 1941), Shaffer Collection.

25 Quoted in Miller, *Pyle*, 169.

26 Miller, *Pyle*, 170.

27 Quoted in *ibid.*, 172.

28 EPC, *Albuquerque Tribune*, January 10, 1942. Sister Margaret Jane Lalor (b. 1902 in Cripple Creek, Colorado) entered the Sisters of Charity on February 1, 1927. A registered nurse, she served in Catholic hospitals in Ohio, Michigan, Colorado, and New Mexico. She worked at St. Joseph Hospital in Albu-

querque from 1939 to 1945 and died at Mount St. Joseph, Ohio, on July 5, 1965. The Pyles were also close to Sister Mary Isidore Linden (b. 1873 in Lansing, Michigan) who entered the Sisters of Charity on April 4, 1900. She served at St. Joseph Hospital from 1939 to 1954, dying in Albuquerque on February 10, 1954. Sister Anita Marie Howe, Sisters of Charity Archivist, to the author, Mount St. Joseph, Ohio, April 25, 1994; *Health City Sun*, January 13, 1939. Recruited by Bishop Jean B. Lamy, the first Sisters of Charity came to work as teachers and nurses in New Mexico in 1865. Kate H. Parker, "I Brought With Me Many Eastern Ways: Euro-American Income-Earning Women in New Mexico, 1850-1880" (Unpublished Ph.D. dissertation, University of New Mexico, 1984), 84, 143-46.

29 Pyle to Cavanaugh, Albuquerque, November 8, 1941, Pyle Collection.

30 *Ibid.*

31 Pyle to Cavanaugh, Albuquerque, November 24, 1941, Pyle Collection; Ella Streger interview in the *Albuquerque Tribune*, January 31, 1953.

32 Quoted in *Miller*, Pyle, 9. Jerry had expressed her love of "good dogs" in Jerry Pyle to Shaffers, Toledo, Ohio, April 20, 1937, Shaffer Collection.

33 Pyle to Cavanaugh, Albuquerque, November 24, 1941, Pyle Collection; EPC, *Albuquerque Tribune*, January 8, 1942.

34 *Miller*, Pyle, 177.

35 EPC, *Albuquerque Tribune*, January 8, 1942. Photos of the Pyles with Cheetah appeared in Miller, *Album*, 63, 87, 114-17.

36 EPC, *Albuquerque Tribune*, January 9, 1942. Pyle purchased his second pet for $100 on December 1, 1941. Expense Account Book, 1940-41, Pyle Collection.

37 EPC, *Albuquerque Tribune*, January 9, 1942.

38 Pyle to Shaffers, Santa Rosa, California, December 26, 1941, Shaffer Collection.

39 Pyle to Cavanaugh, Santa Rosa, California, December 27, 1941; Pyle to Cavanaugh, Portland, Oregon, January 5, 1942; Pyle to Jerry Pyle, Portland, Oregon, January 18, 1942; Pyle to Jerry Pyle, n.p., January 30, 1942; Pyle to Cavanaugh, San Francisco, California, February 5, 1942, Pyle Collection.

40 Jerry Pyle to Willard E. Holt, Albuquerque, December 1941 or January 1942, Willard E. Holt File, Box 2, E. Pyle Collection; Pyle to Cavanaugh, San Diego, California, March 13, 1942, Pyle Collection.

41 Telephone interview, Marguerita Dow, San Angelo, Texas, July 16, 1994.

42 Pyle to Cavanaugh, San Diego, California, March 19, 1942, Pyle Collection. Also see Pyle to Cavanaugh, Phoenix, Arizona, March 23, 1942, Pyle Collection.

43 Quoted in Miller, *Pyle*, 185.

44 Pyle to Shaffers, Palm Springs, California, March 12, 1942, Shaffer Collection.

45 Quoted in Miller, *Pyle*, 188.

46 Pyle to Cavanaugh, San Francisco, California, February 5, 1942; Pyle to Cavanaugh, London, England, August 8, 1942, Pyle Collection.

47 Pyle to Shaffers, Palm Springs, California, March 12, 1942, Shaffer Collection.

48 Quoted in Miller, *Pyle*, 184-85.

49 Quoted in *ibid.*, 185.

50 Quoted in *ibid.*, 186.

51 Pyle to Cavanaugh, San Diego, California, March 13, 1942, Pyle Collection.

52 Quoted in Miller, *Pyle*, 191.

53 Quoted in *ibid.*, 192. Also see the *Albuquerque Journal*, April 15, 1962. Joseph L. Dailey was a fellow native of Indiana who had originally come to Albuquerque as a TB patient. Like so many "lungers" who regained their health in New Mexico, Dailey remained in the state, founding the Rodey and Dailey law firm with Pearce Rodey in 1927. By 1931 fifteen practicing attorneys in Albuquerque were recovered health seekers. *Health City Sun*, June 11 & 19, 1931.

54 Miller, *Pyle*, 193. Judge Kool reported an "astounding increase" in the number of divorce cases during the war. By 1943 he claimed that about half the civil suits heard in his court involved divorces. *Albuquerque Tribune*, October 19, 1943.

55 *Ibid.*, 199.

56 Quoted in *ibid.*

57   Pyle to Shaffers, Clovis, New Mexico, April 5, 1942, Shaffer Collection.

58   Pyle to Pyle Family, Albuquerque, November 4, 1941, Pyle Collection. On November 27, 1941, Pyle withdrew $1,700 from the bank for his planned trip to the Orient. He also withdrew $2,300 for Jerry's expenses while he was to be gone. Expense Account Book, 1940-41, Pyle Collection. Pyle had traveled to the Orient once before, while in college in 1922. Pyle to Pyle Family, In the Pacific, April 1, 1922, Pyle Collection.

59   Pyle to Cavanaugh, San Francisco, California, December 9, 1941, Pyle Collection. The December 7, 1941, attack is well described in Walter Lord, *Day of Infamy* (New York: Henry Holt & Company, 1957).

60   Pyle to Shaffers, Santa Rosa, California, December 26, 1941, Shaffer Collection.

61   Pyle to Cavanaugh, San Francisco, California, December 9, 1941, Pyle Collection.

62   Charles Edman interview. By war's end New Mexico could boast the highest volunteer rate per capita of any state in the Union. Judith Boyce DeMark, ed., *Essays in Twentieth Century New Mexico History* (Albuquerque: University of New Mexico Press, 1994), 8.

63   Pyle to Cavanaugh, San Francisco, California, December 9, 1941, Pyle Collection.

64   Pyle to Shaffers, Portland, Oregon, January 20, 1942, Shaffer Collection.

65   Pyle to Shaffers, Palm Springs, California, March 12, 1942, Shaffer Collection.

66   Quoted in Miller, *Pyle*, 181.

67   Pyle to Shaffers, Palm Springs, California, March 12, 1942, Shaffer Collection.

68   Quoted in Miller, *Pyle*, 181; capital letters in the original.

69   Nichols, *Ernie's War*, 12. Pyle told a close friend that he looked like a "horse's ass" in his Army cap and only wore a military uniform because he wasn't allowed to accompany the Army without one. Pyle to Arthur McCollum, London, England, September 11, 1942, Arthur McCollum Collection, Albuquerque, New Mexico; hereafter cited as the McCollum Collection.

70   *Ibid.*, 14-15.

71   Quoted in Miller, *Pyle*, 188.

72   Pyle to Jerry Pyle, New York, New York, June 18, 1942, Pyle Collection.

CHAPTER 6

1   *Albuquerque Tribune*, October 25, 1944, & April 18, 1945; Richard Collier, *The Warcos: The War Correspondents of World War Two* (London: Weidenfeld & Nicholson, 1989), 140; Charles B. McDonald, *The Mighty Endeavor: The American War in Europe* (New York: DaCapo Press, 1992), 154; Robert H. Adleman & Col. George Walton, *Rome Fell Today* (Boston: Brown & Company, 1968), 129; John Grassner & Dudley Nichols, eds., *Best Film Plays, 1945* (New York: Garland, 1977), xi. G.I., standing for "Government Issue," became the American soldier's nickname in World War II, just as "doughboy" had been his nickname in World War I. For the origin of the former name, see Lee Kennett, *G.I.: The American Soldier in World War II* (New York: Charles Scribner's Sons, 1987), 87-88.

2   Quoted in Collier, *Warcos*, 141. Other war correspondents agreed with Steinbeck's assessment of Pyle. See, for example, Andy Rooney, *My War* (New York: Random House, 1995), 172 & 182. Steinbeck's experiences as a war correspondent were recounted in his *Once There Was a War* (New York: Viking Press, 1958). Pyle's and Steinbeck's wartime coverage was compared (in Pyle's favor) in an editorial in the *Louisville Courier-Journal*, as quoted in the *Albuquerque Tribune*, September 29, 1943. Regarding Steinbeck's famous *Grapes of Wrath*, Pyle privately thought that it "went out of its way to be vulgar, but it is a very important book just the same." Pyle to Pyle Family, Miami, Florida, March 14, 1940, Pyle Collection. Also see Pyle to Cavanaugh, Denver, Colorado, May 29, 1939, Pyle Collection. Pyle reviewed *The Grapes of Wrath* in EPC, *Albuquerque Tribune*, June 21, 1939.

3   Barnett, "Ernie Pyle," 100. One of the best descriptions of Pyle's writing style appeared in Randall Jarrell, "Ernie Pyle," *The Nation*, vol. 160 (May 19, 1945), 573-76. One of the only criticisms of Pyle's writing was made by the "perennial iconoclast," H.L. Mencken. Mencken called the correspondents of World War II a "sorry lot" who were "either typewriter statesmen turning out dope stuff drearily dreamed up, or sentimental human-interest scribblers turning maudlin stuff about the common soldier, easy to get by the censors. Ernie Pyle was a good example. He did well what he set out to do, but

that couldn't be called factual reporting of the war." Quoted in Robert W. Desmond, *Tides of War: World News Reporting, 1940-1945* (Iowa City: University of Iowa, 1982), 462. Judging Pyle with 1990's values, a more recent author has pointed out that Pyle was condescending to women, calling them "gals" and frequently referring to their "giggly ways" in his columns. Michael C.C. Adams, *The Best War Ever: America and World War II* (Baltimore: Johns Hopkins University Press, 1994), 86. Paul Fussell criticized Pyle for concealing much of the horror of war, "reveal[ing] only about one-third of the acutuality." Paul Fussell, *Wartime: Understanding and Behavior in the Second World War* (New York: Oxford University Press, 1989), 287.

4   Tom F. Yeader quoted in the *Albuquerque Tribune*, October 13, 1944.

5   *New York Times*, May 2, 1944. Also see the *Albuquerque Tribune*, September 29, 1943.

6   Miller, *Pyle*, 363. At Pyle's urging Congress passed the so-called "Ernie Pyle Bill" raising soldiers' pay for combat duty. Robert Leckie, *Delivered From Evil* (New York: Harper & Row, 1987), 880; "Ernie Pyle's War," 65n.

7   Quoted in Miller, *Pyle*, 227, and the *Albuquerque Journal*, April 2, 1995. The general also appreciated Pyle's several complimentary columns which made his a household name back in the states. Omar N. Bradley, *A General's Life: An Autobiography* (New York: Simon & Shuster, 1983), 200, 690-91n; Omar N. Bradley, *A Soldier's Story* (New York: Henry Holt & Company, 1951), 147-48. Pyle's columns on Bradley were reprinted in Pyle, *Brave Men*, 209-14; Nichols, *Ernie's War*, 328-29. The Navy also praised Pyle's work in Europe. See the *Albuquerque Tribune*, September 24, 1943.

8   Fussell, *Wartime*, 156.

9   Quoted in Miller, *Pyle*, 246.

10   Cover cartoon (by Sgt.Al Melinger), *Yank: The Army Weekly*, October 6, 1944. Also see Corporal Sy M. Kahn's description of Pyle as the reporter who captured "the real mood of the soldier better than any other newspaper writer." Sy M. Kahn, *Between Tedium and Terror: A Soldier's World War II Diary, 1943-1945* (Urbana: University of Illinois Press, 1993), entry of October 17, 1944, p. 185.

11   Howard (no last name given) to his family, n.p., April 22, 1944, McCollum Collection.

12   This opinion was expressed by many contemporaries, including the *Albuquerque Tribune*, October 18, 1943, and an editorial entitled "Brave Man," *Raton Daily Range*, April 20, 1945.

13   Quoted in Miller, *Pyle*, 411.

14   Jane Easton to Robert Easton, Los Angeles, California, January 4, 1945, in Robert & Jane Easton, *Love and War: Pearl Harbor Through V-J Day* (Norman: University of Oklahoma Press, 1991), 283. For similar reactions to Pyle's columns back home, see Judy Barrett Litoff et. al., *Miss You: The World War II Letters of Barbara Woodall Taylor and Charles E. Taylor* (Athens: University of Georgia Press, 1990), 144, 196, 211, 217, 261.

15   "Ernie Pyle's War," 65.

16   Quoted in the *Albuquerque Tribune*, April 16, 1945.

17   *Albuquerque Tribune*, September 14, 1943; Barnett, "Ernie Pyle," 97; Richard R. Lingeman, *Don't You Know There's a War On?: The American Home Front, 1941-45* (New York: G.P. Putman's Sons, 1970), 302. Pyle's travels in the war zones of Europe and the Pacific are followed in Desmond, *Tides of War*, 136, 295, 302, 311, 317, 318, 321, 350, 363, 371, 374, 377, 434-35.

18   Pyle to Jerry Pyle, London, England, September 26, 1942, Pyle Collection.

19   Pyle to Jerry Pyle, London, England, October 28, 1942, Pyle Collection. Also see Pyle to Jerry Pyle, London, England, October 29, 1942, Pyle Collection.

20   This "refashioning" of the past is discussed in Kennett, *G.I.*, 74.

21   Pyle to Jerry Pyle, North Africa, November 26, 1942, Pyle Collection. Pyle later compared Tunesia's winter season to Albuquerque's. Pyle to Jerry Pyle, North Africa, February 21, 1943, Pyle Collection.

22   Pyle to Jerry Pyle, North Africa, November 26, 1942, Pyle Collection.

23   Ernie Pyle, *Here Is Your War* (New York: Henry Holt & Company, 1943), 19. George Biddle made a similar comparison in his *Artist at War* (New York: Viking Press, 1944), 29.

24   Pyle to Jerry Pyle, North Africa, December 8, 1942, Pyle Collection.

25   *Ibid.*

26   Pyle to Jerry Pyle, North Africa, March 2, 1943, Pyle Collection. Six days later Pyle asked Jerry to "keep Cheetah in old shoes so she won't forget [me]." Pyle to Jerry Pyle, North Africa, March 2, 1943, Pyle Collection. Pyle also "dreamed that Piper had come to life." Quoted in Miller, *Pyle*, 224.

27 See, for example, Pyle to Jerry Pyle, London, England, November 3, 1942, Pyle Collection.

28 Pyle to Cavanaugh, Dublin, Ireland, June 27, 1942, Pyle Collection.

29 Pyle to Shaffers, England, September 18, 1942, Shaffer Collection. Pyle expressed the same wish in Pyle to Arthur McCollum, London, England, September 11, 1942, McCollum Collection.

30 Quoted in Miller, *Pyle*, 221. This typical soldier's nightmare is discussed in Kennett, *G.I.*, 76-77.

31 James R. Toulouse interview. Power of Attorney, Ernest T. Pyle, December 8, 1942. The author thanks attorney James R. Toulouse for sharing a copy of this document in Toulouse to the author, Albuquerque, November 3, 1994.

32 Quoted in Miller, *Pyle*, 231.

33 Marriage Certificate, Ernest T. Pyle and Geraldine Siebolds Pyle, Albuquerque, New Mexico, March 10, 1943. The author again thanks James R. Toulouse for sharing a copy of this document in Toulouse to the author, Albuquerque, November 3, 1994.

34 Quoted in Miller, *Pyle*, 244.

35 Quoted in *ibid.*, 248.

36 Pyle to E.H. Shaffer, Africa, April 8, 1943, Shaffer Collection.

37 *Ibid.*

38 George R. Shaffer interview. To make sure that their March 10 wedding was completely legal, the Pyles repeated the ceremony when he returned to New Mexico that fall. Miller, *Pyle*, 288.

39 Pyle, *Here Is Your War*, 148.

40 Ernie Pyle, *Brave Men* (New York: Henry Holt & Company 1944), 66.

41 EPC, *Albuquerque Tribune*, January 11, 1944. This column was included in Pyle, *Brave Men*, 90.

42 Pyle to Jerry Pyle, France, July 4, 1944, Pyle Collection.

43 "The Story of G.I. Joe" in Gassner & Nichols, *Best Film Plays*, 418. The filming of *G.I. Joe* was described in the *Albuquerque Tribune*, January 25, 1945.

44 Pyle, *Here Is Your War*, 9.

45 *Ibid.*, 56.

46 *Ibid.*, 40. Also see Rudy Faircloth & H. Horace Carter, *Typewriter Soldier* (Tabor City, North Carolina: Atlantic Publishing Company, 1982), 26. On the importance of mail to American morale, see Litoff, *Miss You*, 137-43. A total of 3.5 billion pieces of mail were sent overseas in 1945 alone. *Ibid.*, 139.

47 EPC, *Albuquerque Tribune*, April 25, 1945. This column also appeared in Ernie Pyle, *Last Chapter* (New York: Henry Holt & Company, 1946), 132, and in Nichols, *Ernie's War*, 415-16. Interview, Dick Trauth, Albuquerque, November 22, 1992.

48 Pyle, *Brave Men*, 201.

49 EPC (dated July 20, 1944) included in Nichols, *Ernie's War*, 312-13.

50 Steve McDowell, "A Conversation With Bill Mauldin," *El Palacio*, vol. 98 (Spring 1993), 12 & 15; Gerald W. Thomas, Monroe L. Billington, & Roger D. Walker, eds., *Victory in World War II: The New Mexico Story* (Las Cruces: New Mexico State University, 1994), 107.

51 EPC, *Albuquerque Tribune*, January 15, 1944. This column was reprinted in the *Albuquerque Tribune*, October 26, 1944, and in Pyle, *Brave Men*, 87-90; Nichols, *Ernie's War*, 197-99; parts were quoted in Thomas, et. al., *Victory*, 107.

52 *Albuquerque Tribune*, August 2, 1944.

53 Miller, *Pyle*, 310.

54 Bill Mauldin, *Up Front* (New York: Henry Holt & Company, 1945); *Albuquerque Tribune*, April 11, 1944.

55 McDowell, "Conversation With Mauldin," 11.

56 Mauldin, *Up Front*, 22. Also see Bill Mauldin interviews in Studs Terkel, *"The Good War:" An Oral History of World War II* (New York: Pantheon Books, 1984), 360-64, and in Hal Rhodes, "Illustrated Daily: Remembering Ernie Pyle," KNME-TV, 1983, Special Collections, Zimmerman Library, University of New Mexico. For an example of Pyle's wartime correspondence with Mauldin, see Miller, *Pyle*, 342. Pyle enjoyed Mauldin's cartoons so much that he sent samples home to Jerry for her amusement. Pyle to Jerry Pyle, Italy, March 15, 1944, Pyle Collection.

57 Pyle, *Brave Men*, 54. Also see EPC, *Albuquerque Tribune*, September 11, 1943, entitled "How a Bridge Is Built."

149

58 Pyle, *Brave Men*, 54.

59 EPC,*Farmington Times-Hustler*,April 27,1945. This column also appeared in Pyle,*Last Chapter*,42-45, and, in part, in Nichols,*Ernie's War*, 380-81.

60 EPC, *Albuquerque Tribune*, January 11, 1944. This column also appeared in Pyle, *Brave Men*, 90.

61 EPC, *Albuquerque Tribune*, April 26, 1945.

62 Doris A. Paul, *The Navajo Code Talkers* (Bryn Mawr, Pennsylvania: Dorrance & Company, 1973); Denji Kawano, *Warriors: Navajo Code Talkers* (Flagstaff: Northland Press, 1990).

63 EPC,*Farmington Times-Hustler*, May 18,1945. This column also appeared in Pyle,*Last Chapter*, 134-35.

64 Pyle,*Last Chapter*, 135.

65 Pyle, *Brave Men*, 42-44. Interview, Martin Quintana, Belen, New Mexico,April 2, 1994.

66 *Ibid.*; Pyle, *Brave Men*, 43.

67 EPC,*Albuquerque Tribune*, May 12,1944. This column appeared in Pyle,*Brave Men*,208-9.Also see telephone interview with John W. Truillo, Socorro, New Mexico, September 22,1994.

68 *Ibid.*

69 Pyle, *Brave Men*, 208. Also see Pyle to Jerry Pyle, France, August 9, 1944, Pyle Collection.

70 Miller, *Pyle*, 356-57.

71 *Ibid.*,358.A photo of the recovering English pilot appeared in the*Washington Daily News*,October 16,1944.

72 A photo of Pyle and McCollum in France appeared in Miller, *Album*, 107.

73 Dick Trauth interview; *Albuquerque Tribune*, April 19, 1945; EPC, *Albuquerque Tribune*, April 27, 1945.

74 Pyle to George G. Blaisdell, London, England, May 21, 1944, Zippo Manufacturing Company Museum, Bradford, Pennsylvania; hereafter cited as the Zippo Company Museum.

75 Pyle to George G. Blaisdell, (Albuquerque), October 29,1944, Zippo Company Museum.

76 Pyle, *Brave Men*, 208. Also see the *Albuquerque Tribune*, May 28,1945.

77 Bill Mauldin, "When Bill Mauldin Met Ernie Pyle," *Santa Fe Reporter*, April 17, 1980; McDowell, "Conversation With Mauldin," 56-7.

78 *Albuquerque Tribune*, April 19, 1944. Pyle's column based on this "interview" appeared in Pyle, *Here Is Your War*, 97-99.

79 Nichols, *Ernie's America*, xliv-xlv; italics in the original.

80 E.H. Shaffer to Walker Stone, Albuquerque, (September 3, 1941), Shaffer Collection.

CHAPTER 7

1 EPC (dated September 5, 1944) in Nichols, *Ernie's War*, 358.

2 Pyle to Jerry Pyle, Central Africa, March 13, 1943; Pyle to Jerry Pyle, Sicily, Italy, August 3, 1943; Pyle to Jerry Pyle, n.p., August 15, 1943, Pyle Collection. Also see Shirley (Mount) Hufstedler interview; Stella Mary (Shaffer) Jordon interview; Miller, *Pyle*, 242.

3 Shirley (Mount) Hufstedler interview; Miller, *Pyle*, 148.

4 Shirley (Mount) Hufstedler interview; interview, Robert Cooper, Sandia Peak, May 21,1994; Pyle to Jerry Pyle, Central Africa, March 22, 1943, Pyle Collection.

5 EPC, *Albuquerque Tribune*, November 22,1943.

6 Pyle to Beatrice Bales, Albuquerque, October 5, 1944, Pyle Collection; Miller, *Pyle*, 285-87.

7 EPC, *Albuquerque Tribune*, November 18,1943.

8 EPC,*Albuquerque Tribune*, November 22,1943; Pyle to Cavanaugh,Albuquerque, September 26, 1943, Pyle Collection.

9 EPC,*Albuquerque Tribune*,November 22,1943. Pyle's third appointment was made on September 22, 1943. *Albuquerque Tribune*, April 18,1945.

10 Robert Cooper interview. See the *Albuquerque Tribune*, September 25, 1943, on New Mexico's Victory Fair and its events.

11 Shirley (Mount) Hufstedler interview.

12 Alberts, *Balloons to Bombers*, 67-75. Views of the airfield, practice bombing ranges, and Albuquerque were included in the motion picture *Bombardier*, filmed in 1943. Barron Oder, "From Western Frontier to the Space Frontier: The Military in New Mexico" in DeMark, *Essays*, 117n.

13 EPC, *Albuquerque Tribune*, November 10, 1943.

14 Miller, *Pyle*, 285; E.H. Shaffer, "Columnist Has a Bout With OPA," newspaper clipping, October 6, 1943, Box 6, E. Pyle Collection.

15 EPC, *Albuquerque Tribune*, November 22, 1943. While overseas, Pyle had wondered about the impact of rationing at home in Pyle to Jerry Pyle, North Africa, January 7, 1943, Pyle Collection.

16 Pyle to Cavanaugh, Albuquerque, September 26, 1943; Pyle to Cavanaugh, n.p., November 28, 1943, Pyle Collection.

17 EPC, *Albuquerque Tribune*, November 20, 1943.

18 *Ibid.*

19 *Albuquerque Tribune*, January 15, 1944; Edward D. Shaffer interview; Robert Cooper interview.

20 EPC, *Albuquerque Tribune*, November 20, 1943.

21 The tragic experience of New Mexican troops in the Bataan Death March is recounted in Dorothy Cave, *Beyond Courage: One Regiment Against Japan, 1941-45* (Las Cruces: Yucca Tree Press, 1992). Several New Mexican survivors of the Death March were interviewed in Donald Knox, *Death March: The Survivors of Bataan* (New York: Harcourt Brace Jovanovich, 1981).

22 EPC, *Albuquerque Tribune*, November 17, 1943. Later studies have documented that over 1,400 New Mexicans served in the 200th, of which 272 came from Bernalillo County. Thirty percent of the 200th were Hispanic or Native American. One hundred and seventy-five families had one or more relatives captured in the 200th, and the regiment's casualty rate equaled forty-seven percent. Eva Jane Matson, *It Tolled for New Mexico: New Mexicans Captured By the Japanese, 1941-1945* (Las Cruces: Yucca Tree Press, 1994), 3-4, 11, 13, 16, 155.

23 EPC, *Albuquerque Tribune*, November 17, 1943. On the Bataan Relief Organization, see Matson, *It Tolled for New Mexico*, 23, 26-33; Cave, *Beyond Courage*, 257-67; Janie Meuli interview. Janie Meuli was a founding member of the BRO.

24 Pyle to Charles C. Broome, Albuquerque, October 28, 1944, Bond Drives File, Box 2, E. Pyle Collection; *Albuquerque Tribune*, November 10, 1944. Given his skittishness of audiences, Pyle turned down many speaking requests, including a proposed lecture tour that would have paid him $25,000. *Albuquerque Tribune*, September 20, 1943.

25 Pyle, "Buy Bonds and Save Soldiers' Blood," *Albuquerque Tribune*, November 20, 1944; Pyle to Jerry Pyle, Washington, D.C., November 8, 1943, Pyle Collection. Pyle had written a similar article from Italy in 1943. *Albuquerque Tribune*, September 14, 1943. The Pyles also contributed funds to the Albuquerque Community Chest, the Tuberculosis Association, and, probably, the Carrie Tingley Hospital for Children. Expense Account Book, 1940-41, Pyle Collection; Miller, *Pyle*, 390.

26 *Albuquerque Tribune*, November 22, 1944.

27 *Brave Men* was reviewed in the *Kansas City Star*, November 18, 1944; *Pittsburgh Press*, November 19, 1944; *New York Times*, November 20, 1944; *New York Herald Tribune*, November 21, 1944; *Washington News*, November 21, 1944. General Dwight D. Eisenhower thanked Pyle for sending him a copy of *Brave Men* in Eisenhower to Pyle, Supreme Headquarters, Allied Expeditionary Force, December 9, 1944, Box 2, E. Pyle Collection. Pyle had met Eisenhower in London as early as September 24, 1942. Captain Harry C. Butcher, *My Three Years With Eisenhower* (New York: Simon & Schuster, 1946), 122. Secretary of State E.R. Stettinius, Jr., sent his copy of *Brave Men* to Pyle and requested that it be autographed. E.R. Stettinius, Jr., to Pyle, Washington, D.C., January 20, 1945, Pyle Collection. 687,450 copies of the book were sold in the country. Lingeman, *Don't You Know?*, 277.

28 *Albuquerque Tribune*, November 21, 1944, December 6 & 19, 1944, February 7, 1945. An ad to promote *Brave Men* appeared in the *Albuquerque Tribune*, November 24, 1944.

29 *Albuquerque Tribune*, December 1944. A bookstore in Washington, D.C., had ordered 400 copies of the book, but only received 100. The store sold its 100 copies in six hours. *Washington Daily News*, November 28, 1944.

30 *Albuquerque Tribune*, December 8, 1944. Pyle's *Here Is Your War* and *Brave Men* were among seventy books sent to Europe by the U.S. government to counteract Nazi propaganda against the United States. *Albuquerque Tribune*, May 22, 1945.

31 *Albuquerque Journal*, March 1 & May 6, 1953.

32 *Albuquerque Tribune*, May 29, 1945.

33 *Albuquerque Tribune*, June 6, 23, & 25, 1945, & July 20, 1965.

34 Nichols, *Ernie's War*, 14.

35 *New York Times*, April 9, 1944.

36 *Albuquerque Tribune*, August 2, 1944.

37 *New York Times*, December 17, 1944.

38 Arthur Miller, *Timebends: A Life* (New York: Grove Press, 1987), 281. The final screen play was written by Leopold Atlas, Guy Endore, and Philip Stevenson. It was later published in Gassner & Nichols, *Best Film Plays*, 381-425. Philip Stevenson had lived in Santa Fe and Taos art colonies from 1930 to 1936. Active in several leftist causes and groups, he wrote a 1,500-page, four-book epic about the Gallup coal miners strike of 1933. Connie Capers Thorson & James L. Thorson, "Gomorrah on the Puerco: A Critical Study of Philip Stevenson's Proletarian Epic *The Seed*" in Robert Kern, ed., *Labor in New Mexico: Unions, Strikes, and Social History Since 1881* (Albuquerque: University of New Mexico Press, 1983), 147-75. Stevenson's controversial leftist ideas were hardly reflected in *The Story of G.I. Joe*.

39 Miller, *Timebends*, 282-83.

40 *Ibid.*, 282.

41 *Ibid.*

42 *Ibid.*, 283.

43 *Ibid.*, 282.

CHAPTER 8

1 Quoted in Miller, *Pyle*, 285.

2 Quoted in *ibid.*, 286.

3 *Albuquerque Tribune*, December 30, 1944.

4 Pyle to Shaffers, Africa, April 8, 1943, Shaffer Collection; Pyle to Beatrice Bales, Albuquerque, October 5, 1944, Pyle Collection; Nichols, *Ernie's War*, 27.

5 Pyle to Cavanaugh, Albuquerque, October 21, 1943, Pyle Collection; "Aftermath," *Life*, vol. 15 (November 15, 1943), 58, 60, 62, 64, 69; Barnett, "Pyle."

6 Miller, *Pyle*, 285.

7 *Ibid.*, 305 & 317; *Albuquerque Tribune*, January 10 & February 11, 1944. *Here Is Your War* was reviewed twice in the *Albuquerque Tribune* on October 28, 1943, the day it went on sale in Albuquerque. Also see Lingeman, *Don't You Know?*, 275.

8 Pyle to Beatrice Bales, Albuquerque, October 5, 1944, Pyle Collection.

9 *Albuquerque Tribune*, January 8, 1945.

10 *Ibid.*

11 EPC, *Albuquerque Tribune*, February 7, 1945.

12 Pyle to Cavanaugh, Albuquerque, October 29, 1944, Pyle Collection.

13 Pyle to Jerry Pyle, Italy, January 12, 1944, Pyle Collection.

14 Pyle to Jerry Pyle, London, England, April 27, 1944, Pyle Collection.

15 Pyle to Jerry Pyle, San Francisco, California, January 13, 1945, Pyle Collection.

16 Pyle to Cavanaugh, London, England, May 26, 1944, Pyle Collection.

17 Miller, *Pyle*, 353. Pyle was pictured with his new stove in Miller, *Album*, 108.

18 *Albuquerque Tribune*, January 1, 1945. Even those Pyle wrote about received gifts from his readers. When, in the late 1930s, Pyle wrote about a woman prospector in Nevada, the woman received over 400 letters plus flowers, fruit, cake, potatoes, and several offers of marriage. Pyle to Pyle Family, San Francisco, California, January 1938, Pyle Collection. During the war, when Pyle mentioned that six pilots on an aircraft carrier had no wrist watches, a jewelry company in St. Louis sent the watches. *Albuquerque Tribune*, May 28, 1945. The citizens of Indianapolis went so far as to raise $6,000 for cigarettes for American troops, although Pyle didn't "remember ever saying [there was a shortage]

and as a matter of fact, we have plenty of cigarettes." Pyle to Pyle Family, n.p., June 1, 1943, Pyle Collection.

19 Marjorie Binford Woods, "Ernie Pyle Most Prayed-for Man In America, Says Personal Secretary," newspaper clipping, September 30, 1944; E.H. Shaffer, "Columnist Has a Bout With OPA," newspaper clipping, October 6, 1943, Box 6, E. Pyle Collection.

20 EPC, *Albuquerque Tribune*, February 7, 1945; Miller, *Pyle*, 47. Pyle knew Earhart from his days as an aviation columnist. Earhart thought so much of Pyle that she once declared, "Not to know Ernie Pyle is to admit that you yourself are unknown in aviation." Quoted in Harden & Hobson, *A Wing and A Prayer*, v. Pyle praised Earhart's flying ability in a column dated August 9, 1930, included in *ibid*., 63-65.

21 Pyle to Pyle Family, n.p., June 1, 1943, Pyle Collection.

22 Shirley (Mount) Hustedler in "We the People" radio script, KGGM, July 15, 1945, Box 4, E. Pyle Collection; Rosamond Goodman interview in Marjorie Binford Woods, "Ernie Pyle Most Prayed-for Man In America, Says Personal Secretary," newspaper clipping, September 30, 1944, Box 6, E. Pyle Collection; Pyle, *Miller*, 372. An entire room in Goodman's apartment was said to be piled high with gifts for Pyle.

23 Quoted in Pyle, *Miller*, 369.

24 Pyle to Jerry Pyle, London, England, May 7, 1944, Pyle Collection; *New York Times*, May 2, 1944; *Albuquerque Tribune*, May 2, 1944; *Santa Fe New Mexican*, May 2, 1944.

25 Quoted in Miller, *Pyle*, 321.

26 *New York Times*, May 3, 1944, & April 21, 1945; *Albuquerque Tribune*, April 20, 1945; *Santa Fe New Mexican*, April 30, 1945. Years earlier, Pyle had declared that Raymond Clapper's "speech, his clothes, his manner of life are all just plain American, without any of the eccentricities that make some public figures such colorful newspaper copy." EPC, *Albuquerque Tribune*, November 22, 1940.

27 *New York Times*, November 8, 1944; *Indianapolis Times*, November 13, 1944; *Albuquerque Tribune*, November 7 & 13, 1944; Sanders, "Hoosier Vagbond," 17-18. Harvard University had planned to give Pyle an honorary Master of Arts degree on June 28, 1945. Miller, *Pyle*, 388.

28 *Albuquerque Tribune*, October 7, 1944.

29 *Albuquerque Tribune*, October 7 & 25, 1944; [*University of*] *New Mexico Lobo*, November 3, 1944; *New York Times*, October 8, 23, & 25, 1944. Commencement was kept simple following the death of UNM President James F. Zimmerman just five days prior to the ceremony.

30 General Commencement, October 25, 1944, University of New Mexico Archives, Special Collections, Zimmerman Library, University of New Mexico.

31 Sanders, "Hoosier Vagbond," 18.

32 Shirley (Mount) Hufstedler interview; Larry Wilson interview, Albuquerque, November 4, 1994. Wilson, a member of this graduating class, took photos of Pyle and spoke to him briefly after the ceremony. He soon shipped out to New York for military training. Photos of Pyle at the ceremony were included in [*University of*] *New Mexico Lobo*, November 3, 1944; *Albuquerque Tribune*, October 25, 1944; Miller, *Album*, 119. Pyle's honorary degree and an autographed copy of a commencement program are in Box 2, E. Pyle Collection.

33 Interview, Mary Elena Davis, Albuquerque, August 3, 1994.

34 *Albuquerque Tribune*, October 7, 1944.

35 *Albuquerque Tribune*, April 18, 1945; *Santa Fe New Mexican*, April 18, 1945; Pyle to Jerry Pyle, n.p., February 2, 1945, Pyle Collection. The bill to establish Ernie Pyle Day was introduced by State Representatives J.A. Montoya and Mrs. Will Rogers of Albuquerque. Governor John J. Dempsey signed it on April 11, 1945. *Albuquerque Tribune*, April 19, 1945.

36 Miller, *Pyle*, 371-72.

37 *Ibid.*, 372.

38 Pyle to Cavanaugh, Albuquerque, October 21, 1943, Pyle Collection.

39 George Shaffer interview.

40 "1918-Armistice Day-1938" editorial, *Albuquerque Tribune*, November 11, 1938.

41 "Armistice Day" editorial, *Albuquerque Tribune*, November 11, 1939.

42 *Albuquerque Tribune*, April 4, 1944.

43 *Ibid*. This edition of the *Tribune* included editorials about Shaffer from around the state, including

those from the *Las Vegas Optic*, the *Carlsbad Current-Argus*, and the *Santa Fe New Mexican*. According to the latter, Shafe was "the best liked man in New Mexico journalism."

44 Pyle to Jerry Pyle, London, England, October 11, 1942; Pyle to Jerry Pyle, North Africa, March 2, 1943; Pyle to Jerry Pyle, April 8, 1943; Pyle to Jerry Pyle, May 19, 1943; Pyle to Jerry Pyle, Central Africa, May 26, 1943; Pyle to Jerry Pyle, Sicily, Italy, August 3, 1943; Pyle to Cavanaugh, n.p., November 28, 1943. Jerry's work was described in Clarence E. Redman, "That Girl, [Kirtland Air Field] Bombsight," December 1943, Vertical Files, Ernie Pyle Branch Library, Albuquerque, New Mexico. A photograph of Jerry at her job was included in this article. Reflecting the Pyles' interest in privacy, the picture's caption read: "Reproduction of this photograph or article is prohibited unless authorized by *Bombsight*." Pyle urged Jerry to hire an Hispanic maid so she could practise her Spanish. Both Ernie and Jerry had attempted to learn some Spanish during their trip to South America in late 1938. Pyle to Pyle Family, Guayaquil, Ecuador, October 12, 1938.

45 E.H. Shaffer to Walker Stone, Albuquerque, (September 3, 1941), Shaffer Collection.

46 Stella Mary (Shaffer) Jordon interview; Shirley (Mount) Hufstedler interview; Kenneth Mount (Earl Mount's son) interview in Hal Rhodes, "Illustrated Daily: Remembering Ernie Pyle," KNME-TV, 1983, Special Collections, Zimmerman Library, University of New Mexico; Pyle to Cavanaugh, London, England, May 26, 1944, Pyle Collection; *Miller, Pyle*, 354; Fussell, *Wartime*, 231.

47 Pyle received as many as five letters at one time from Sister Margaret Jane. Pyle to Jerry Pyle, Sicily, Italy, August 3, 1943, Pyle Collection. Also see Pyle to Arthur McCollum, London, England, September 11, 1942, McCollum Collection.

48 Pyle to Jerry Pyle, Portland, Oregon, January 18, 1942; Pyle to Cavanaugh, Italy, March 24, 1944; Pyle to Jerry Pyle, Pacific, February 9, 1945, Pyle Collection; Miller, *Pyle*, 397n.

49 Pyle to Cavanaugh, London, England, August 8 & September 13, 1942, Pyle Collection.

50 Staff Sergeant Arthur W. Everett, Jr., quoted in Miller, *Pyle*, 304.

51 Quoted in A. Miller, *Timebends*, 283.

52 Quoted in Miller, *Pyle*, 374.

53 Quoted in *ibid.*, 375.

54 Quoted in *ibid.*, 376.

55 Quoted in *ibid.*, 377.

56 Pyle quoted in *ibid.*, 378.

57 *Ibid.*

58 Nichols, *Ernie's War*, 27.

59 Quoted in Miller, *Pyle*, 378.

60 Pyle to Cavanaugh, Evansville, Indiana, September 17, 1940, Pyle Collection.

61 Paul Lancaster, "Ernie Pyle: Chronicler of 'The Men Who Do the Dying,'" *American Heritage*, vol. 32 (February/March 1981), 38.

62 Roosevelt, *This I Remember*, 314. Eleanor Roosevelt had praised Pyle's *Here Is Your War* in "My Day," her daily newspaper column. *Washington Daily News*, November 5, 1943.

63 Quoted in *Ernie's America*, xlvi.

64 *Ibid.* Seeing Pyle after the fall of Paris, General Bradley noted that "Tragedy had at last sponged him dry." Bradley, *Soldier's Story*, 410.

65 Quoted in Lancaster, "Chronicler," 38. Pyle had uttered similar words when he returned to Europe in late 1943. EPC, *Albuquerque Tribune*, November 10, 1943.

66 Pyle to Jerry Pyle, London, England, April 27, 1944, Pyle Collection.

67 Quoted in the *Santa Fe New Mexican*, April 18, 1945.

68 *Ibid.* Pyle had announced his intentions of covering the war in the Pacific in his interview with *BRO Bulletin* editor Paul McCahon in October 1944. See "Ernie Pyle," *BRO Bulletin*, vol. 2 (October 31, 1944), 4.

69 Quoted in Miller, *Pyle*, 145.

70 *Ibid.*, 226.

71 Quoted in *ibid.*, 231.

72 *Ibid.*, 273.

73 Quoted in *ibid.*, 315. Photos of Pyle standing in the debris following this incident were included in Miller, *Album*, 96.

74 Quoted in Miller, *Pyle*, 328.

75 Colonel Samuel L. Myers quoted in *ibid.*, 331. Colonel Myers accompanied Pyle on the invasion.

76 Quoted in *ibid.*, 336.

77 Nichols, *Ernie's War*, 25; James H. "Jimmy" Doolittle, *I Could Never Be So Lucky Again: An Autobiography* (New York: Bantam Books, 1991), 407-8; Bradley, *A General's Life*, 279; Dwight D. Eisenhower, *Crusade in Europe* (Garden City: Doubleday, 1949), 272; Kennett, *G.I.*, 175-76; McDonald, *Mighty Endeavor*, 332-35.

78 Quoted in Miller, *Pyle*, 350-51.

79 *Ibid.*, 351.

80 Collier, *Warcos*, 196. Although he didn't mention the odds of Pyle's survival, General Eisenhower sent Pyle a note that read: "I hear that you are going to the Pacific and I hope you will enjoy your new assignment. Good luck." Eisenhower to Pyle, Supreme Headquarters, Allied Expeditionary Force, December 9, 1944, Box 2, E. Pyle Collection. A photo of Pyle with Bradley and Eisenhower appeared in Miller, *Album*, 105. According to Pyle, "If I could pick any two men in the world for my father except my own dad, I would pick General Omar Bradley or General Ike Eisenhower." Quoted in *ibid.*

81 Quoted in Miller, *Pyle*, 275.

82 Quoted in *ibid.*, 375.

83 Pyle visited several wounded correspondents, including Bill Strand and Richard Tregaskis in Italy. Miller, *Album*, 97; Richard Tregaskis, *Invasion Diary* (New York: Random House, 1944), 217-18. Clapper's death was reported in *Albuquerque Tribune*, February 3, 1944; Pyle to Pyle Family, Italy, February 10, 1944, Pyle Collection.

84 These New Mexicans included Dan Burrows, Arthur McCollum, Earl Mount, Shirley Mount, and Ruth Baldwin. *Gallup Independent*, April 18, 1945; *Albuquerque Tribune*, April 19, 1945, & April 18, 1955, & April 18, 1958; Arthur McCollum interview in *Albuquerque Journal*, July 29, 1969; Earl Mount interview in *Albuquerque Tribune*, July 15, 1965; *Albuquerque Tribune*, April 19, 1995; telephone interview, Ruth Baldwin, Albuquerque, January 18, 1994.

85 Pyle to Cavanaugh, Albuquerque, December 12, 1944; Pyle to Pyle Family, Pasadena, California, December 23, 1944, Pyle Collection.

86 This photo appeared in Miller, *Album*, 122.

87 *New York Times*, November 24, 1945; *Albuquerque Journal*, April 24, 1946. The *New York Times* reported that Pyle had made "well over" half a million dollars in the last two years of his life. *New York Times*, April 19, 1945.

CHAPTER 9

1 This photo appeared in the *Albuquerque Tribune*, December 21, 1944, & November 23, 1945; Miller, *Album*, 123.

2 Quoted in Miller, *Pyle*, 383. Also see Pyle to Pyle Family, Pasadena, California, December 23, 1944, Pyle Collection.

3 Pyle to William R. Lovelace, Hollywood, California, December 27, 1944, File MHA-FL-826, New Mexico Medical History Archives, Health Sciences Center Library, University of New Mexico, Albuquerque, New Mexico.

4 Miller, *Pyle*, 383; Nichols, *Ernie's War*, 28.

5 Quoted in Miller, *Pyle*, 383-84.

6 *Albuquerque Tribune*, January 8, 1945.

7 Pyle to Jerry Pyle, San Francisco, California, January 10, 1945, Pyle Collection.

8 *Ibid.*

9 Quoted in Miller, *Pyle*, 389-90.

10 *Ibid.*, 391-92.

11   Quoted in *ibid.*, 395.

12   Pyle's columns on these several New Mexicans also appeared in his *Last Chapter*, 32, 35, 42-45, 132, 134-35; Nichols, *Ernie's War*, 376-77, 380-81, 415-16.

13   *Albuquerque Tribune*, April 24-28, 1945.

14   EPC, *Farmington Times-Hustler*, March 23, 1945; Pyle, *Last Chapter*, 43.

15   Edward D. Shaffer interview. Dr. Randolph V. Seligman of Albuquerque was also aboard a ship off shore. Randolph V. Seligman interview in the *Albuquerque Tribune*, July 17, 1965. Sergeant Thomas Padilla, Jr., of Albuquerque was photographed with Pyle on Okinawa just before the reporter's death. *Albuquerque Tribune*, April 27, 1945.

16   Quoted in Miller, *Pyle*, 406-7.

17   Quoted in *ibid.*, 407.

18   Quoted in *ibid.*, 410.

19   Quoted in *ibid.*, 411.

20   *Ibid.*

21   Quoted in *ibid.*, 414.

22   EPC (dated April 9, 1945) in Nichols, *Ernie's War*, 405. Also see James & William Belote, *Tyhoon of Steel: The Battle for Okinawa* (New York: Harper & Row, 1970), 63.

23   *Ibid.*, 62-63.

24   Quoted in Miller, *Pyle*, 419.

25   Pyle to Jerry Pyle, Pacific, April 8, 1945, Pyle Collection.

26   *Ibid.*

27   *Albuquerque Tribune*, April 18 & August 2 (editorial), 1945.

28   Quoted in Miller, *Pyle*, 408-9.

29   Milton Chase interview in the *Albuquerque Tribune*, May 1, 1956.

30   Miller, *Pyle*, 421.

31   Milton Chase interview in the *Albuquerque Tribune*, July 12, 1965.

32   Miller, *Pyle*, 252-53.

33   EPC (dated June 26, 1944) in Nichols, *Ernie's War*, 293-94. This column was later reprinted in the *Albuquerque Tribune*, July 8, 1994.

34   EPC, *Albuquerque Tribune*, May 11, 1945.

35   Miller, *Pyle*, 425.

36   *Ibid.*; John Valentine, "Ernie Pyle Speaks to a New Generation," *Wall Street Journal*, April 17, 1985.

37   Witnesses told of Pyle's death in the *Albuquerque Tribune*, April 28, 1945. General Edwin H. Randle told of meeting Pyle on Ie Shima and later learning of Pyle's death in his *Ernie Pyle Comes Ashore and Other Stories* (Clearwater, Florida: Eldnar Press, 1972), 1-9. Also see Belote & Belote, *Tyhoon of Steel*, 177-78, 183; Robert Leckie, *Okinawa: The Last Battle of World War II* (New York: Viking, 1995), 125-26.

38   *Newsweek*, vol. 25 (April 30, 1945), 78.

39   *Albuquerque Tribune*, July 11, 1945. Joe A. Parras of Albuquerque was on Ie Shima when Pyle was killed. *Albuquerque Tribune*, August 6, 1965. Learning of Pyle's death, a saddened George G. Blaisdell of the Zippo Manufacturing Company sent 600 specially engraved lighters to the officers and crew of the *U.S.S. Cabot*, the last ship Pyle had sailed on. Peggy Errera (Communications Coordinator, Zippo Manufacturing Company) to the author, Bradford, Pennsylvania, October 28, 1994; *Albuquerque Tribune*, April 28, 1945; Captain W.W. Smith (of the *U.S.S. Cabot*) to George G. Blaisdell, In the Pacific, November 7, 1945, Zippo Company Museum.

40   *Santa Fe New Mexican*, April 12, 1945; *Albuquerque Tribune*, April 13, 1945. For public reaction to Roosevelt's death, see Bernard Asbell, *When F.D.R. Died* (New York: Signet Books, 1962), 87-97.

41   Pyle and Roosevelt both received the American Legion's Distinguished Service Medal at the Legion's national convention later in 1945. *New York Times*, November 20, 1945.

42   Many of these statements were included in the *New York Times*, April 19, 1945. An average serviceman's reaction appears in James J. Fahey, *Pacific War Diary, 1942-45* (Boston: Houghton Mifflin, 1992), entry of April 21, 1945, page 311.

43   *Albuquerque Journal*, April 19, 1945.

44   *Albuquerque Tribune*, April 19, 1945.

45   Quoted in Miller, *Album*, 151. Also see the *Albuquerque Tribune*, April 18, 1945.

46   *New York Times*, April 19, 1945; Bradley, *Soldier's Story*, 410. Bradley later dedicated a bronze plaque in Pyle's honor in Bloomington, Indiana. *New York Times*, October 6, 1953.

47   *Albuquerque Tribune*, April 18, 1945; *Santa Fe New Mexican*, April 18, 1945; *Silver City Daily Press*, April 18, 1945; *Las Cruces Sun-News*, April 18, 1945; *Portales Daily News*, April 18, 1945; *Clovis New Journal*, April 18, 1945; *Carlsbad Daily Current-Argus*, April 18, 1945; *Gallup Independent*, April 18, 1945; *Roswell Morning Dispatch*, April 19, 1945; *Albuquerque Journal*, April 19, 1945; *[University of] New Mexico Lobo*, April 20, 1945.

48   See, for examples, *Albuquerque Tribune*, April 19, 20, 23, & 28, 1945; *Clovis New Journal*, April 19, 1945; *Raton Daily Range*, April 20, 1945; *Roy Record*, April 20, 1945; *Albuquerque Journal*, April 23, 1945; *Roswell Morning Dispatch*, April 28, 1945.

49   *Albuquerque Tribune*, April 23, 1945.

50   *Albuquerque Tribune*, April 18, 1945; *Santa Fe New Mexican*, April 18, 1945; *Albuquerque Journal*, April 19, 1945; *El Paso Times*, April 19, 1945.

51   *New York Times*, April 21, 1945; *Albuquerque Tribune*, April 23, 1945. A joint letter by 51 G.I.'s in *Stars & Stripes* also supported this resolution. *New York Times*, April 28, 1945.

52   *Albuquerque Tribune*, April 18, 1945.

53   *New York Times*, April 19, 1945; *Santa Fe New Mexican*, April 19, 1945.

54   *Albuquerque Tribune*, April 19, 1945.

55   James Toulouse interview; Janie Meuli interview.

56   *Albuquerque Tribune*, April 17, 1995; *Health City Sun*, May 4, 1945; Eleanor Jette, *Inside Box 1663* (Los Alamos: Los Alamos Historical Society, 1977), 90. The *Health City Sun* printed a poem in memory of Pyle entitled "Last Assignment." Written by Robert S. Greene, it appeared in the newspaper's May 18, 1945, edition.

57   Quoted in the *New York Times*, April 19, 1945. Also see Kahn, *A Soldier's Diary*, entry of April 22, 1945, p. 256.

58   *Albuquerque Tribune*, April 18, 1945. One hundred and forty-nine correspondents were also listed as missing, wounded, or prisoners of war by this date. Some 800 reporters (including 24 women) had been accredited by the U.S. military during World War II. By war's end their casualty rate equalled 22 percent, as compared to five percent for all Americans in combat roles. Norman Polmar & Thomas B. Allen, *World War II: America at War, 1941-1945* (New York: Random House, 1991), 876.

59   Matson, *It Tolled For New Mexico*, 6. Of New Mexico's dead, 2,032 served in the Army, and 231 served in the Navy. *Ibid.*

60   See, for example, *Roy Record* editorial, April 20, 1945.

61   EPC, *Albuquerque Tribune*, April 28, 1945. This column later appeared in Nichols, *Ernie's War*, 417.

62   *Albuquerque Tribune*, April 28, 1945.

63   George R. Shaffer interview; *Albuquerque Tribune*, April 18, 1945; *Santa Fe New Mexican*, April 18, 1945.

64   *Albuquerque Tribune*, April 18, 1945; *Albuquerque Journal*, April 26, 1945. Local groups included the Albuquerque Kiwanis Club.

65   Nichols, *Ernie's War*, 34.

66   *New York Times*, April 19, 1945.

67   Miller, *Pyle*, 427.

68   On Senator Cutting's memorial service, see the *Albuquerque Journal*, May 10 & 11, 1935; Richard Lowitt, *Bronson M. Cutting: Progressive Republican* (Albuquerque: University of New Mexico Press, 1992), 311.

69   *Albuquerque Journal*, May 14, 1945.

70   Quoted in *ibid.*

71   *Ibid.* Pyle's favorite song was said to be "Lili Marlene." Valentine, "Pyle Speaks," 30.

72   *Albuquerque Journal*, May 11, 1945.

73 EPC, *Albuquerque Tribune*, October 18, 1943; Pyle, *Home Country*, 245.

74 See, for example, Pyle, *Here Is Your War*, 79-106. The last combat plane Pyle flew in was a B-29. *Albuquerque Tribune*, May 12, 1945.

75 *Albuquerque Tribune*, April 18, 1955. Community Services in Memory of Ernie Pyle Program, University of New Mexico, Albuquerque, New Mexico, May 13, 1945; copy in author's possession.

76 *New York Times*, July 3 & 4, 1945.

77 Nichols, *Ernie's America*, xlvii.

78 Quoted in the *Albuquerque Tribune*, July 5, 1945.

79 *Albuquerque Tribune*, July 16, 1945; "We the People" radio script, KGGM, July 15, 1945, Box 4, E. Pyle Collection. Davidson made this bust of Pyle when Ernie traveled through New York on his way home to New Mexico in 1944. Davidson recalled three days of work in his studio "amid bourbon, tobacco fumes and a steady throng of visitors ... in a regular hullabaloo." Jo Davidson, *Between Sittings: An Informal Autobiography* (New York: Dial Press, 1951), 339.

80 Quoted in Liggett, "That Girl," 10.

81 *Albuquerque Journal*, November 24, 1945.

82 *Ibid.*

83 "Poe" Jones telegram to Cavanaugh, Albuquerque, November 23, 1945, Pyle Collection; Jerry Pyle Obituary, *Newsweek*, vol. 26 (December 3, 1945), 80; Miller, *Pyle*, 427-28.

84 "Jerry Pyle" editorial, *Albuquerque Tribune*, November 24, 1945.

85 The Tingleys also died within months of each other. Clyde Tingley died on December 24, 1960, while his wife, Carrie, died less than a year later, on November 7, 1961. *Albuquerque Tribune*, December 24, 1960, & October 25, 1968.

86 *Albuquerque Tribune*, November 24, 1945; *Silver City Daily Press* November 28, 1945; *New York Times*, November 28, 1945; *Albuquerque Journal*, February 16, 1949.

87 Nichols, *Ernie's War*, 36.

88 Interview, Elsa Smith Thompson, Albuquerque, December 28, 1993. It was said that Cheetah still raised her ears when Pyle's name was spoken. *Albuquerque Journal*, November 24, 1945. When Lee Miller visited Pyle's house after the journalist's death, he reported that Cheetah "heard me typing at Ernie's desk [and] ran into the room. There she stood for a minute or two, listening to this once familiar sound and eyeing me in perplexity." Miller, *Pyle*, 243n. Jerry's nurse, Ella Streger, cared for the pet until its death in October 1951. *Albuquerque Tribune*, January 31, 1953. A gravestone marks the faithful dog's grave in the Pyles' backyard.

89 *Silver City Daily Press*, April 19, 1945; *Albuquerque Tribune*, April 18, & August 2, 1945. When asked if she wanted Pyle buried in New Mexico, Jerry had said, "No, Ernie is where he would want to be—with his friends." Her words were later quoted in the *Albuquerque Tribune*, July 3, 1947.

90 Committee members included Erma Fergusson, William A. Keleher, Ethel Moulton Bond, Dan Burrows, Gus Bruskas, Fred White, Cale Carson, and Keen Rafferty, chairman of UNM's Department of Journalism. *Albuquerque Journal*, May 3, 1945. Keleher also listed James P. Threlkeld, an Albuquerque bookstore owner. William A. Keleher, *Memoirs: 1892-1969, A New Mexico Item* (Santa Fe: Rydal Press, 1969), 229.

91 *Albuquerque Tribune*, April 28, 1945.

92 *Albuquerque Tribune*, April 25 & May 2 & 4, 1945; *Albuquerque Journal*, May 3 & 5, 1945.

93 *Carlsbad Daily Current-Argus*, April 19, 1945.

94 *Albuquerque Journal*, May 3, 1945.

95 Quoted in Nichols, *Ernie's War*, 36.

96 Quoted in the *New York Times*, August 22, 1945.

97 Margaret Dees to the Editor, *Albuquerque Tribune*, April 7, 1949.

98 A photo of the beach, opened in 1931, appears in Charles D. Biebel, *Making the Most of It: Public Works in Albuquerque during the Great Depression, 1929-1942* (Albuquerque: Albuquerque Museum History Monograph, 1986), 61.

99 *Albuquerque Journal*, February 14, 1968. The Ernie Pyle Junior High School is now the Ernie Pyle Middle School.

100 *Albuquerque Tribune*, October 16, 1950.

101 Interview, Rodney W. Shoemaker, Albuquerque, August 26, 1994. In addition to delivering news-papers to Pyle's house as a boy, Shoemaker later worked at the Ernie Pyle Theatre. An Ernie Pyle Theatre was also opened in Tokyo, Japan, to entertain American occupation troops stationed there following the war. *New York Times*, February 24, 1946.

102 *New York Times*, May 30, 1945. Dwight Eisenhower and hundreds of wounded soldiers also watched an early showing of the film in Washington, D.C. Butcher, *Three Years With Eisenhower*, 874.

103 *Albuquerque Tribune*, July 7, 1945; Nichols, *Ernie's War*, 35.

104 *Albuquerque Tribune*, July 12, 1945; *Albuquerque Journal*, July 12, 1945. The movie starred Burgess Meredith, Robert Mitchum, Freddie Steele, Wally Cassell, Jimmy Lloyd, Jack Reilly, and Bill Murphy. Gassner & Nichols, *Best Film Plays*, 381.

105 *Albuquerque Journal*, July 13, 1945.

106 *Albuquerque Tribune*, July 12, 1945.

107 *Ibid.*; *Albuquerque Tribune*, July 13, 1945; *Albuquerque Journal*, July 13, 1945.

108 *Albuquerque Tribune*, July 11, 1945.

109 *Albuquerque Tribune*, July 19, 1945. Typical ads for the movie appeared in the *Albuquerque Tribune*, July 11 & 12, 1945.

110 See *The Story of G.I. Joe* movie ads in the *Santa Fe New Mexican*, July 24, 1945; *Farmington Times-Hustler*, August 10, 1945; *Clovis News Journal*, September 5 & 7, 1945; *Gallup Independent*, September 22, 1945; *Carlsbad Daily Current-Argus*, September 24, 1945; *Las Cruces Sun-News*, October 7, 1945; *Raton Range*, November 9, 1945; *Silver City Daily Press*, November 28, 1945.

111 *New York Times*, October 6 & 14, 1945; Manny Farber, "The Story of G.I. Joe," *New Republic*, vol. 113 (August 13, 1945), 190; James Agee, "The Story of G.I. Joe," *The Nation*, vol. 160 (September 15, 1945), 264-66.

112 William O'Neill, *A Democracy at War: America's Fight at Home and Abroad in World War II* (New York: The Free Press, 1993), 258. Also see Lance Bertelsen, "San Pietro and the 'Art' of War," *Southwest Review*, vol. 74 (Spring 1989), 247; Bernard F. Dick, *The Star-Spangled Screen: The American World War II Film* (Lexington: University Press of Kentucky, 1985), 140-42; Clayton R. Koppes & Gregory D. Black, *Hollywood Goes to War: How Politics, Profits, and Propaganda Shaped World War II Movies* (New York: The Free Press, 1987), 304-9; Lingeman, *Don't You Know?*, 205. The film was reissued as late as 1970. *Albuquerque Tribune*, August 22, 1970.

113 Keleher, *Memoirs*, 230.

114 Pyle to Jerry Pyle, London, England, February 9, 1941, Pyle Collection.

115 Keleher, *Memoirs*, 230.

116 *Ibid.*, 231-32; *New York Times*, May 8, 1947.

117 Elsa Smith Thompson interview. Librarian Elsa Smith Thompson opened the Ernie Pyle Library as well as five other branch libraries in later years. The house had been kept up by its caretaker, E.J. Cain. *Memphis Press*, September 5, 1947.

118 *Albuquerque Tribune*, April 7, 1947.

119 EPC, *Albuquerque Tribune*, April 16, 1941. Also see Jim Belshaw, "Ernie Pyle's House Retains His Spirit," *Albuquerque Journal*, April 16, 1995.

120 Elizabeth Long (librarian) to Mary Walker (KOB radio), Albuquerque, October 5, 1948, Ernie Pyle Branch Library Collection; *Albuquerque Tribune*, October 18, 1948, & October 11, 1950, & April 17, 1962; *[University of] New Mexico Lobo*, October 19, 1948; *Denver Post*, April 19, 1970; *Outlook*, November 4, 1981; *Los Alamos Monitor*, August 14, 1986; *Albuquerque Journal*, December 14, 1991, & April 16, 1995.

121 Keleher, *Memoirs*, 232.

122 Wayne Bower at the Scotish-American Military Society's annual Ernie Pyle memorial celebration, Ernie Pyle Branch Library, Albuquerque, August 3, 1994. Annual statistics on the library's number of volumes and users are kept on file at the branch.

123 Most of these items were donated by Ella Stegner and the Mount family. *[University of] New Mexico Lobo*, October 19, 1948. Ernie Pyle's black protable typewriter is on display at the National Archives. *Albuquerque Journal*, July 6, 1995.

124 *Albuquerque Tribune*, October 18, 1948, & October 11, 1948; Keleher, *Memoirs*, 232.

125 Isabel Wiley Grear, "Street of Memories," *Coronet*, vol. 21 (April 1947), 47. Also see Dorothy L. Pillsbury, "A Little White House on a Hilltop Where People Stop a While," *Christian Science Monitor Magazine Section* (November 26, 1949), 16.

126 *Albuquerque Tribune*, October 11, 1950.

127 *Ibid.* The Reverend N.B. Saucier, who officiated at Pyle's funeral on Ie Shima, was among the many who visited the branch library in the summer of 1950. *Albuquerque Tribune*, July 29, 1950.

128 Joe Garland entry, Ernie Pyle Branch Library Guest Book, October 29, 1991.

129 J.L. Schneider entry, Ernie Pyle Branch Library Guest Book, August 14, 1982.

130 *Albuquerque Tribune*, August 15, 1949. The article was also reprinted in Fitzpatrick, *This Is New Mexico* (1948 edition), 273-78; *New Mexico Magazine*, vol. 54 (November 1976), 18 & 41-45.

131 *Albuquerque Tribune*, October 9, 1972.

132 Interview, Ann McRedmond, Albuquerque, December 28, 1993. Unfortunately, the canceled checks (a good source of information regarding Pyle's daily life) were discarded. Only one sample of a torn check with Pyle's signature remains. It is in Special Collections at the University of New Mexico.

CHAPTER 10

1 Quoted in Miller, *Pyle*, 119.

2 Quoted in the *Silver City Press*, April 18, 1945.

3 Ernie Pyle to the Editor, *Albuquerque Tribune*, November 9, 1943.

4 A photo showing the many new homes built to the west of Pyle's house by 1947 was included in the *Memphis Press*, September 5, 1947.

5 Simmons, *Albuquerque*, 377. Population statistics are from Jerry L. Williams, *New Mexico in Maps* (Albuquerque: University of New Mexico Press, 1986), 153-55. Also see Robert T. Wood, "The Transformation of Albuquerque, 1945-72" (Unpublished Ph.D. dissertation, University of New Mexico, 1980).

6 *New Mexico Magazine*, vol. 20 (January 1942), 56.

7 Pyle to Cavanaugh, London, England, May 26, 1944, Pyle Collection.

8 Quoted in Miller, *Pyle*, 326.

9 Quoted in *ibid.*, 389-90.

10 Ross Calvin Diary, November 8, 1939, entry, Box 4, Calvin Collection. Calvin called on Jerry shortly after she had moved into the Pyles' new house on Girard Avenue. Ross Calvin Log Book, January 27, 1941, entry, Calvin Collection.

11 EPC, *Albuquerque Tribune*, January 15, 1944; Pyle, *Brave Men*, 87-90.

12 Pyle and Shafe also encouraged the career of Edward C. Rightley, an Albuquerque student who won a Scripps-Howard Scholarship in 1939. The two newspapermen visited this appreciative young man in his home for nearly an hour. Mary S. Rightley to the Editor, *Albuquerque Tribune*, April 23, 1945.

13 Shirley (Mount) Hufstedler interview; Shirley Mount quoted in "We the People" radio script, KGGM, July 15, 1945, Box 4, E. Pyle Collection; *Albuquerque Tribune*, July 15, 1965, & October 30, 1979; "Alumni Profile," [*University of New Mexico*] *Mirage* (Summer/Fall 1993), 14-15.

14 Don Whitehead of the Associated Press quoted in Miller, *Pyle*, 296-97. Also see Jones, "Small, Shy Guy"; interview, (Ret.) General Theodore Antonelli, Albuquerque, June 15, 1993. Pyle wrote of then-Lieutenant Antonelli in Pyle, *Here Is Your War*, 216.

15 For example, Pyle dealt with Scripps-Howard officials who questioned whether Shaffer was physically able to continue in his role as editor of the *Albuquerque Tribune*. John Sorrells (Scripps-Howard Executive Director) to Pyle, New York, New York, April 25, 1941; Pyle to Jerry Pyle, Los Angeles, California, November 12, 1941, Pyle Collection; Pyle to Liz Shaffer, n.p., May 6, 1941, Shaffer Collection.

16 Rodney Shoemaker, who married McCollum's step-daughter, Beverly, kindly showed this inscription to the author during his interview of August 26, 1994. Also see Charles Edman interview; Earl Mount interview in *Albuquerque Tribune*, July 15, 1965; McCollum interview in *Albuquerque Journal*, July 29, 1965.

17 Pyle to Pyle Family, Albuquerque, n.d.; Pyle to Cavanaugh, Dublin, Ireland, June 27, 1942; Pyle to Cavanaugh, Italy, March 24, 1944, Pyle Collection.

18 EPC, *Albuquerque Tribune*, January 10, 1942.

19 Pyle to Jerry Pyle, Washington, D.C., November 11, 1943; Pyle to Jerry Pyle, Italy, January 12, 1944, Pyle Collection.

20 In an earlier instance, Pyle had written to Governor Tingley "just passing on a hope" that a certain crippled girl "might get a job at Carrie Tingley Hospital." Pyle reported that he later received a long telegram from Tingley "saying that the girl is now working at Tingley Hospital." Pyle to Shaffers, Oklahoma City, Oklahoma, March 29, 1939, Shaffer Collection.

21 *Albuquerque Journal*, November 24, 1945.

22 Quoted in *Albuquerque Tribune*, April 18, 1945.

23 *Carlsbad Current-Argus*, March 29 & May 20, 1938.

24 *Albuquerque Tribune*, January 19, 1954, & January 21 & April 18, 1955.

25 *Albuquerque Tribune*, September 22, 1954, & March 3, 1967. Contributors included Dan Burrows, W.E. Knott, Jr., Jack Korber, Howard Major, H. Means, Sr., H. Means, Jr., E.R. Werner, C.T. French, and the Mims & Knott Cattle Company.

26 "Ernie Pyle's New Mexico," film clip, *Army-Navy Screen Magazine*, no. 65, 1945; Special Ernie Pyle Number, *New Mexico Magazine*, vol. 23 (June 1945). The latter featured a reprint of Pyle's "Why Albuquerque?" article of 1942.

27 *Albuquerque Tribune*, April 18, 1946, July 20, 1950, April 18, 1955, April 17, 1965; *Albuquerque Journal*, April 17, 1970. Pyle's previously unpublished columns appeared in the *Albuquerque Tribune* between July 19, 1965, and August 6, 1965.

28 This series began with a column in memory of Pyle by Bill Mauldin and ended with a column by fellow war correspondent Wade Jones. *Santa Fe Reporter*, April 17, 1980, & January 5, 1983.

29 *Albuquerque Tribune*, April 18, 1995.

30 *Albuquerque Tribune*, August 2, 3, & 5, 1946, August 2, 1948, July 21, 1949, July 20, 1950, & August 3, 1989; *Albuquerque Journal*, August 4, 1948; Janie Meuli interview. Documents declaring August 3, 1976, Ernie Pyle Day in Albuquerque and in New Mexico (as part of the 1976 Bicentennial Celebration) are found in the Ernie Pyle Branch Library.

31 *Albuquerque Tribune*, August 3 & 5, 1960.

32 *Albuquerque Tribune*, March 24 & 27, 1971.

33 Hal Rhodes, "Illustrated Daily: Remembering Ernie Pyle," KNME-TV, 1983, Special Collections, Zimmerman Library.

34 Pyle's acclaimed column on the combat death in Italy of Captain Henry T. Waskow appeared on the front page of newspapers across the nation, including the *Albuquerque Tribune* and the *Washington Daily News*, on January 10, 1944. The *Tribune* wrote two editorials about this column (January 10 & 20, 1944), calling it "one of the greatest narratives of English literature." Also see Miller, *Pyle*, 297-300. Considered a classic of World War II journalism, the column has been reprinted in many places, including Pyle, *Brave Men*, 106-107; Nichols, *Ernie's War*, 195-97; Frederick S. Voss, *Reporting the War: The Journalistic Coverage of World War II* (Washington, D.C.: Smithsonian Institute, 1994), 102-103; and, most recently, Jack Stenbuck, ed., *Typewriter Battalion: Dramatic Frontline Dispatches from World War II* (New York: William Morrow, 1995), 129-31. A biographical sketch of Waskow's life and military service appeared in the *Houston Chronicle*, February 6, 1994.

35 *Albuquerque Journal*, June 12, 1992. William Derringer wrote these dramatic readings. Actor William Windom created a one-man show based on Pyle's life before and during World War II. While quite successful elsewhere since the 1970's, Windom has yet to appear in this role in New Mexico. *Rocky Mountain News*, January 6, 1978; *Los Angeles Times*, February 17, 1985; *Wall Street Journal*, April 17, 1985.

36 Thomas et. al., *Victory*, 106. Only two other men received separate chapter treatment in *Victory*: Bill Mauldin and Robert H. Goddard.

37 *Albuquerque Tribune*, October 27, 1950.

38 Ernie Pyle Festival Program, Dana, Indiana, August 2-4, 1985, Ernie Pyle Branch Library. Dana is currently expanding its Ernie Pyle State Historic Site, raising funds from both individuals and large groups, including the Scripps-Howard Foundation which contributed a quarter of a million dollars to the Pyle memorial. *Editor & Publisher*, vol. 127 (September 10, 1994), 21.

39 *Albuquerque Tribune*, April 17, 1995; *Albuquerque Journal*, April 19, 1995. A video of this special event was broadcast on C-Span television in a program entitled "A Tribute to World War II Journalist Ernie Pyle." The video was shown several times over the 1995 Memorial Day weekend.

BIBLIOGRAPHY

COLLECTIONS & MUSEUMS

Father Roger Aull File, Silver City Museum, Silver City, New Mexico.
Ross Calvin Collection, Special Collections, Zimmerman Library, University of New Mexico, Albuquerque, New Mexico.
Cornelious Cosgrove Whitehill File, Silver City Museum, Silver City, New Mexico.
Erna Fergusson Papers, Special Collections, Zimmerman Library, University of New Mexico, Albuquerque, New Mexico.
Arthur McCollum Collection, Albuquerque, New Mexico.
New Mexico Medical History Archives, Health Sciences Center Library, University of New Mexico, Albuquerque, New Mexico.
Ernie Pyle Collection, Indiana University, Bloomington, Indiana.
Ernie Pyle Collection, Special Collections, Albuquerque Public Library, Albuquerque, New Mexico.
Ernie Pyle File, Ernie Pyle Branch, Albuquerque Public Library, Albuquerque, New Mexico.
Ernie Pyle File, Main Branch, Albuquerque Public Library, Albuquerque, New Mexico.
Ernie Pyle State Historical Site, Dana, Indiana.
Edward H. Shaffer Collection, Albuquerque, New Mexico.
Zippo Manufacturing Company Museum, Bradford, Pennsylvania.

ORAL HISTORIES

Interviews by the Author:
    (Ret.) General Theodore Antonelli, June 15, 1993
    George Baldwin, January 18, 1994
    Ruth Baldwin, January 18, 1994
    Louise (Abeita) Chewiwi, November 5, 1994
    Robert Cook, May 21, 1994
    Mary Elena Davis, August 3, 1994
    Charles Edman, September 4, 1994
    Shirley (Mount) Hufstedler, September 12, 1993
    Janie Meuli, December 12, 1994
    Ann McRedmond, December 28, 1993
    Martin Quintana, April 2, 1994
    Betty Sabo, August 26, 1994
    Edward D. Shaffer, July 22, 1993
    George R. Shaffer, December 28, 1993
    Stella Mary (Shaffer) Jordon, September 9, 1993
    Rodney W. Shoemaker, August 26, 1994
    James R. Toulouse, October 31, 1994
    Elsa Smith Thompson, December 28, 1993
    Dick Trauth, November 22, 1992
    John Trujillo, September 22, 1994
    Larry Wilson, November 4, 1994
Interviews by Others:
    Bill Mauldin in McDowell, Sam. "A Conversation With Bill Mauldin." *El Palacio*, vol. 98 (Spring 1993), 10-15, 55-59.

Bill Mauldin in Rhodes, Hal. "Illustrated Daily: Remembering Ernie Pyle." KNME-TV, 1983.

Bill Mauldin in Terkel, Studs. *"The Good War:" An Oral History of World War II*. New York: Pantheon Books, 1984.

Arthur McCollum, *Albuquerque Journal*, July 29, 1965.

Earl Mount, *Albuquerque Tribune*, July 15, 1965.

Kenneth Mount in Rhodes, Hal. "Illustrated Daily: Remembering Ernie Pyle." KNME-TV, 1983.

Ella Streger, *Albuquerque Tribune*, January 31, 1953.

NEWSPAPERS & MAGAZINES

Albuquerque Journal
Albuquerque Tribune
Bataan Relief Organization Bulletin
Carlsbad Daily Current-Argus
Clovis News Journal
Denver Post
Editor & Publisher
El Paso Herald
El Paso Times
Farmington Times-Hustler
Gallup Independent
Hatch Courier
Health City Sun
Houston Chronicle
Indianapolis Times
Kansas City Star
[Kirtland Air Field] Bombsight
Las Cruces Sun-News
Los Alamos Monitor
Los Angeles Times
Memphis Press
Mountainair Progressive

New Mexico Magazine
[New Mexico State Teachers College] Mustang
Newsweek
New York Times
Pittsburgh Press
Portales Daily News
Raton Daily Range
Rocky Mountain News
Roswell Morning Dispatch
Roy Record
San Diego Union
Santa Fe Examiner
Santa Fe New Mexican
Santa Fe Reporter
Silver City Daily Press
Silver City Enterprise
Stars & Stripes
Taos Review
Time
[University of New Mexico] Lobo
Wall Street Journal
Washington Daily News
Yank: The Army Weekly

MOVIES, SHORT FEATURES, TELEVISION BROADCASTS, & RADIO SCRIPT

"Ernie Pyle's New Mexico," film clip, *Army-Navy Screen Magazine*, no. 65, 1945.

Rhodes, Hal. "Illustrated Daily: Remembering Ernie Pyle." KNME-TV, 1983.

The Story of G.I. Joe.

"A Tribute to World War II Journalist Ernie Pyle." C-Span television broadcast, April 28, 1995.

"We the People" radio script, KGGM, Albuquerque, New Mexico, July 15, 1945.

ERNIE PYLE'S BOOKS, ARTICLES, & COLLECTED COLUMNS

Ainsworth, Ed, editor. *Ernie Pyle's Southwest*. Palm Desert, California: Desert-Southwest, 1965.

Harden, Mike, & Evelyn Hobson, editors. *On A Wing and A Prayer:The Aviation Columns of Ernie Pyle*. Dana, Indiana: The Friends of Ernie Pyle, 1995.

Nichols, David, editor. *Ernie's America: The Best of Ernie Pyle's 1930s Travel Dispatches*. New York: Vintage Books, 1989.

_____, editor. *Ernie's War: The Best of Ernie Pyle's World War II Dispatches*. New York: Random House, 1986.

Pyle, Ernie. *Brave Men*. New York: Henry Holt & Company 1944.

_____. *Ernie Pyle in England*. New York: Robert M. McBride & Company, 1941.

_____. *Here Is Your War*. New york: Henry Holt & Company, 1943.

_____. *Home Country*. New York: William Sloane Associates, 1947.

_____. *Last Chapter*. New York: Henry Holt & Company, 1946.

_____. "Why Albuquerque?" *New Mexico Magazine*, vol. 20 (January 1942). Reprinted as Special Ernie Pyle Number, *New Mexico Magazine*, vol. 23 (June 1945).

MEMOIRS, DIARIES, ORAL HISTORIES, BIOGRAPHIES & AUTOBIOGRAPHIES

Abousleman, Michel D., editor. *Who's Who in New Mexico: Biographical Sketches of Contemporary New Mexicans*. Albuquerque: The Abousleman Company, 1937.

Anderson, H. Allen. *The Chief: Ernest Thompson Seton & the Changing West*. College Station: Texas A & M Press, 1986.

Biddle, George. *Artist at War*. New York: Viking Press, 1944.

Bradley, Omar N. *A General's Life: An Autobiography*. New York: Simon & Shuster, 1983.

_____. *A Soldier's Story*. New York: Henry Holt & Company, 1951.

Butcher, Captain Harry C. *My Three Years With Eisenhower*. New York: Simon & Schuster, 1946.

Caporaso, Anthony. *The Miracle of Father Aull*. New York: Pageant Press, 1958.

Davidson, Jo *Between Sittings: An Informal Autobiography* New York: Dial Press, 1951.

Doolittle, James H. *I Could Never Be So Lucky Again: An Autobiography*. New York: Bantam Books, 1991.

Eisenhower, Dwight D. *Crusade in Europe*. Garden City: Doubleday, 1949.

Ellis, Anne. *Sunshine Preferred*. Lincoln: University of Nebraska Press, 1984.

Fahey, James J. *Pacific War Diary, 1942-45*. Boston: Houghton Mifflin, 1992.

Fisher, Irene. *Bathtubs and Silver Bullets*. Albuquerque: Albuquerque Historical Society, 1976.

_____. *More Bathtubs, Fewer Bullets*. Albuquerque: Albuquerque Historical Society, 1977.

Hoopes, Roy. *Americans Remember the Home Front: An Oral Narrative of the World War II Years in America*. New York: Berkeley Books, 1992.

Jette, Eleanor. *Inside Box 1663*. Los Alamos: Los Alamos Historical Society, 1977.

Kahn, Sy M. *Between Tedium and Terror: A Soldier's World War II Diary, 1943-1945.* Urbana: University of Illinois Press, 1993.

Kalloch, Eunice, & Ruth K. Hall. *The First Ladies of New Mexico.* Santa Fe: The Lightning Tree Press, 1982.

Keleher, William A. *Memoirs: 1892-1969, A New Mexico Item.* Santa Fe: Rydal Press, 1969.

_____. *New Mexicans I Knew: Memoirs, 1892-1969.* Albuquerque: University of New Mexico Press, 1983.

Knox, Donald. *Death March: The Survivors of Bataan.* New York: Harcourt Brace Jovanovich, 1981.

Litoff, Judy Barrett, et. al. *Miss You: The World War II Letters of Barbara Woodall Taylor and Charles E. Taylor.* Athens: University of Georgia Press, 1990.

Lowitt, Richard. *Bronson M. Cutting: Progressive Republican.* Albuquerque: University of New Mexico Press, 1992.

Luhan, Mabel Dodge. *Edge of Taos Desert.* Albuquerque: University of New Mexico Press, 1987.

Mauldin, Bill. *Up Front.* New York: Henry Holt & Company, 1945.

_____. "When Bill Mauldin Met Ernie Pyle." *Santa Fe Reporter* (April 17, 1980), 20.

Meltzer, Milton. *Dorothea Lange: A Photojournalist's Life.* New York: Farrar, Straus, Giroux, 1978.

Miller, Arthur. *Timebends: A Life.* New York: Grove Press, 1987.

Miller, Lee G. *An Ernie Pyle Album: Indiana to Ie Shima.* New York: William Sloane Associates, 1946.

The Story of Ernie Pyle. New York: Viking Press, 1950.

Murrow, Edward R. *This Is London.* New York: Simon & Schuster, 1941.

Nymeyer, Robert. *Carlsbad, Caves, and a Camera.* Teaneck, New Jersey: Zephyrus Press, 1978.

Priestley, J.B. *All England Listened.* New York: Chilmark Press, 1967.

_____. *Rain Upon Godshill: A Further Chapter of Autobiography.* New York: Harper & Brothers, 1939.

Randle, General Edwin H. *Ernie Pyle Comes Ashore and Other Stories.* Clearwater, Florida: Eldnar Press, 1972.

Rooney, Andy. *My War.* New York: Random House, 1995.

Roosevelt, Eleanor. *This I Remember.* New York: Harper & Brothers, 1949.

Steinbeck, John. *Once There Was a War.* New York: Viking Press, 1958.

Sperber, A.M. *Murrow: His Life and Times.* New York: Freundlich Books, 1986.

Terkel, Studs. *"The Good War:" An Oral History of World War II.* New York: Pantheon Books, 1984.

Tregaskis, Richard. *Invasion Diary.* New York: Random House, 1944.

Utley, Robert M. *Billy the Kid: A Short and Violent Life.* Lincoln: University of Nebraska, 1989.

BOOKS, ARTICLES, & DISSERTATIONS

Adams, Michael C.C. *The Best War Ever: America and World War II*. Baltimore: Johns Hopkins University Press, 1994.

Adleman, Robert H., & Col. George Walton. *Rome Fell Today*. Boston: Brown & Company, 1968.

"Aftermath," *Life*, vol. 15 (November 15, 1943), 57-8, 60, 62, 64, 69.

Agee, James. "The Story of G.I. Joe." *The Nation*, vol. 160 (September 15, 1945), 264-66.

Alberts, Don E. *Balloons to Bombers: Aviation in Albuquerque, 1882-1945*. Albuquerque: Albuquerque Museum History Monograph, 1987.

Asbell, Bernard. *When F.D.R. Died*. New York: Signet Books, 1962.

Austin, Mary. *Land of Little Rain*. Boston: Houghton, Mifflin, 1903.

Barnett, Lincoln. "Ernie Pyle." *Life*, vol. 15 (November 15, 1943), 95-98, 101-102, 105-108.

Belote, James & William. *Tyhoon of Steel: The Battle for Okinawa*. New York: Harper & Row, 1970.

Belshaw, Jim. "Ernie Pyle's House Retains His Spirit." *Albuquerque Journal*, April 16, 1995.

Bertelsen, Lance. "San Pietro and the 'Art' of War." *Southwest Review*, vol. 74 (Spring 1989), 230-5.

Biebel, Charles D. *Making the Most of It: Public Works in Albuquerque during the Great Depression, 1929-1942*. Albuquerque: Albuquerque Museum History Monograph, 1986.

Blum, John Morton. "The G.I. in the Culture of the Second World War." *Ventures*, vol. 8 (1968), 51-56.
_____. *V Was For Victory: Politics and American Culture During World War II*. San Diego: Harcourt Brace Jovanovich, 1976.

Braudy, Lee. *The Frenzy of Renown: Fame and Its History*. New York: Oxford University Press, 1986.

Brown, John Mason. "Brave Man." *Saturday Evening Post*, vol. 28 (April 28, 1945), 20-22.

Bryan, Howard. "Adopted Homeland Treasures Journalist's Memory." *Albuquerque Tribune*, August 3, 1983.

Calvin, Ross. "Man Determines." *New Mexico Quarterly*, vol. 35 (Autumn 1965), 287.

_____. *Sky Determines*. New York: Macmillan, 1934; Silver City: High-Lonesome Press, 1993.

Cave, Dorothy. *Beyond Courage: One Regiment Against Japan, 1941-45*. Las Cruces: Yucca Tree Press, 1992.

Collier, Richard. *The Warcos: The War Correspondents of World War Two*. London: Weidenfeld & Nicholson, 1989.

DeMark, Judith Boyce. *Essays in Twentieth Century New Mexico*. Albuquerque: University of New Mexico Press, 1994.

Desmond, Robert W. *Tides of War: World News Reporting, 1940-1945*. Iowa City: University of Iowa, 1982.

Dick, Bernard F. *The Star-Spangled Screen: The American World War II Film*. Lexington: University Press of Kentucky, 1985.

Dickens, Elizabeth. "Please Omit Flowers," *The New Yorker*, 15 (March 18, 1939), 52-53.

Easton, Robert & Jane. *Love and War: Pearl Harbor Through V-J Day*. Norman: University of Oklahoma Press, 1991.

"Ernie Pyle's War." *Time*, vol. 44 (July 17, 1944), 65-66, 68, 70, 72.

Etulain, Richard W. *Contemporary New Mexico, 1940-1990*. Albuquerque: University of New Mexico Press, 1994.

Faircloth, Rudy, & H. Horace Carter. *Typewriter Soldier*. Tabor City, North Carolina: Atlantic Publishing Company, 1982.

Farber, Manny. "The Story of G.I. Joe," *New Republic*, vol. 113 (August 13, 1945).

Fergusson, Harvey. *Rio Grande*. New York: Alfred A. Knopf, 1933.

Fitzpatrick, George, editor. *This Is New Mexico*. Santa Fe: Rydal Press, 1948; Albuquerque: Horn & Wallace, 1962.

Flynn, Kathryn A. *Treasures of New Mexico Trails: New Deal Art and Architecture*. Santa Fe: Sunstone Press, 1995.

Freeman, Don. "The Ernie Pyle House." *Travel & Leisure*, vol. 16 (February 1986), E14-E15.

Fussell, Paul. *Wartime: Understanding and Behavior in the Second World War*. New York: Oxford University Press, 1989.

Gassner, John, & Dudley Nichols, eds. *Best Film Plays, 1945*. New York: Garland, 1977.

Gibson, Arrell Morgan. *The Santa Fe and Taos Colonies: Age of the Muses, 1900-1942*. Norman: University of Oklahoma Press, 1983.

Grear, Isabel Wiley. "Street of Memories," *Coronet*, vol. 21 (April 1947), 47.

Hough, Richard, & Denis Richards. *The Battle of Britain: The Greatest Air Battle of World War II*. New York: W.W. Norton, 1989.

Hoyt, Edwin P. *The G.I.'s War: The Story of American Soldiers in Europe in World War II*. New York: McGraw-Hill, 1988.

Jarrell, Randall. "Ernie Pyle." *The Nation*, vol. 160 (May 19, 1945), 573-76.

Kawano, Denji. *Warriors: Navajo Code Talkers*. Flagstaff: Northland Press, 1990.

Kennett, Lee. *G.I.: The American Soldier in World War II*. New York: Charles Scribner's Sons, 1987.

Ketchum, Richard M. *The Borrowed Years, 1938-1941: America On the Way to War*. New York: Random House, 1989.

Knightley, Phillip. *The First Casualty: The War Correspondent As Hero, Propagandist and Myth Maker*. London: Quartet Books, 1982.

Koppes, Clayton R., & Gregory D. Black. *Hollywood Goes to War: How Politics, Profits, and Propaganda Shaped World War II Movies*. New York: The Free Press, 1987.

Lancaster, Paul. "Ernie Pyle: Chronicler of 'The Men Who Do the Dying.'" *American Heritage*, vol. 32 (February/March 1981), 30-40.

Leckie, Robert. *Delivered From Evil*. New York: Harper & Row, 1987.

167

_____. *Okinawa: The Last Battle of World War II*. New York: Viking, 1995.

Liggett, Lila Noll. "'That Girl' of Ernie Pyle's." *The Woman With Woman's Digest* (July 1945), 9-11.

Lingeman, Richard R. *Don't You Know There's a War On?: The American Home Front, 1941-45*. New York: G.P. Putnam's Sons, 1970.

Matson, Eva Jane. *It Tolled For New Mexico: New Mexicans Captured by the Japanese, 1941-1945*. Las Cruces: Yucca Tree Press, 1994.

McDonald, Charles B. *The Mighty Endeavor: The American War in Europe*. New York: DaCapo Press, 1992.

McNamara, John. *Extra! U.S. War Correspondents in Action*. Plainview, New York: Books for Libraries Press, 1973.

Nash, Gerald D. *The American West in the Twentieth Century: A Short History of an Urban Oasis*. Albuquerque: University of New Mexico Press, 1977.

_____. *The American West Transformed: The Impact of World War II*. Bloomington: Indiana University Press, 1985.

_____. *World War II and the West: Reshaping the Economy*. Lincoln: University of Nebraska Press, 1990.

O'Neill, William. *A Democracy at War: America's Fight at Home and Abroad in World War II*. New York: The Free Press, 1993.

Parker, Kate H. "I Brought With Me Many Eastern Ways: Euro-American Income-Earning Women in New Mexico, 1850-1880." Unpublished Ph.D. dissertation, University of New Mexico, 1984.

Paul, Doris A. *The Navajo Code Talkers*. Bryn Mawr, Pennsylvania: Dorrance & Company, 1973.

Peeler, David P. "Unlonesome Highways: The Quest for Fact and Fellowship in Depression America." *Journal of American Studies*, vol. 18 (1984), 185-206.

Pillsbury, Dorothy L. "A Little White House on a Hilltop Where People Stop a While." *Christian Science Monitor Magazine Section*, (November 26, 1949), 16.

Polmar, Norman, & Thomas B. Allen. *World War II: America at War, 1941-1945*. New York: Random House, 1991.

Powell, Lawrence Clark. "Southwest Classics Reread: *Sky Determines* by Ross Calvin," *Westways*, vol. 63 (September 1971).

Ream, Glen O. *Out of New Mexico's Past*. Santa Fe: Sundial Press, 1980.

Redman, Clarence E. "That Girl," *[Kirtland Air Field] Bombsight*, (December 1943), 7-8.

Robertson, Edna, & Sarah Nestor. *Artists of the Canyons and Caminos: Santa Fe, The Early Years*. Salt Lake City: Gibbs M. Smith, 1982.

Roeder, George H., Jr. *The Censored War*. New Haven: Yale University Press, 1993.

Rothman, Sheila M. *Living in the Shadow of Death: Tuberculosis and the Social Experience of Illness in American History*. New York: Basic Books, 1994.

Sanders, Steve. "Hoosier Vagbond: Ernie Pyle." *Indiana [University] Alumni*, vol. 47 (July/August 1985), 17-21.

Sando, Joe S. *The Pueblo Indians*. San Francisco: Indian Historian Press, 1976.

Schneider-Hector, Dietmar. *White Sands: The History of a National Monument*. Albuquerque: University of New Mexico Press, 1993.

Severin, Werner J. "Cameras with a Purpose: The Photojournalists of [the] F.S.A." *Journalism Quarterly*, vol. 41 (1964), 191-200.

168

Simmons, Marc. *Albuquerque: A Narrative History*. Albuquerque: University of New Mexico Press, 1982.

_____. *Ranchers, Ramblers and Renegades: True Tales of Territorial New Mexico*. Santa Fe: Ancient City Press, 1984.

Spidle, Jake W., Jr. *Doctors of Medicine in New Mexico: A History of Health and Medical Practice, 1886-1986*. Albuquerque: University of New Mexico Press, 1986.

Stein, Meyer L. *Under Fire: The Story of American War Correspondents*. New York: Julian Messner, 1968.

Stenbuck, Jack, editor. *Typewriter Battalion: Dramatic Frontline Dispatches from World War II*. New York: William Morrow, 1995.

Thomas, Gerald W., Monroe L. Billington, & Roger D. Walker, editors. *Victory in World War II: The New Mexico Story*. Las Cruces: New Mexico State University, 1994.

Thompson, Zan. "A Homecoming of Sorts for Columnist Ernie Pyle." *Los Angeles Times* (February 17, 1985).

Thorson, Connie Capers, & James L. Thorson. "Gomorrah on the Puerco: A Critical Study of Philip

Stevenson's Proletarian Epic *The Seed*" in Robert Kern, editor, *Labor in New Mexico: Unions, Strikes, and Social History Since 1881*. Albuquerque: University of New Mexico Press, 1983.

Trimmer, Maurice. "Ernie Pyle Called Albuquerque 'Home'." *New Mexico Magazine*, vol. 38 (October 1960), 4 & 34.

Valentine, John. "Ernie Pyle Speaks to a New Generation." *Wall Street Journal* (April 17, 1985).

Van Orman, Richard A. *A Room for the Night: Hotels of the Old West*. New York: Bonanza Books, 1966.

Voss, Frederick S. *Reporting the War: The Journalistic Coverage of World War II*. Washington, D.C.: Smithsonian Institute, 1994.

Weigle, Marta, editor. *New Mexicans in Cameo and Camera: New Deal Documentation of Twentieth-Century Lives*. Albuquerque: University of New Mexico Press, 1985.

Weigle, Marta, & Peter White. *The Lore of New Mexico*. Albuquerque: University of New Mexico Press, 1988.

Williams, Jerry L. *New Mexico in Maps*. Albuquerque: University of New Mexico Press, 1986.

Wood, Robert T. "The Transformation of Albuquerque, 1945-72." Unpublished Ph.D. dissertation, University of New Mexico, 1980.

INDEX